The Dying Patient in Psychotherapy

The Dying Patient in Psychotherapy

Desire, Dreams and Individuation

Joy Schaverien

First published 2002 by
PALGRAVE MACMILLAN
Houndmills, Basingstoke, Hampshire RG21 6XS and
175 Fifth Avenue, New York, N. Y. 10010
Companies and representatives throughout the world

PALGRAVE MACMILLAN is the global academic imprint of the Palgrave Macmillan division of St. Martin's Press, LLC and of Palgrave Macmillan Ltd. Macmillan® is a registered trademark in the United States, United Kingdom and other countries. Palgrave is a registered trademark in the European Union and other countries.

ISBN 0–333–76342–4

This book is printed on paper suitable for recycling and made from fully managed and sustained forest sources.

A catalogue record for this book is available from the British Library.

10   9   8   7   6   5   4   3   2   1
11   10   09   08   07   06   05   04   03   02

Printed and bound in Great Britain by
Creative Print & Design (Wales), Ebbw Vale

In memory of Hyman Schaverien
1910–99

'Like a projectile flying to its goal, life ends in death. Even its ascent and its zenith are only steps and means to this goal.'

(Jung, 1935b, p. 408)

'Those, like myself, who accompany the dying know just how much we receive as a gift simply by accepting the commitment to embark on this ultimate experience in a human relationship that is proffered to us by the dying patient.'

(de Hennezel, 1997, p. 131)

Contents

List of Dreams

Preface

During the course of our lives certain people touch us in a particular way; they make some difference in our lives. The effects of a meeting may be evidently life-changing but sometimes it is merely a passing remark or a momentary gesture that leaves a lasting imprint. It is similar in the work of the psychotherapist. We are privileged to meet people at transitional times in their lives; they seek help because something is amiss for them. We come to share a little of their life's journey; it is as if our paths run parallel for a while, and so we travel together. Then, inevitably, we part, each of us a little changed by the encounter. When, during the course of this, the person who has come, seeking help, is faced with a life-threatening illness, this is brought acutely into focus. It was so with James. James came into my consulting room and my life, making an immediate impact, and by the time he died, two and a half years later, we had both been changed by the encounter. This book is the story of his journey, but it is also the story of my journey in his company and what I learned from the territory that we travelled together.

Joy Schaverien

Acknowledgements

This book is dedicated to the memory of 'James'. Although his true identity must remain hidden, I am indebted to him for sharing a little of his journey and for his permission to write about it. I am grateful to his family for their permission to publish.

During the analysis, on which this book is based, the support of Warren Colman, Shielagh Finlay, Katherine Killick and Andrew Samuels was indispensible. However, writing has been a solo enterprise. I take full responsibility for all inclusions and omissions, but there are a number of people who have helped along the way. The Omega Foundation provided a grant which gave me that most valuable commodity for a writer – time. My thanks to Ralph Goldstein for his belief in the project, and to Alison Caunt for her encouragement as a sensitive and insightful commissioning editor at Palgrave Macmillan. I am grateful to Tessa Dalley, Renos Papadopoulos, Penny Pickles and the anonymous reader for Palgrave for their comments on the penultimate draft. Jane Schaverien and Peter Wilson also, read and commented on that draft and contributed in numerous ways throughout; to them, and to Damien Wilson and Galia Wilson, my very special gratitude.

JOY SCHAVERIEN

Definition of Terms

The terms for the person in analysis, psychotherapy or counselling reflect sensitive professional issues.

> Analysand: Person undergoing psychoanalysis.
> Patient: A person receiving or registered to receive medical treatment.
>> Origin Middle English: from old French, via Latin: *patient* 'suffering', from the verb *pati.*
> Client: A person or organisation using the services of a lawyer or other professional person or company. The term originally indicated a person under the protection and patronage of another (*The New Oxford Dictionary of English.*)

The term 'analysand' clearly the most appropriate, is cumbersome so I use it interchangeably with the term 'patient'. 'Patient', meaning a person who is suffering, is more in keeping with the treatment offered in depth psychology than the term 'client'.

> 'Analyst': an abbreviation of psychoanalyst – (Jungian) and 'psychotherapist' are also used interchangeably.

Introduction

This book is intended primarily for professionals: analysts, psychotherapists and counsellors, working with patients facing a life-threatening illness, as well as those from other disciplines who work in palliative care. However it it will be of wider interest; relevant to psychotherapists and counsellors concerned with the management of the psychotherapeutic frame and the erotic transference. The general reader, affected by the issues under consideration, may be interested in the glimpse it gives into the usually private world of the analyst's consulting room. The latter reader may choose to skip the theoretical chapters and just read the narrative of the analysis.

It is my intention to elucidate the aims and methods of psychotherapy and to show how the process that Jung called individuation continues to the end of life. The narrative centres on one person who had been psychologically isolated for most of his life. This person, to whom I have given the pseudonym James, gave me his permission to write about him, indeed had he lived longer it is likely he would have written his own story. In the interest of confidentiality, certain aspects of the story have been fictionalised. Names, places and distinctive characteristics have been disguised, but this does not detract from either the psychological authenticity of the story or the purpose of the account. The aim is to draw out certain general theoretical points and to demonstrate how the boundaries of the analytic frame are significant in maintaining the therapeutic relationship. If this is successfully negotiated, previously blocked psychological potential is liberated.

The process becomes more complicated when the patient is suddenly confronted with a life-threatening illness. The path of such an illness is inevitably unpredictable so the analytic frame has to be adapted. Hospital and home visits are alien to the formal analytic structure but these may become necessary if psychotherapy is to continue. Therefore working analytically with someone who is seriously ill presents particular challenges.

Death and rebirth are often applied as metaphors for the therapeutic process. In depth psychology a symbolic death of one part of the self is understood to herald the birth of a new aspect. However when, in the course of long-term analysis or psychotherapy, the patient develops a terminal illness death is no longer a mere metaphor, it becomes a concrete reality. The potential outcome changes, the process of individuation may be spontaneously speeded up and, as death approaches, it intensifies. This serves to challenge the psychotherapeutic boundaries and calls for careful monitoring of the countertransference.

The single case study as research

In books and articles that are written to illustrate some aspect of psycho-analytic or psychotherapy theory the convention is to present case vignettes. In this book the case that illustrates, and from which the vignettes are drawn, remains the same throughout. The single case study is an accepted research method in psychotherapy (McLeod, 1994, 2000). It offers the benefit of continuity, bringing out general theoretical points in a sequential narrative. In this account the initial engagement in analysis is revealed, followed by its deepening as the erotic transference comes to dominate, in all its multitude of facets; then gradual separation/differentiation as consciousness takes over from the unconscious state. The order of the chapters is faithful to the chronological sequence of the material and the dreams are reported in the order in which they occurred. Thus a pattern is discernable, as conscious acknowledgement of one theme leads to the next. This is the benefit of recounting vignettes from one single case rather than disparate parts of different analyses.

Inner world and outer world

An account of analysis or psychotherapy is the story of a person's inner world, but despite its private and bounded nature it does not take place in a vacuum. Analysis operates at the interface between the inner and outer worlds, the personal and the cultural. Psychoanalytic theory is based on the idea that the pattern of interpersonal relating is shaped by the very earliest experiences. Patterns learned in childhood or infancy may be unconsciously repeated in adult life. The aim is to bring these earlier patterns to consciousness, thereby presenting the opportunity for a different way of being in the world. The undivided attention of the analyst and the confidentiality of the setting evoke the mother–child bond. Therefore analysis is often characterised by regression, as early patterns of relating become manifest within the therapeutic relationship.

When writing about the origins of such patterns there is a tendency to appear to blame the parents or parenting adults, but this is not my intention. When the parents appear in this narrative, in disguised and altered form, the reader is asked to remember that it is not the actual parents but their inner-world representation in the adult that is under discussion. Family members and close friends feature in the inner world of the adult, they are also the closest real people in a person's life. They are personified in memory and imagination. However the inner-world representation is not an objective truth. If you and I experience the same event we are likely to form very different perceptions of it. So it is with childhood memories. For example a parent might be surprised to learn that their child was traumatised by an incident that they perceived in a benign light. However it is the child/now adult's viewpoint that is of interest in analysis rather than the objective truth of the situation. Jung writes that:

> The unconscious creative force . . . wraps itself in images. When therefore we read: "His mother was a wicked witch," we must translate it as: the son is unable to detach his libido from the mother imago, he suffers from resistances because he is tied to the mother (Jung, 1956, p. 222).

The liberation of this creative force is the central story in this book. Whilst untangling the past from the present involves speaking to a stranger (the analyst) about personal and intimate life events, it is important to remember that the analyst is both, a real and a not, real person in the life of the analysand. For a while the analyst may seem to play a very important part, but as the inner-world elements are rearranged and the projections we reintegrated into the personality, this changes and eventually the analyst is left behind. I hope to demonstrate that, far from taking the person away from their family, psychotherapy eventually facilitates the deepening of the patient's relationships with the real people in their life.

In this regard the reader may be left with questions about the details of James's real family, and his early development but these will have to remain unanswered for reasons of confidentiality. Thus although the case study tells a very revealing story, it should be borne in mind that it is the analyst's story – a version of events that occurred within the analytic frame.

Countertransference

Countertransference is a technical term for the analyst's response to the whole of the analytic situation (Little, 1950; Heimann, 1949). In the narrative chapters of this book my own thoughts and feelings are recorded, so as well as being a case study in the conventional sense, it is also a case study of an analyst at work. Recording my own experiences as I accompanied James reveals the thought processes, conflicts and dilemmas that daily confront the analyst. Far from this being the cold, inhuman process caricatured by the media, it will become evident that the analyst struggles daily with their own emotional responses and has to judge what is right or ethical in any particular situation. This is of course the rationale for a thorough training analysis; it helps the analyst to differentiate their own patterns from those of the patient. This attention to the private workings of the analyst's mind demonstrates how countertransference is an integral aspect of the analytic method.

The boundaried frame is central in facilitating a depth psychological process, and so the analyst's process is not disclosed to the patient. The reasons for this will become clear as the story unfolds. For example discussion of the analyst's emotions would distract from the patient's material, possibly burdening her or him with concerns about the analyst's well-being. Moreover disclosure may seem seductive, offering the hope of a more intimate engagement than is possible, or indeed ethical. Even so the stereotype of the analyst as a mirror, merely reflecting back that which is projected onto her or him, is an oversimplification. A mirror offers only a cold and frozen reflection, and although there are times when the analytic method may seem to be thus, it is far from the whole story. Analysis is a complex and technically skilled process, but it is also a human endeavour that calls into play the analyst's humanity.

Exploitation of the patient by sexual, or other forms of abuse of power, is all too common. Acting out of the analytic frame is a topic that engages the media as well as professional ethics committees. Therefore it is vital that understanding of the difference between thought and deed is developed. In psychotherapy, although intense emotions may emerge it would be an abuse of power to act on them, and this is the case even if the patient appears to want it. This calls for conscious monitoring of the countertransference and thoughtful consideration of the boundaries.

Desire

This book does not offer a philosophical discourse about the nature of desire, nor is it a philosophical treatise on the links between death and desire, such as elucidated by Dollimore (1998). Unlike my previous book, *Desire and the Female Therapist,* it does not offer a feminist analysis of the topic of desire either. The desire in the subtitle refers strictly to desire as it manifests itself in clinical practice. Although not explicitly discussed it is a theme that is threaded through the account of the transference and countertransference dynamic, and it is revealed in the patient's dreams.

Dreams

Dreams play a central role in the narrative of this analysis and there is detailed discussion of them in Chapters 4, 5 and 6. The interpretation of these dreams is based on understandings reached at the time they were presented. However when I was reconsidering them for the book, further understandings emerged and these too are included. A sequence of dreams might at first seem opaque. However, like pictures, viewed in retrospect they may reveal the paradoxically chaotic logic of the psyche. The dreams, as they were reported are presented in italics. The associations made by the patient and analyst are presented in normal type.

As indicated above, this book is divided into theoretical and narrative chapters. Most of the narrative chapters cover roughly three-month periods, separated by breaks in the analysis. The reader can choose how to read the book. The general reader may prefer to skip the theory and read the narrative as a story. This reader might begin with Chapter 2, skip Chapters 1, 4 and 7 and end with Chapter 17. Chapter 1, is a review of the literature on psychotherapy with the dying patient; Chapter 4 discusses dream theory and Chapter 7 the erotic transference and countertransference. The final chapter (Chapter 18) provides some general thoughts for psychotherapists working with patients who are facing a terminal illness. It also addresses some practical issues with regard to supervision and fees. Finally, it is hoped that this book will raise questions for further research in this area.

Part One
The Therapeutic Relationship

1 Psychotherapy with the Dying Patient

> Our psyche is . . . not indifferent to the dying of the individual. The urge, so often seen in those who are dying, to set to rights whatever is still wrong might point in the same direction (Jung, 1935b: p. 411).

The aim of this book is twofold: to elucidate a psychological approach to death and dying; and, following on from *Desire and the Female Therapist* (Schaverien, 1995), to further develop an understanding of the meaning and purpose of the erotic transference and countertransference dynamic. These themes are explored within a closely observed therapeutic relationship, highlighting boundary issues encountered in psychotherapy when awareness of death is an imminent reality, rather than a distant prospect. Whilst the book is principally about psychotherapy in the shadow of the hovering awareness of death, it is essentially about love, life and vitality. In this chapter the literature on psychotherapy with people who are facing death is reviewed, with particular attention to boundaries.

Central to analytical psychology is the concept of individuation. This is a way of understanding psychological development that continues throughout life. It is 'a process of differentiation . . . having for its goal the development of the individual personality' (Jung, 1913, p. 448). When all goes well we are rarely conscious of it, but, if the path of individuation is blocked, it is the depth psychological project to liberate this potential. The analytic frame provides the contained setting in which previously disowned or unconscious elements in the psyche may become conscious. These are gradually and imperceptibly integrated into the personality and a sense of autonomy develops, enabling the person to feel more centrally an agent in their own life. When, in the midst of this process, the patient is diagnosed as having a life-threatening illness the whole endeavour enters a new dimension. As the threat of imminent death gains acceptance, the process becomes more urgent and resistances may be relinquished.

Psychotherapists, analysts and counsellors are increasingly confronted in their private practices with people affected by cancer, HIV-related illnesses and other life-threatening conditions. In an established psychotherapeutic relationship the onset of a life-threatening illness may have a profound affect on the analyst as well as the patient. Whilst there are many similarities for the analyst, this is different from working in an institution such as a hospital or hospice where the terminally ill are the client group. Unlike colleagues who work in palliative care, the analyst in private practice has not chosen this line of work; it is more a case of the work choosing them.

Working with the dying does not merely pose a technical problem but it does bring technical issues to the fore. Confronted with common humanity in the face of death the conventional analytic frame may come to seem particularly rigid and the therapist may begin to question the usual way of working. The psychotherapist is changed a little by each therapeutic encounter, but none more so than when the patient is confronting death. The experience of working with a dying patient is unusually engaging; it makes very particular demands and calls for a flexible approach. Physical illness does not stay within prescribed boundaries and inevitably the structure of the analytic frame has to be adapted to accommodate the deterioration of the patient's health. As with all changes to the frame, these alterations to the formal structure of the therapeutic environment need to be consciously considered. It is important to attend to the meaning, both actual and perceived, of changes made to accommodate the altered state of the patient. However there is little to be found in the literature that directly discusses the conflicts that such a situation arouses in the psychotherapist.

When treating someone living with the diagnosis of a terminal illness the analyst inevitably becomes intimately engaged in the person's day-to-day hopes, fears and uncertainty about the progress of the disease, and in the later stages analysis continues in the full knowledge that the outcome will be death. This is an unusual situation and material relating to it will, if possible, need to be processed within the dynamics of the therapeutic relationship. In this situation, perhaps more than in any other, attention to inner-world material will be mediated with awareness of the reality of the outer-world situation. This raises the question of what can be regarded as therapeutic when the patient has limited time left. Psychotherapists faced with a dying patient may justifiably complain that this was not addressed in their training as this is one area that provokes little interest until it is brought – often unsolicited – into the consulting room. It is a subject, like death itself, that is often avoided until the day it must be faced.

When the threat of imminent death emerges a particularly intense form of transference–countertransference engagement may constellate (Schaverien, 1999a). It is as if the powerful archetypal state that death evokes, holds both patient and analyst in thrall. When plants are about to die they sometimes throw off seeds in a last effort at regeneration, it is as if the creative process intensifies in the last stages of life. It seems as if unconsciously, something within the patient responds to the urgency of the situation in a similar way. The life force seems to intensify and the individuation process speeds up as the psyche, propelled by an unconscious awareness of the impending end of life, reorders priorities. Gordon (1971) observes something similar when she makes a link between the creative process and dying in her detailed exploration of symbolic aspects of death and rebirth in different cultures.

Similarly, when conducting an analysis with an elderly patient Wharton (1996, p. 36) was 'impressed by the drive to truly live as death draws near.' Feinsilver (1998), who worked with a woman whose analysis continued until the day before she died, writes that during the last months of her analysis 'she entered into a . . . phase of remarkable mobilisation of transference issues along with a striking ability to analyse what came up' (ibid., p. 1146). Clearly this intensification of the process is not uncommon and may partly account for the special status some such patients attain in their analysts' working lives.

The case at the centre of this book is one example, but it is clear that it is not unique. I have observed similar experiences among colleagues, and it seems that those who are moved to write about psychotherapy with the dying, do so because the experience has deeply affected them. Not all who face imminent death involve the analyst in this way, but certain people, perhaps those who need to compensate for unlived aspects of their lives, seem to draw the analyst into an almost irresistible process.

It is the psychotherapist as person who is affected, and therefore when writing about such work it would be disingenuous to hide behind the role. In order to convey the experience with authenticity, a degree of self-exposure is inevitable. The wounded healer archetype, the need to heal a wounded aspect of their own psyche, is a well-known aspect of the analyst's motivation for their work (Guggenbuhl-Craig, 1971; Samuels, 1985a; Sedgwick, 1994). The terminal illness of the patient brings this sharply into focus. The psychotherapist who truly engages with this process is obliged to confront the inevitability of their own death. This glimpse of mortality may heighten identification with the patient. However it may also lead to other subtle concerns: there may be anxiety about being a good enough analyst or unconscious denial of the impending loss of the patient.

This situation, as no other, takes the analyst to the limits of their experience. This is one time in psychotherapy where, the patient journeys physically and psychologically to a place where, no matter what depth of analysis the psychotherapist has experienced, they have yet to travel. This is accompanied by the certain knowledge that one day they too will travel this path. This may be awe-inspiring and the power imbalance of the therapeutic relationship may subtly shift. Writing about losses experienced in old age, Hubback (1996) warns against a form of idealisation that places the elderly patient automatically in the place of a wise woman or man because of their advanced years. Younger people who are about to die may evoke similarly complex feelings, and they too may be idealised or feared because of the power attributed to their 'special' status.

Death or illness of the analyst

Very often the end of analysis is discussed in terms of a symbolic death, but when actual death intervenes its very real implications as well as its symbolic dimensions need attention. In this book the topic is the patients' illness but sometimes analysts too become seriously ill. This is highlighted in Haynes' (1996) moving account of the sudden death of her analyst. As an analyst herself she was in a position to consider the effects of this from the viewpoint of both analysand and analyst. She addresses the personal impact of ending analysis in this way and also some of the professional issues it raised with regard to her own analytic practice. It is well known that, in the prelude to the termination of therapy, previously denied or repressed material presses to the fore. When the analyst dies suddenly this process is disrupted.

It is different if the analyst or patient becomes seriously ill, and awareness of the proximity of death may give an opportunity to work through an ending. Feinsilver's (1998) courageous account addresses this from the analyst's position. When his own cancer recurred he decided that it would be best for his patients to confront the truth about his situation. Furthermore he reflects that 'normal therapeutic processes [were enhanced] by both patient and therapist sharing the news of [his] life-threatening illness' (ibid., p. 1132). He also writes that one of the benefits of his illness was that it caused him to be intensely aware of his priorities in life. This seems to confirm the view that the prospect of death mobilises the psyche. It seems that, no matter which side of the couch we find ourselves, confronting our worst fears when they emerge so starkly within the analytic encounter does indeed intensify life.

Social attitudes towards death

Young and Cullen's (1996) sociological study provides a picture of attitudes towards death and dying at the end of the twentieth century. They conducted interviews at regular intervals with a group of people living in the East End of London who had been diagnosed as having cancer. Their study highlights the ways in which this group of people approached the end of their lives. The effects on those caring for the dying were included in the study and the authors found that, irrespective of whether the carers were family members, neighbours or professionals, they often made tremendous efforts for very little reward. They propose that this may be due to the fact that, in the face of the death of another, we all face our own death. They write:

> Death is the common experience which can make all members of the human race feel their common bonds and their common humanity. The presence of death, for all its terror and bitterness . . . can generate the mystical sense of unity with other people that transcends the boundaries of the body and the self (ibid., p. 201).

This conveys the apparent paradox of the awesome normality of death that confronts carers and the bereaved. A number of personal accounts of the experience of dying have been written by close relatives or by people facing death. The philosophical treatise by Wilber (1991), a psychotherapist, was written as a way of coming to terms with the illness and eventual death of his wife. Her own words complement his and so the reader can gain insight into the experiences of both patient and carer. In recent years several accounts have been written by journalists, which show how the previously taboo topic in Western society is being paid increasing attention in the public arena. Perhaps this reflects a social change in attitudes towards death and dying. At the time of his father's final illness Morrison (1993) was moved to write a memoir of his father's life. This portrait of a bold, outrageous, dominant and amusing man, presented from the viewpoint of a child growing up in the 1950s, is a celebration of a life, with all its imperfections. Morrison candidly observes the changing roles of father and son as his father sank gradually from life into death. This account indicates the transformation from power to powerlessness that is so common as life ebbs away.

Two intensely moving accounts by journalists have done much to normalise the perception of cancer and to bring discussion of it into the open. By confronting the struggles of the process they have brought dying from the closeted sick room and hospital right into the living rooms of ordinary people. This is where it used to take place in days gone by but, in Western society, more recently, death and dying have been hidden away. Picardie (1998) and Diamond (1998), both had regular newspaper columns in which they described living with cancer. Their books give a vivid insight into the roller coaster of hope and despair, the painful treatments and the relentless progress of the disease. These are personal rather than professional accounts but there is much of relevance to psychotherapy. Diamond's attitude towards counselling and psychotherapy, is far from complimentary but it is worth noting because analysts need to confront the limits of what they have to offer in the face of a life-threatening disease. The intense emotions conveyed in these books, evoked by living with the constant threat of death, clearly have implications for psychotherapists working with the dying.

Until recently there were only a few well-known works on counselling the dying. Eissler (1955), writing mainly for psychiatrists, addressed this topic, followed by Bowers *et al.* (1964) in the USA. The pioneering work of Dame Cicely Saunders (1959), who founded the Hospice movement, altered the way in which the dying were treated. She recounts how her work was the legacy of a dying man with whom she fell in love when she was a young nurse. Kubler-Ross's (1969) immense contribution was to introduce a psychologically minded approach to understanding the need to talk about death with dying people, as well as their families and carers. The research and writings of Murray Parkes (1972), which began in the 1950s and continued in the subsequent decades, gradually changed the public perception of the bereaved. The loss of attachment figures is now acknowledged, by general medical practitioners as well as counsellers and psychotherapists, as a significant life event that has profound psychological consequences.

More recent publications on the topic include the republication in 2000 of Kastenbaum's 1972 work, which traces the psychology of death from childhood through the life stages; Orbach (1999) on psychotherapy with the dying, and a sociological study by Lawton (2000). None of these addresses the central theme of this book: the boundary issues and stresses on the psychotherapeutic frame that the diagnosis of a life-threatening illness evokes.

The psychotherapist's role with the dying patient is an ambiguous one. Family members and medical and nursing staff have to deal with the often distressing physical aspects of a serious illness; the psychotherapist does not, and therefore may appear to be in a privileged position. Certainly psychotherapists are privileged to work intimately with people during this awesome transition in their lives, but it is also true that the psychological can be 'messy' as well as distressing. Analysts working with the inner world of the patient may be deeply affected and at times even, infected by the patient's hopes and terrors. Although this is a privilege it can also be an awesome responsibility. It drives the analyst – patient relationship to the borderline of the personal and professional. This is evident in various moving accounts of work in palliative care.

Palliative care – the analytic attitude and the witness

Jung observed that 'the psyche is not indifferent to the dying of the individual. The urge, so often seen in those who are dying, to set to rights whatever is still wrong might point in [this] direction' (Jung, 1935. p. 411). Based on their work in palliative care, Kearney (1996) and de Hennezel (1997) discuss how the pain of unresolved emotional suffering may keep patients hanging onto life. Through vivid clinical vignettes they demonstrate how, when the particular emotional block is at last confronted, patients may be able to let go and die peacefully. Sometimes all that is needed is the opportunity to talk through their concerns with family or professional carers. However Kearney (1997, 2000) stresses that sometimes emotional pain cannot be alleviated and so it is not always possible to bring life to a peaceful conclusion. Both these writers stress the importance of teamwork in palliative care; workers who are confronted with their own powerlessness in the face of death need the support of colleagues. Psychotherapists working in private practice do not have this collegial support and therefore provisions need to be made for peer discussion or supervision.

De Hennezel (1997), a psychologist, reveals just how closely the therapist may be drawn into the world of the dying patient. None-the-less a distinction is maintained between the role of the professional carer and that of friends and family. The reader travels with her as she 'accompanies' individuals at the end of their life's journey:

Accompanying someone involves engaging with that person; it is a matter of heart. Above all, it is about one's common humanity. One cannot retreat behind one's white coat, whether one is a doctor, a nurse or a psychologist. This does not mean, however, that there are no limits (ibid., p. 130).

The fact that she maintains a boundaried role permits her to work in this way. One of her psychotherapist colleagues, surprised at the extent of her emotional involvement, asked her about therapeutic distance. Inspired by this challenge she wrote:

All the safeguards and rigid rules of the analytic world – don't touch, don't speak – melted in a single mass. I had to move up close, listen to my own intuition, speak with my heart, lay my hands where it hurt, the way I would have done with anyone in that situation (ibid.).

However, as we saw above, she stresses that there are limits. It seems that she maintained the analytic attitude and this enabled her to become closely involved. This is the point: it is only possible to be present in this way if professional distance is simultaneously maintained. It is essential to understand the purpose of therapeutic boundaries before they can be adapted. For example, before physically touching a patient it is important to check whether the touch is really for the benefit of the patient. It may be an unconscious attempt by the therapist to console her- or himself (Scaife, 1993). It is essential to be aware of the power imbalance and the limits of what is appropriate. It is also important to have some sense of how the gesture might be interpreted by the patient. This is a particularly sensitive issue when someone with whom a boundaried psychotherapeutic relationship has already been established becomes ill.

For those at the end of their lives the need for a 'witness' is often a crucial factor, and maintaining an analytic attitude permits the therapist to hold this position. In palliative care it is increasingly common for the skills of arts therapists to be used. Art therapy (Connell 1998; Pratt and Wood, 1998) and music therapy (Lee, 1996; Aldridge 1999), involves the application of psychodynamic techniques in conjunction with art or music. Very often arts therapists work in situations where maintenance of the psychotherapeutic frame is under constant pressure. In this situation the therapist's witnessing function is significant, as Wood (1990, 1998) points out. In her work with patients living with or dying from AIDS related-illnesses it is sometimes not possible to have more than a single session, and she demonstrates how highly significant the art therapist as witness can be in such a situation. Beaver (1998), working with male prisoners infected with HIV, describes how, although it might seem impossible to create a psychotherapeutic environment in a prison setting, she managed to adapt her approach to allow space for the men to articulate their hopes and fears. In adapting to such settings these therapists show that, even when an analytic frame is impossible, a boundaried psychotherapeutic attitude can be maintained.

Another understated aspect of work in palliative care is the repeated sense of loss experienced by the therapist. Beaver (ibid.) reminds us that the individuals whose stories she recounts would have died by the time the book to which she was contributing was published. This is the case with all the books and articles discussed here and highlights the repeated losses experienced by those working in palliative care, This inevitably takes an emotional toll on the professional.

Children

An analytic attitude and a boundaried approach is just as necessary when working with children. If it is hard to come to terms with the diagnosis of a terminal illness in an adult it is even more so in the case of children. Most of the books written about working with dying children are illustrated with the children's pictures (for example Bertoia, 1993; Sourkes, 1995). Susan Bach's (1990) research on the drawings of seriously ill children spanned many years and is probably the most extensive exploration of the art of the dying child (Goldstein, 1999). However it is Judd's (1989) work that is most relevant when considering boundaries and therapeutic distance.

In her painfully detailed account of the treatment and eventual death of a small boy suffering from cancer, Judd makes a clear distinction between the role of the psychotherapist and that of the family. Psychotherapy with seriously ill children closely involves the parents and other carers, and the ways in which the psychotherapeutic boundaries are maintained takes account of their needs. Judd demonstrates how psychotherapy can offer an opportunity for unbearable or unspeakable feeling to be conveyed by interpreting coded messages from the child. Her aim was to complement the care of the family by facilitating the expression of feelings that might have been unbearable for them. The analytic attitude seemed to offer a particular form of comfort by providing an understanding of the depth of emotion the child was experiencing. Drawing on 'Freud's 1920 notion of the "shield" that protects us from psychic trauma', she makes the point (which has a bearing on the case that follows later in this book) that 'the parents and the patient can and, do use necessary defences, while the therapist, and perhaps the reader, can afford this intense pain because the contact is not constant' (ibid., p. 102). It is only possible for the therapist to maintain contact with feelings that might otherwise become unbearable because of the professional distance that is maintained at the same time as being involved. This is the challenge of such work, which will become clear as the account in this book develops.

Psychotherapy and analysis with adults

A number of detailed accounts by Jungian analysts and psychoanalysts demonstrate how the last stages of life can be eased by psychological understanding. Jung's interest in dreams and development at different stages of life led him to write about both actual death and also death as a metaphor for psychological processes (Jung, 1935). This legacy has continued and Jungians have had a particular interest in depth psychological processes connected with dying, particularly as they are revealed in dreams (Bosnak, 1989; Von Franz, 1984; Jaffe, 1958).

There are a few single case study books on the topic of the dying patient, and perhaps part of their significance is that the process of writing involves the psychotherapist's own individuation process. Wheelwright (1981), writing 20 years after the experience, recounts how she was asked by a colleague to work with a married woman of 37-years-old who had a diagnosis of cancer. As a woman in her sixties at the time, Wheelwright writes that she was interested in this challenge for professionals and personal reasons, and that the work was like a mutual research project (ibid., p. 9). The referral was made after the diagnosis and her stated purpose was to help the patient 'with the process of individuation' (ibid., p. 8). This was distinct from the concerns of the family and other professionals who were absorbed with the considerable outer-world problems. Wheelwright describes the boundaried nature of the analysis but also conveys the love that was clearly present, as well as the distress caused by the physical deterioration of the patient. She makes the point that in a situation like this it can be helpful for a woman to work with a woman analyst.

Bosnak's (1989) account of the analysis of a man with AIDS is also a single case study. The analyst and analysand were both in their thirties, and the book traces the tragic dawning of the realisation that the patient would not recover from his illness. The dreams of the patient were the focus of the work and the therapeutic relationship centred on the process of recording, reporting and amplifying the dream material. The analysand moved to the town where the analyst was based in order to work with him. Bosnak's openness about the effect on his own life reveals the powerful manner in which such a patient can engage the analyst.

In Ulanov's (1994) single case study the onset of the cancer occurred when her patient, Nancy who was in her late thirties and married, was about to finish a six-year analysis. When Nancy's speech failed due to the effects of a brain tumour she drew pictures and these are shown in the book. The bond between Ulanov and Nancy is vividly conveyed: 'Nancy was not my first experience of death as psychotherapist . . . . Nonetheless, her circumstances pulled on me as few others, because of the long work we had done together and continued to do . . . because of the person she was, her gentleness and toughness, her constant reaching for the center' (ibid., p. 91).

As well as conveying the love evidently involved in the therapeutic inter-actions these books address the genuine problems of boundary issues. These demand particular attention when the analytic frame is disturbed by medical interventions, the deterioration of the patient and meetings with the family.

The two journal articles discussed next were written by psychoanalysts. However it is interesting to note that theoretical differences did not alter the fact that the analytic frame was adapted. This is because irrespective of the analyst's theoretical orientation, at the point at which the patient is unable to travel to sessions the only alternative to adapting the frame would be to terminate the analysis. The solution to this problem is different in each case in response to the physical circumstances and the nature of the therapeutic relationship. It seems that differences in theoretical orientation fade when analysts are faced with the human task of travelling alongside someone who is dying.

Minerbo (1998) discusses the relative merits of continuing to maintain the boundaried analytic frame versus providing supportive psychotherapy. She describes how, in the fifth year of an eight-year analysis, her patient became ill with cancer. At first the patient, a 48-year-old married woman with three children, responded to treatment and was therefore able to attend the analytic sessions, but in the seventh year she was confined to complete bed rest. At that point the decision was made to replace the sessions with phone calls. Minerbo never saw the patient again, but by means of phone calls the analysis continued for six months, three times a week, until the day before the patient died. In this way Minerbo was spared the distress of witnessing the patient's physical deterioration. This meant that at times she could be in denial of the state of the patient, however at other times she was very nearly overwhelmed with emotion.

McDougall's (2000) patient was a 40-year-old mother of two children who approached her with some urgency after a diagnosis of cancer. Although they had never worked together the patient had consulted McDougall on one occasion some years previously and had clearly held her in mind. In the first session of what was to become a three-year analysis the patient expressed her fear of an imminent bone marrow transplant, which meant that she would be confined alone in a sterile room for three weeks. McDougall offered her telephone sessions during that time, telephone sessions were subsequently permitted during breaks. The fax machine was later incorporated as a way of continuing the analytic process during breaks and at weekends. McDougall permitted this contact because she was clearly touched by the patient's predicament. She suggests that this helped to repair the negative experiences the patient had with her own mother. This she equates with the cancer: 'Since cancer is envisioned as a deathlike enemy in the interior of one's own body, it is readily equated with a fantasized "internal mother" who is attacking her daughter from within' (ibid., p. 47). Although she maintains that psychoanalysis cannot cure cancer she asserts that,

> By exploring and putting into words the nature of the projections for which the cancer becomes the focus, . . . there is much evidence to support the contention that when the patient is helped both somatically and psychically, her chances of survival are notably increased (ibid., p. 48).

There was a strong erotic bond, which McDougall understood in developmental terms as the girl child's love for her mother. It is clear that in this case the pressures of eros and the life force accelerated as the patient was about to die. This seems to indicate pressure from the psyche towards individuation; this patient had to come to life before she could die.

It is notable that in four of the above cases both analyst and patient were female. Significantly, these patients were also married and their husbands were centrally involved. This was different from the patient described later in this book; like Bosnak's analysand, he did not have a partner at the time and therefore the analytic partnership became central to his life. The man–woman pairing added to an erotic transference in which infantile regression was at first undifferentiated from heterosexual passion.

A similar erotic intensity seems to have constellated in the case described by Lee (1996), a music therapist who writes about his work with a musician with AIDS. Unusually, and perhaps controversially, his book is accompanied by a CD recording of the patient playing a piano during the sessions. In some sessions therapist and patient played duets together and in others the patient played alone and the therapist listened. Clearly this was not an analytic encounter, but it is evident that the love that developed in this therapeutic relationship tested the boundaries to their limits. Like my patient James, Lee's patient was a single man whose life seemed to have lacked fulfilment. Lee describes how the imminent death of the patient intensified the process, and at that point he relinquished the therapeutic stance and agreed to the patient's request to befriend him. Thus in response to the demands of the patient and his illness the therapist could be understood, in analytic terms, to have acted out. This is an example of the tremendous conflicting emotions that may arise in the analyst when confronted with a seriously ill patient. It highlights the way in which the analyst may be drawn into an archetypally charged state where rational thinking is not easily maintained. It is particularly distressing for the analyst when the patient has not lived his or her life to the full or is dying relatively young. Furthermore, when the patient has no partner added pressures are placed on the analyst and the desire to relinquish the analytic stance may be difficult to resist.

This raises serious questions about the nature of the therapeutic ending when the patient is dying. Clearly there are no rules, and as we have seen above each case has to be assessed at the time and in the full knowledge of the situation in question. In may be that in some cases befriending the patient may be the most therapeutic solution, whilst in others it may be appropriate for the analyst to withdraw when the work seems to be complete. In cases such as those described by Wheelwright, Bosnak, Ulanov, Minerbo and McDougall and that which I shall discuss in this book, it may be in the interest of the patient to continue psychotherapy to the end. But there are no rules, and few guidelines, and it has to be a matter of judgment in each case.

2 Intimacy Revealed: Establishing a Therapeutic Relationship

> Our house is our corner of the world. As has often been said, it is our first universe, a real cosmos in every sense of the word. If we look at it intimately, the humblest dwelling has beauty (Bachelard, 1964, p. 4).

As James lay dying he was in his house, in a bright room surrounded by his plants and cared for by members of his family. At that time I wrote: 'James is housed. He is at home. He says, "I am more alive now than I have ever been". In some part he attributes this to the effects of psychotherapy.' The fact that he was housed reflects the successful outcome of one of the main themes of our work together. His body was at rest in a house – the spiritual parallel of this was that his soul too was housed.

This chapter records the first three months of James's analysis, introduces his psychological history and presenting problems, and outlines the main themes that were to develop as our work together progressed. At the end of this period James was unexpectedly diagnosed as suffering from lung cancer. The aim of this chapter is to give a sense of the analysis prior to diagnosis.

James was referred by his general medical practitioner for psychotherapy and I first met him late one December evening. The previous night he had contacted the Samaritans because he had felt so isolated and desperately lonely that suicide had seemed to be the only option. (The Samaritans, founded by Chad Varah, is a voluntary organisation that provides a confidential 24-hour telephone line for people contemplating suicide.)

Despite his desperation James's was initially ambivalent about the psychotherapeutic process. This was evident in his first telephone call to me. He began by telling me that Dr X had suggested he contact me. We arranged an appointment but he then became hesitant. He was unsure whether he could come because he did not know if he should drive when taking the anti-depressant medication prescribed by Dr X, nor if he could borrow his parents' car to get to my consulting room. He said he would have to phone Dr X to check whether it would be alright to drive. Five minutes later he phoned to say that he would come at the appointed time.

The First Session

After this I had expected a young man in his early twenties, and was surprised to meet a slim man in his mid forties with a mass of curly black hair that was greying at the temples. He was informally dressed and his accent, which gave the impression of a public school education, contrasted with his general demeanour. His appearance was rather dishevelled and fitted in with the sense of depression and desperation he communicated as his story unfolded. He sat in the chair, ignoring the couch, and without looking at me began to talk rapidly.

James recounted his history with great intensity. He was divorced and his ex-wife and three teenage children were living in France, his wife's home country and also that of his mother. He described how he had felt suicidally depressed throughout his life. He had never been able to settle anywhere except during the brief years of his marriage. At that time he had had a home, but ever since his marriage had broken up twelve years previously he had not had a significant relationship or a place of his own to live. He had stayed with friends until they became fed up with him, and then he had resentfully returned to stay with his parents. It became increasingly evident that this paralleled his psychological state; when he was in a relationship he had been 'housed' and when that had broken down he had been unable to 'house' himself. He explained that when he married he had been 'joined at the hip' to his wife. This indicated the level of regressed dependence he had experienced within that relationship and it also gave some sense of the pattern that was to emerge in the transference. It was as if he 'fell into the therapeutic relationship'; it seemed to offer the promise of a psychological home.

Recently he had been living in a flat while the friend who owned it was away, but he had been unable to pay the bills and therefore had had to leave. Although he had enough money he had felt psychologically blocked and unable to write the necessary cheques. It was similar with jobs; they had always gone wrong because, as he put it, 'I throw a spanner in the works.' His most recent job was an example. He had been employed at a senior level in an international company where he was well respected. He had been both surprised and delighted to be appointed to this very prestigious firm and for a while all had gone well. However his responsibility within the company involved travelling abroad and it had recently necessitated his filling out some documents. He had encountered the same sort of block as with the household bills; – he had been completely unable to take the necessary action. It had proved impossible for him to admit his difficulties to his senior colleagues and he had been terrified that his omission would bring litigation to the company and censure to himself. As a result he had become anxious and then depressed, and being incapable of returning to work and confronting the situation he had returned to his parents' home.

He had resented this and would not communicate with his parents. He had also avoided approaches from other members of his family and work colleagues, and so spoke to no one. Psychologically paralysed he had taken to his bed and reverted to the depressed state that had intermittently haunted him for most of his adult life. He had become totally isolated. At that point he had gone to see his GP, who had prescribed anti-depressants and referred him to me. At the end of the first session he agreed to attend twice a week.

Although the cancer that was diagnosed three months later must have already been active in him, no one knew that James was terminally ill. It is of course obvious that when we embark on an analytic voyage (McDougall, 1995) with someone we can never predict the direction the journey will take. Certainly neither James nor I could have predicted that he was to die two and a half years later.

At the beginning of the second session James's ambivalence was still evident. He began by saying that he had hoped that he would be able to come for a few sessions, get some advice and go away again. However he seemed relieved when I said that the problems he had presented the previous week were not likely to be resolved by a few quick sessions. Despite his relief he introduced a further obstacle. He had failed an alcohol breathalyser test and was waiting to hear whether the police would prosecute him. As his driving license could be revoked he might have to consider seeing someone nearer to his home. He asked, 'Is it advisable to change therapists if things are going OK between us?' I replied that we would work with whatever arose but that it seemed to me he was in immediate need of therapy. Again he appeared relieved. He seemed to be testing the safety of investing in therapy at the same time as leaving an escape route.

He recounted how he had begun but not finished many things in his life – university courses, marriage and jobs. I suggested that he was telling me of a pattern in his life and was now wondering whether he would be able to stay with the psychotherapy. This seemed to free him to speculate that if he lost his license it would be possible to cycle.

After these preliminaries he appeared satisfied with the safety of the analytic container, and during the following sessions he recounted his history with a sense of urgency. He was the eldest of the four children of a French mother and an English father. When he was a small boy he had moved with his parents and sisters, to this country, to live in the family house where he was now living in isolation from his parents. His brother was born when he was sixteen. A telling memory recounted at this time was of being four years old and looking down the lane from the house where he then lived. He had wondered where the path would lead; it seemed to stretch so very far. This memory from the time when he had been on the threshold of life seemed to be a metaphor for the beginning of the analytic journey. In retrospect there is the added poignancy of the knowledge that his life's journey was moving towards its conclusion.

Boarding school

James had been sent to boarding school at the age of eight. The way in which this was communicated made it clear that the wound was still fresh; it seemed as though he had been waiting to tell his story since that time. As he spoke he appeared to relive the excitement of the preparations. There was a tremendous build-up and for several days in advance his mother helped him to prepare and pack. He was treated as special; as the only son in the family at that time, he was told that he alone had been chosen for this exciting event whilst his sisters were to stay at home. He understood that this was in preparation for his role as a man in the world and the message was that he was special. However the reality of boarding school was quite different. He was totally unprepared for the appalling realisation, on his arrival, of utter loneliness and abandonment.

He was homesick and cried all night, hidden under the bedclothes, away from the gaze of the other boys. There was no one to witness his distress, no one knew how unhappy he was. From that time onwards there was never anyone to mediate his experiences. In the analysis he responded immediately to this aspect of the relationship, to having a witness. He said: 'This is what I have been looking for all my life but I did not know what it was.' At last there was someone to understand and give words to the state of perpetual loneliness that had haunted him since that time.

One event that was to have profound psychological significance was a race he ran soon after starting at that school. He was very small in stature and all the other boys were bigger than he was, but with a supreme effort and against all the odds he won. Having won he looked around and realised that there was no one with whom to celebrate his victory. He was profoundly disappointed; he desperately wished that his parents had seen his triumph. Immediately after the race he developed flu symptoms and a high temperature and was put to bed in the school sanatorium. His parents were contacted but they were told that his illness was not serious and there was no need for them to come. As he tearfully recounted this he re-experienced the loneliness and despair he had felt. He became aware that, even at the time he had realised that he was ill because he wanted his parents to come to him. When they had not he had felt truly abandoned and soon cut himself off from his feelings. So it was that he had learned not to cry. In retrospect it is possible to see that this set the precedent for his inability to complete anything; there was no point if there was no one with whom to share his successes.

Thus it was that his special role as the only son in the family was replaced by life as an insignificant boy in a vast male institution. A child in a boarding school is expected to conform to the collective values of the institution. Jung writes that 'Individuation is a natural necessity . . . its prevention by levelling down to collective standards is injurious to the vital activity of the individual' (Jung, 1913, p. 448). This seems to encapsulate James's experience of boarding school: he was longer a special individual, the only boy in the family, but merely a member of a collective – a group of boys and men. His emotional life was not valued, and at this early developmental stage it had catastrophic psychological consequences. When James returned home for vacations he was unable to communicate his suffering to his family and therefore felt that no one really knew him. The sense of betrayal and isolation which began at this time, were to influence the rest of his life. He had never been able to communicate his distress at what he experienced as complete abandonment by his mother. Thus began the lifelong pattern of giving up when success was potentially within his grasp.

By the time of my winter break, which came two weeks after our first appointment, James had already engaged in analysis. A therapeutic alliance had been established and the process of recounting his history had evoked a regression to dependence, such that he was concerned about how he would manage in my absence. I too was worried about how he would survive. At that stage my conscious concern was a response to his expressed suicidal thoughts. However it was also a countertransference response that resonated with his history of repeated separations. Later, especially as he became progressively more ill, this became a constant theme of the breaks in therapy. As time passed I was increasingly faced with two questions. Would he survive? Would I see him again?

The mother

After the break the analysis resumed with similar regressed intensity. I came to understand how his relationships with women had been affected by the shadow of his unrequited longing for his mother. His time at boarding school had not been the first separation from his mother. Rather that experience had seemed to replay and compound the effects of a separation at the age of four months, when he had been sent to live with his grandparents for a month due to his mother's ill-health. The combination of these events had left him with a deep yearning for his mother but also a vengeful anger which came to the fore almost immediately the analysis began.

James remembered reading *The Count of Monte Cristo* when he was at school. He had identified with the hero, who had been unjustly thrown into prison and isolated from the world. When he escaped from prison and returned at last to marry his childhood sweetheart he discovered that she had married someone else. Forever after he was bent on revenge for the injustice that had been perpetrated against him. James felt that this was very much like him; boarding school had been the prison and he too was bent on revenge for the betrayal he had experienced. The implication seemed to be that James's childhood sweetheart had been his mother.

The acknowledgement of his anger seemed to release a chain of memories of a time when he had been close to his mother. There had once been a deep bond between them and he was sad that he was now unable to get close to her. As he was speaking of this he was unexpectedly overcome, touched by a memory of his mother singing and tears overwhelmed him. He remembered how beautifully she had sung when he was very young, and he speculated that she might have sung when she was pregnant with him. When he sadly reflected that she no longer sang the sense of loss was palpable. (That evening, when he returned home, he talked with his mother about his early years.)

When he was at prep school he too had had a very good singing voice. He recalled singing *There is a Green Hill Far Away* and being surprised and unsettled to realise that his teacher was visibly moved. It could be speculated that this hymn had provided a channel for expression of his homesickness. However it was significant that he had been disturbed by the realisation that he could touch another human being emotionally and it became increasingly evident that he did not know what to do in such situations.

It seemed that this train of memories was evoked by his feelings about the beginning of analysis. Here at last he could express his grief at the loss of the mother of his early childhood. It is not uncommon for boys who are sent to boarding school at an early age to yearn for an idealised mother. The separation is a rupture that comes too early. Later, in adolescence, separation from the internalised mother (the maternal imago) is not possible because there has been too little actual closeness. From then on all women seem tantalising; offering the hope of the idealised love object but also the constant threat of abandonment. This contributes to a pattern of women being idealised and then denigrated – loved and hated. This pattern had affected all of James's relationships with women and it soon came to be replayed in the transference. I was sometimes experienced as the yearned for home/mother/lover, alternating in quick succession with the boarding school/rejecting mother. Boarding school could be understood as an object of negative transference – loveless and cold.

Snow

The contrast between the warmth James desired and the coldness he had experienced for much of his life came to the fore as he was leaving at the end of one early session. He turned and asked: 'Does it get cold in here when it snows?' Commenting on how effective the heater seemed to be, he observed that it would probably be warm in here. This seemed to indicate that he was experiencing a sense of emotional warmth within the therapeutic relationship. Soon after that it snowed heavily and most people cancelled their sessions, but James arrived on time, saying that it had been a challenge to get through.

The cold was associated with his memory of the move to his parents' present house when he was a small boy. It had been a very cold winter and the snow had lain on the ground for weeks. His mother had hated it and would have preferred to remain in the warmth of her home in the South of France. James remembered the physical discomfort of the cold, which had been compounded by a feeling of emptiness. He recalled waking one night feeling alone and fearing that his parents would die. He had called out in his distress but no one had come to comfort him and he had cried alone all night. This early experience had prefigured the boarding school, suggesting that James's sense of abandonment, whilst associated primarily with boarding school, originated in an earlier developmental stage. His comment about the snow seemed to be an expression of the hope that he might at last find some respite from his life-long sense of isolation and emotional coldness.

The Father

James had a great affinity for the very fine houses that had belonged to his family for generations. He loved and hated with equal intensity the historical town house where his parents still lived. It was surrounded by exceptionally beautiful gardens and had been built by his paternal great-grandfather, an industrialist. It was his understanding that the reason he had been sent away to boarding school was to prepare him for inheriting it and the family business. However when he was 16 his father, assuming that his son was not interested, had sold the business. The house had also been sold to a distant member of the family, on condition that his parents could live in it for the rest of their lives. The garden had been donated to the city council as a public amenity. James had been devastated: the only point he had been able to find in his exile and suffering at boarding school had been snatched from him. He had lost the home he loved and to which he had planned to return. Furthermore his brother had been born at that time and consequently he had lost his status as the only son in the family. Moreover he had been faced with earning his own living, for which he had been totally unprepared. It seemed that his fury at this injustice had psychologically paralysed him and thereafter he had never stayed in a job, completed a course or lived in one place for any length of time.

One of a father's functions is to introduce his son to the world and to help him find a role in life (Samuels, 1985b; Perry, 1991), but James had felt denigrated by his father's actions. His role in the family firm, and therefore his potential as a man, had been negated. This had been compounded by the birth of another boy child, whom James had seen as replacing him. Psychologically it seemed that just at the point when he should have been moving into the outside world he had been dashed back to the maternal realm, but there had been no place for him there either.

James's depression could be understood as masking the fury he felt at these injustices. He talked of revenge, describing himself as like the Count of Monte Cristo, returning after years of exile to wreak his revenge on those who had wronged him. This revenge was directed at his parents; he was now living in their house but he hardly spoke to them and refused to eat their food. Unconsciously it seemed that he was punishing them by inflicting his suffering on them; they were witnesses to it but they could offer nothing. James knew that he must leave his parents' house but he was unable to do so. This house stood for so much in his history that he found it impossible to detach himself from it. Its significance was threaded throughout the analysis.

Intimacy and distance

James, describing his perception of the space between people, said that it was as though people had bubbles around them to keep others at a distance; he felt that his was an awfully big bubble. I reflected on this and asked how he felt about the distance between him and me. His response was that the distance between us was OK at present, but if I were to move closer he would move away. At the conscious level he was referring to physical distance and that I was safe only if I remained in my chair, at a predictable distance from him. However I understood the underlying message to be that I was touching him emotionally, but were I to move emotionally closer to him it would be too much. This became evident in a series of sessions when he began to discuss his sexuality.

James began one day by saying 'I want to off-load', which seemed like a warning to me to listen and not intervene. He remarked that, yesterday I had talked more than I usually do, and when I queried how he had experienced that he said 'I was aware that you were trying to say something for my own good and I looked away because I was thinking about what you said.' He then went on to announce, 'I'm auto-erotic, auto-sexual'. I saw this as having both a conscious meaning and an unconscious one. I understood that the underlying message was that he felt troubled by the relationship between us, and that the interpretation I had made in the previous session had impinged on him. Until then it was as though he had been unaware that he was talking to someone, but on that occasion I had spoken more than usual and so he had noticed, to his frustration, that I was a person, separate from him, not under his control. I often felt rather like a non-person with him and so the statement that he was auto-erotic fitted with this – he could do it himself. His noticing that there were two people present meant that he realised that he did not know how to be with me.

This conformed to the history of his relationships with women. James had had a number of sexual encounters since the break-up of his marriage but he had often unwittingly rejected women he found attractive. There was a lack of subtlety in his negotiations regarding intimacy and distance – it was all or nothing. He began to recount his sexual history. This was clearly difficult for him; he described his first love, a girl he had met at a school dance. It had been very romantic, but he had dropped her suddenly and without explanation after only two weeks because other boys had teased him, saying that they were sweet together. He had not been able to take that. He was in the middle of this story when the time came to end the session, so I stopped him.

In the next session I gave him my Spring break dates and the bill, to which he seemed to pay no attention. Then he continued where he had left off in the previous session. He had been writing his sexual history and had brought it with him, attached to a clipboard. He read from it without looking at me. It was a history of passionate attachments; he had invested every-thing in these idealised relationships, but then had either withdrawn or been rejected. When he was in his twenties he had shared a bed with a young woman for several weeks. She had evidently been attached to James, and he had lain awake wanting her sexually but unable to make the necessary move. He had realised that he needed something first but had not known what it was. It seemed to me that he needed maternal holding before he could be sexual in a relationship.

I was profoundly moved by this account, which felt like a tragic missed opportunity. At the end of the session I once again had to stop him in mid-flow. James's engagement with the process was intensifying. There was a strongly erotic atmosphere and I became aware that I was reluctant to end the session; I identified with the woman in his story. This caused me to reflect that it was likely that she had not wanted him to leave her. Thus it began to become clear that my feelings were countertransference. It fol-lowed that, as well as the story he was reporting, he was telling me that he wanted to move towards me but did not know how to do so.

The next day, when James entered the room I noticed that he looked very pale. This was because he was enraged. In a very angry outburst he told me: 'You wanted emotion – now you get it. You did not notice yesterday I was furious – really angry – you wanted to control me and no one controls me!' He had felt so angry when he left that he had had to stop the car. He said: 'I've always had doubts about psychotherapy – you just sit there and you completely missed the point. I'm not coming back – I can do this myself. This is the most intimate relationship I have had in my life and you just sit there and talk about holiday dates.'

It appeared that the fixed ending time of the session combined with the practical arrangements for my break had been too much for James. Added to the intimate material he was revealing, this seemed a cruel insult to his self-esteem. He seemed to be telling me that he that he had attempted some form of intercourse with me, but this had just confirmed that it was better to remain auto-erotic.

Eventually the tirade stopped, and after a pause I suggested that he was telling me how very painful it had been when I had cut short his account of his intimate relationships. I also confirmed that I had heard him when he said that this was the most intimate relationship he had had in his life. It seemed that he felt hurt to be reminded of the limits of our relationship, especially when there was going to be a break. It reminded me of his pattern of rejecting women who got close to him; perhaps he might want to reject me because I was becoming important to him.

There was a silence and an almost immediate change in his demeanour. He said 'You have persuaded me – I will come back.' He relaxed and then said 'I can talk about anything here – that's right isn't it?' Then he talked about sexual fantasies that were troubling him. At the end of the session he admitted that he had needed to get angry with me: 'I wanted to hurt you and see what happened – to get you to kick me out.' After this session he seemed much relieved and a period of positive transference followed.

Reflections on transference and countertransference

Observing my own responses I realised that I was beginning to feel very engaged with James. An indication of this was that I was often reluctant to end the sessions on time, although I always did so. When he confessed that this was the most intimate relationship he had had in his life I understood this as transference regression to the mother of infancy. Even so I was profoundly moved. There had clearly been an early emotional bond with his mother but it appeared that James had not felt held since then, although it was significant that there had been such a time. Combined with this 'maternal erotic transference' (Wrye and Welles, 1994) there was a sexual attraction. The transference weaves a complex spell that operates simultaneously at different levels that were all constellating in this therapeutic relationship. There was the infant–mother bond and the adolescent love of the Oedipal phase, and at the same time there was the reality of the man–woman dynamic and an attraction that had a basis in reality – I was aware of James as a man and of a mutual sexual attraction evoked by irrefutable fact that we were both adults in an intimate situation. It is the task of analysis to facilitate the development of a conscious attitude, which gradually enables each of these facets of the transference to be understood as belonging to a different developmental phase.

Later James told me that, among his first impressions of me, was that I reminded him of his first serious girl friend. Thus the transference, which was infantile in origin, was complex and composed of evocations of other early attachments. The disparate elements of the psyche that had been invested in different women during James's life now seemed to constellate in the transference, and to evoke a positive attraction and sense of belonging. This was significant because it soon became almost unbearable for James to stay in analysis and this attachment generated the impulse to leave, but ultimately it enabled him to stay.

As well as the transference a certain synchronicity added to my sense of James as special. It is, in my experience, rare that an analysand's material overlaps with one's own life, but when it does it can be a powerful factor in bringing the real relationship to the fore. As James recounted his history I realised that certain events in his life had touched my own. We were of similar age and his boarding school was in the part of the country where I grew up. When he was recounting experiences at his preparatory (first boarding) school he mentioned a boy by name; his mother had been kind to James on out-of-school visits. This boy was a second cousin of mine. Furthermore when James was telling me of the places he had lived I realised that we had lived quite near each other in a different part of the country, and he described political activities with which I too had been closely involved. As far as I know James remained oblivious to these coincidences, but because they were meaningful to me it is almost certain that they played a part at an unconscious level. A situation such as this brings the analyst-as-person to the fore. A decision has to be made about whether disclosure of such links would benefit the patient. In this case I decided against disclosure as I could not see that James would benefit from having this information. He was vulnerable and this would have impinged on the complex transference, which was already well established.

Inevitably it affected the countertransference and compounded my already strong attachment to him. If I had disclosed the connections to him it would have met my own need but not his. When the analyst-as-person is brought into the situation in this way there can be a temptation to breach the analytic boundaries. The potential for sexual acting out was contained in such a situation. There was an attraction and it might have been seductive to disclose a real intimate connection when intimacy was being replayed within the therapeutic bounds. In retrospect these synchronous events could be seen as having had a purpose: they drew me to James and gave me a sense of him as a man outside the consulting room.

My intention in this chapter has been to convey a sense of the considerable erotic involvement in this particular analysis. From the start there was clearly a fit and the analysis started at depth. There was a real mutual attachment that constituted a bond, which later helped to sustain the relationship when it might have otherwise broken down. The individuation process and the therapeutic relationship were well established by the end of the first three months, prior to the diagnosis of cancer that was to colour the rest of the analysis. Already both positive and negative feelings had been expressed and were beginning to become conscious. Furthermore the positive counter transference – the love I felt for him – came to serve an additional purpose once the terminal illness was diagnosed: it enabled me to accompany him in a way that might otherwise have proved difficult.

3 The House and Boarding School: Intimacy and Exile

> Thanks to the house, a great many of our memories are housed, and if the house is a bit elaborate, if it has a cellar and a garret, nooks and corridors, our memories have refuges that are all the more clearly delineated. All our lives we come back to them in our daydreams. A psychoanalyst should therefore turn his attention to this simple localization of our memories (Bachelard, 1964, p. 8).

This evocation by Bachelard of the house as a repository of memory and a sense of place offers a way of understanding its significance as an image in the psyche. People need a shelter; be this a cave or a castle there is an instinct to create safety and warmth, to make a hearth. Even in circumstances of physical deprivation, construction of a refuge is imperative. The very term refugee implies that shelter is a primary need of human kind. It is probably because of this that the house frequently emerges in dreams, in pictures and in the imaginal world as an unconscious representation of the state of the psyche. 'The house is our corner of the world . . . it is our first universe, a real cosmos in every sense of the word' (ibid., p. 4).

The house may symbolise the spaces that are inhabited in emotional life as well as embodied living. If there has been a time when a person has been – so to speak – 'housed', then within the psyche there will be an image of a place of safety that continues to be an emotional refuge in times of crisis. 'In the house itself, the family sitting room, a dreamer of refuges dreams of a hut, of a nest, or of nooks and corners in which he would like to hide away' (ibid., p. 30). The house is an archetypal image, a metaphor for a sense of psychological at-homeness, or homelessness.

Inhabiting

During analysis it soon becomes evident that people who have not been 'housed' safely lack an inner refuge. This is less to do with actual houses than with the sense of at-homeness generated by the shelter of the primary caretaker of infancy and childhood. Early psychological or physical abandonment leaves a scar that may immediately become evident in the transference. This is an observation of analysis in general, but I shall turn again to our central story to illustrate the point. The significance for James of moving into a house of his own was linked to the meaning of the house in his psyche. Therefore some of the recurrent themes of his analysis that were introduced in Chapter 2 will be revisited.

It will be recalled that as a baby James had been sent away from his mother to be cared for by his grandparents. Then as a small boy he had been sent away to boarding school. It became clear that he had experienced both these as abandonment. As a result his home became a longed for and rather idealised image of his existence before the age of eight. His memories of the grand family home alternated with those associated with the cold and unforgiving boarding school:

> Boarding schools don't 'build character' or 'make the man', they break the child, and replace it with a coat of armour filled with fear, loneliness and alienation (a former pupil of a major public school, quoted in Duffell, 2000, p. 31).

This characterised the way in which James had lived his life. Armoured against the pain of relationships, he had kept his true self hidden within the protective bubble that he had described as maintaining the space between him and other people. Part of his inner conflict was the tension between the vulnerable child and the adult bent on revenge. Unable to inhabit the house of his memory, James had become alienated from his 'self'.

The uninhabited house may fall into disrepair, but when it is occupied again it may be restored and enlivened. James identified with the hero in *The Count of Monte Cristo*. In the story, when the hero returns from his years of deprivation and degradation in an isolated dungeon his circumstances are transformed by the inheritance of unlimited opulence. He is not free to enjoy this but rather uses the power it brings to avenge each of his betrayers in turn. This desire for revenge is common in the psychology of the boarding school survivor. However the nostalgic attachment that James felt for the houses in which he had once lived was also a thread of connection to the healthy part of his personality. The following description from *The Count of Monte Cristo* of the overnight transformation of a house that had been uninhabited for years resonates with his engagement in analysis:

> This house, which had appeared only the night before so sad and gloomy . . . awakened from its long sleep, like the Sleeping Beauty in the wood, lived, sang, and bloomed like the houses we have cherished, and in which, when we are forced to leave them we leave a part of our souls (Dumas, 1844 [1990], pp. 628–9).

In real life such a transformation rarely if ever happens overnight; it is a gradual process that can take months or even years and, to pursue our metaphor, it is similar with inhabiting the human psyche. Analysis offers an opportunity for transformation; as the transference ignites the fire of eros it awakens long repressed desires and half-forgotten memories of past homes or states of emotional homelessness. In analysis, therefore, the metaphorical houses where we have 'left part of our souls' are revisited and restored.

Transference and the analyst's room

The house may also offer a metaphor for the analyst's consulting room. When patients enter analysis they enter a space that is set apart from the distractions of everyday life and dedicated to the imaginal world. The bounds of psychotherapy make it possible for the analyst to travel with the patient on a voyage of discovery. For 50 minutes the time and the undivided attention of the analyst is devoted to this one person; to her or his view of the world and life's experiences. To continue with Bachelard's metaphor, it can be as though the room opens out or closes in as the contents of the attics and cellars of the person's buried memories are investigated. In a sense the person riffles through the treasures and terrors that have lain hidden away for years. The contents of the psychological attics and cellars of each person are as different and as similar as the contents of the real ones.

From the analyst's point of view, when someone crosses the threshold the room is transformed; the space is affected by the past history of the person with whom it is shared for 50 minutes. Upon entering, each person reproduces their expectations of how the house will greet them; the threshold of the room can evoke hope for one and trepidation for another. There may be an atmosphere of closeness that transforms the room into an intimate hearth, or of coldness and distance that is chilling. For one the terror associated with some traumatic past event may be re-evoked upon entering the room, whilst for another some past abandonment, unremembered but reconstructed in its present re-enactment, can make the room seem like a huge cavern. The analyst is the temporary keeper of the house, holding the threads of meaning and relatedness.

Transference

As the transference engaged James he moved swiftly into the analytic house. The conflicting feelings that were at the root of his fear of the pain of truly living became live. His question, about whether the heater in my room was effective when it snowed revealed his unconscious desire to find a warm and nurturing environment. Later, as we shall see, many other facets of his psyche were played out in the room. The analytic house is forever changing, never static.

The normal unconscious knows how to make itself at home everywhere, and psychoanalysis comes to the assistance of the ousted unconscious, of the unconscious that has been roughly or insidiously dislodged. But psychoanalysis sets the human being in motion, rather than at rest. It calls on him to live outside the abodes of his unconscious, to enter into life's adventures, to come out of himself (Bachelard, 1964, p. 10).

Analysis did indeed set James in motion; it 'called to him' to 'come out of himself', out of exile and into community. James had been in exile; his life had been spent psychologically alone. Now, with the analyst as witness, he began to recount the story of his life, as if for the first time, and to take it seriously. It became clear that a part of his being was still lost in the vast institution to which he had been banished at eight years of age. A tremendous sense of loss became live in the present as the depths that had remained hidden to him for years opened up through the transference. Within the first three months the therapeutic relationship had become 'the most intimate relationship I have had in my life'. This attachment immediately evoked an echo of the mother–child bond. The effect of this was a reciprocal attachment, which is not surprising. As Bachelard writes, 'There does not exist a real intimacy that is repellent. All the spaces of intimacy are designated by an attraction. Their being is well-being' (ibid., p. 12). Intimacy and distance were a constant theme. As memories associated with his mother became conscious it became clear that James was still attached by a thread to the mother of his early years. Gradually this revealed the meaning of his investment in continuing to live with his parents in their house.

The house and transference

Each one of us then should speak of his roads, his crossroads, his roadside benches: each one of us should make a surveyor's map of his lost fields and meadows (ibid., p. 11).

Houses appeared in the account of James's life, in his imagination and fantasies. People had failed James but the houses of his childhood had remained constant, and when he recalled them they evoked a yearning nostalgia. It was houses rather than people that seemed to symbolise intimacy in James's inner world. Yet, except for the brief time when he was married, he had 'never been housed'. The problem was that the houses of James's memories were very grand. His love for these beautiful places was vividly conveyed when he described how, as a child, he had delighted to play in their vast grounds. As he recounted their pleasures it was clear that it was there that he had 'left a part of his soul'. It seemed that these houses symbolised maternal protection and shelter as well as his place in the world. Thus the house in which he grew up became the symbol of the mother for whom he yearned.

When James was a boy the biggest houses in the French town where he had lived had seemed to him tiny and he had wondered how people could live in them. This was the view of a financially privileged child but, despite assumptions to the contrary, affluence is not always a benefit. When, due to altered circumstances, the family house in the UK was sold James had been devastated. His anticipated status in the world had become unattainable and this was experienced as a great betrayal. When James embarked on life he was unable to invest in a place other than that of his childhood promised land. Psychologically he was ill-equipped for earning a living or for residing in an ordinary house, but his aspirations no longer matched the reality of his situation. Any residence to which he could now realistically aspire paled into insignificance beside the magnificence of his childhood homes. Unable to accept anything of a lesser scale, everything seemed hopeless and James surrendered to the life of the imagination at the expense of living. The associated depression and underlying fury at times overwhelmed him.

Exile and boarding school

> Those original solitudes, the childhood solitudes leave indelible marks on certain souls. Their entire life is sensitised for poetic reverie, for a reverie which knows the price of solitude (Bachelard, 1960, p. 99).

For the adult, who as a child was banished at six, seven or eight years of age into a boarding school, the solitude to which he may return is rarely one of poetic reverie. Rather the boarding school child continues to reside in a place of lonely abandonment. The rude imposition of such an institution places the child in the position of exile. Forever after, that, seeking a place of safety, the person is perpetually searching for the place from whence he came. James had returned to his home during the holidays but had been unable to tell anyone about his distress. His physical need for shelter had been accommodated but, even when he had been with others he had been unable to authentically communicate with them. This sense of exile had continued into his adult life; he was arrested at the point of abandonment. Lacan (1977, p. 62) evokes this when he writes of a 'centrifugal tracing', a returning to the site of abandonment. This unconscious retracing is a perpetual quest, to repair a life that has been suddenly disrupted.

The tragedy is that very often the mother is as distressed as the child, but she complies with the expectations of the British class system. Duffell describes his own experience when his mother left him at boarding school:

> Crying was not done in those days, neither by mother nor child. Tears of loneliness were never permissible in front of other children, but you might get away with it in two places where there was some privacy – under the sheets or in the toilets. At my school, however, the

toilets were doorless, to guard against other equally prohibited activities (Duffell, 2000, p. 33).

Duffell describes the difficulty of speaking about this trauma because of the common assumption that boarding school is a badge of social privilege. It is the wealthy who can afford to send their children away to boarding school, and this puts tremendous social pressure on what he calls 'the survivor' not to make a fuss. The accounts in Duffell's book reveal two categories of survivor: those who continue within the system and enter the army, the law or banking, and those who are paralysed by the experience and, usually unconsciously, continue to fight the system. James was one of the latter. He was exceptionally bright and seemed destined for one of the top universities, but he had failed to fulfil this promise. We came to understand his unconscious motivation for giving up all the projects, courses and jobs he had begun in life through a particularly vivid example. As a mature student he had embarked on a course, and for one particular assignment he had been given an A grade. His tutor had been so impressed with the essay that he had sought James out to discuss it. James had reacted by tearing up the essay and leaving the course, thereby transforming his success into failure. Until he came into analysis he did not understand why he should have reacted so strongly. It seemed that unconsciously he had felt that to succeed, and hence to fulfil his potential, would have been to collude with the system he despised.

Duffell shows that this too is typical when he describes boarding school survivors' bewilderment at their paradoxical responses to the world. According to one of these survivors:

> I connect my debilitating 'fear of failure' with the fact that so much was 'expected' and one is not allowed to be just anybody. [Instead of going to university] I suffered a kind of paralysis, avoiding challenge, not able to compete, unable to fulfil my 'promise' (ibid., p. 59).

The demands of institutional life, met at the expense of the inner world of the child, marks the person for the rest of their lives. The boarding school child is sent away from hearth and home, and parents, siblings, pets and all that is familiar is lost. When he or she returns in the holidays there is barely time to feel at home before the ritual of packing for the new term starts again (ibid.)

In terms of 'the simple localization of [his] memories' (Bachelard, 1964, p. 8) with which this chapter began, in James's mind there was either the parental home/mother that he had loved and lost, or a lonely image of a cold boarding school. Instead of refuge, his memory carried the pain of loss and abuse that he had suffered in the stark male institution. There was no hearth, no place of intimacy in which to rest. Hopelessness came to dominate his life. As a boy he had been powerless, unable to change his situation. As he grew up his fury at these injustices had turned inward and he continued to feel powerless. He had been unconscious of just how angry he had been until it began to emerge in the transference.

It became clear that the breaks in analysis evoked the abandonment he had experienced at the end of each vacation. The associated expectation that intimate attachments would cause pain and were therefore dangerous had resulted in the severing of all his intimate relationships. This was replayed in analysis as the unconscious fear that the therapeutic relationship would be severed by the breaks, resulted in behaviour that was rejecting and hostile. It reached its extreme when the analysis nearly broke down completely, as will be described in Chapter 8. During James's analysis long extinguished hopes and dreams, now came to life. It was as if analysis became for James an interim home; a place to experience multiple emotions and to grieve for past losses and injuries. The significance of the meaning of houses became conscious and James realised he was psychologically homeless; living with his parents but pretending to be far away. He gradually came to recognise that this was an outdated way of being and was no longer relevant to his present life. Thus the glimmer of hope of a move and the possibility of a relationship became a reality after a lifetime of emotional exile. The tragedy was that, as he began to come emotionally alive, James's life expectancy was drastically reduced.

The house and the body

> The house as a home arouses strong, spontaneous associations with the human body and human thought (Circlot, 1962, p. 153).

As well as a metaphor for the psyche the house may become a metaphor for the body. Embodied living is a form of inhabiting; the body is the location of the self. This becomes evident when someone is seriously ill, because in stories about the house, anxieties about the body and its deterioration are ever present. As James's illness progressed, talk of what was happening to his house or his car reflected his growing awareness of the fragility of his embodied existence. The concrete reality of the physical world became a metaphor for the psychological, and the psychological for the physical.

It was not until a few months before he died that James was at last able to find himself a place to make a home. This was clearly an important part of the resolution of his life's journey. Analysis enabled him to find a psychological home within himself, which freed him to leave the parental shelter and to establish a separate identity. This was a significant aspect of his individuation, but it was hard won, as the following chapters will show.

Part Two

Dreams and the Erotic Transference and Countertransference

4 Dreams

In the early stage of analysis the natural healing potential of the psyche is set in motion. One indication that a process of psychological transformation has commenced can be found in the dreams reported by the patient. Later in this chapter we shall consider the first dream James related in his analysis – a 'big dream' from long ago. At this stage attention to the form and presentation of the dream takes precedence over the content; the beginning of the transference is revealed in the manner and timing of its delivery rather than in the dream narrative. In Chapter 5 two dreams associated with the diagnosis and treatment of a life-threatening illness will be discussed, while in Chapter 6 a sequence of dreams will be considered in order to show the manner in which the transference becomes manifest in dream narratives. First, however, we shall investigate some background theory that elucidates the psychological significance of dreams.

Freud

Freud considered all dreams to be meaningful. His view of the psyche was that traumatic events or wishes that are unacceptable to the conscious mind are repressed and become unconscious. Very often these relate to infantile sexuality. In later life these repressed memories, unconsciously press to the fore and find form in obsessional thoughts or actions. It is the psycho-analytic task to restore the unconscious origins of these 'symptoms' to consciousness. One means of gaining access to these repressed drives and memories is through the free association method. This is derived from Freud's earlier work with hypnosis. In free association the patient is encouraged to lie on the couch and to report all the thoughts that come to mind without censoring them (Freud, 1900, pp. 101–2). The chains of associations are traced and sometimes lead to the underlying unconscious wish or traumatic memory. Another pathway is through the dreams of the patient.

By exploring his own dreams and those of his adult patients Freud came to realise that dreams enfold complex meanings in coded form. Whilst some relate to forgotten childhood memories, others are evoked by more recent incidents. Freud noted that condensation takes place, and very often the processing of the associated thoughts and feelings takes more space than the original account of the dream. It is when the manifest content is unpacked and supplemented by what Freud called 'dream-thoughts' that its latent meaning is revealed. 'The dream-thoughts and the dream-content are presented to us like two versions of the same subject-matter in two different languages' (ibid., p. 277). This approach to dreams is sometimes considered to be reductive, as if everything in a dream can be explained, and so it is of note that while Freud believed that most aspects of a dream could be analysed, he wrote that it is 'never possible to be sure that a dream has been completely interpreted' (ibid., p. 279).

Whilst Freud saw the dreams as being woven from the residues of the day, from responses to bodily sensations or childhood memories, Jung considered that these were merely the first, most accessible layer of the unconscious. Another 'collective' layer lies beneath the personal unconscious and archetypal themes arise from this collective unconscious and take form in dreams, myth and images. Although some consider these to have a biological foundation (for example Stevens, 1995), in my opinion it is more helpful to view them as the products of culture. Like Freud, Jung regarded dreams as a central means of 'opening up an avenue to the unconscious' (Jung, 1928, p. 3), but he viewed the dream as a 'thing in itself'. For Jung, dreams are the 'facts of the unconscious' and therefore cannot always be decoded or fully depotentiated. There are times when all we can hope for is to attain a conscious attitude in relation to them. This fits his view that 'in analysis we must be very careful not to assume that we know all about the patient' (ibid.) Thus ultimately it is the patient who is the expert on himself and the doctor must respect this.

Jung's trust in the autonomy of the psyche, given the right circumstances, led to the concept of active imagination. This differs from Freud's free association method in that the material presented by the patient is amplified rather than decoded. Active imagination is not limited to the processing of dreams; it is a form of reverie, whilst awake, of imagery spontaneously arrived at or induced by associations or elaboration. Thus when processing a dream the dreamer might be encouraged to engage in reverie, whereby the dream is developed and new avenues may be opened up. Sometimes dreams may be amplified with reference to relevant myths or fairy tales introduced by the patient or, when appropriate, the analyst.

Dreams and the body

When considering analysis in the case of physical illness, the relation of psyche to soma is clearly of interest. Freud noted that simple external events such as a cover falling off the bed or the ringing of an alarm clock, might become incorporated into a dream. Similarly 'internal (subjective) sensory excitations' such as ringing in the ears or impressions left on the retina by changes in light might be incorporated in the dream narrative. Words or names heard during the day are sometimes, like visual images, repeated in a dream, often in apparently bizarre contexts (Freud, 1900, p. 33). These are simple and easily explained impingements. More complicated is the question of whether the psyche knows, at some unconscious level, when a physical disease is present. Dreams have been considered significant in this regard from the earliest times. Freud refers to Hippocrates and Aristotle, both of whom suggested that the presence of disease in the body might first be revealed in a dream (ibid., pp. 3, 33).

Jung provides many accounts of dreams that appear to indicate the presence of some bodily disturbance or disease. He also gives examples of dreams that might be considered prophetic, and so it is important to make a distinction. In ancient times dreams were believed to be prophetic, therefore in some cultures dreams were recounted daily and accorded a social and political function. Jung writes of cultures in which the leader was believed to get his thoughts 'straight from heaven' via dreams (Jung, 1928, p. 5). Today dreams are less integrated into Western culture and so it is unusual to give them attention in the way that psychoanalysis does. However recent experiments in 'social dreaming' attend to dreams as indicative of the state of a group. (Bion, 1968; Lawrence, 2000). Members of social dreaming groups meet, usually in the morning prior to the work of the day, and report their dreams. The dreams are listened to and respected, but they are not interpreted or decoded on a personal level. As the dreams are recounted their connections become evident and the unconscious preoccupations of the group gradually emerge. Thus dreams become a significant means of attending to the group unconscious, adding to the depth of relating to the task of the meeting in question.

Jung recounts an example of a prophetic dream. An acquaintance of his dreamed that 'he stepped out into space from the top of a mountain' (Jung, 1960, p. 81). Jung was concerned about the meaning of this dream and told his acquaintance that his unconscious could be warning him to take care on dangerous mountaineering expeditions. Just 'a few months later while climbing a mountain he actually did step off into space and was killed' (ibid.) The sceptic might dismiss the link as an interesting coincidence, but there are many other examples of prophetic dreams, especially in the Jungian literature. This raises the question of whether they take us any further towards understanding the human psyche. It is important to acknowledge that there is a problem with this whole area of investigation, which is compounded by the fact that the discussion is nearly always informed by the benefit of hindsight. The inexplicable nature of such events means that respect for the dream as 'a thing in itself' entails a suspension of disbelief.

Some of the writings on this topic take us to the edge of pure speculation. Jaffe (1958), a Jungian analyst and close collaborator of Jung, collected many accounts of mysterious experiences and folk tales bordering on the paranormal. There are many examples of synchronicity and this is a reminder that mysteries cannot always be explained. Synchronicity is the acausal connecting principle of which Jung wrote at length. He noticed that certain

experiences bring together a real outer-world incident and some inner experience in a way that is beyond coincidence. This he attributed to the acausal
connecting principle of the universe (Jung, 1955). The main lesson to be
derived from this is that it is important to keep an open mind about such
incidents, particularly when the psychological consequences of bodily
deterioration are of paramount interest, as in James's case. There are no
examples of prophetic dreams in this book, but the dream sequences that
are recounted reveal the changing relation of James to his body and his
awareness of the progress of the disease.

Since the time of Freud and Jung, laboratory research on sleep and
dreaming has led to a far greater understanding of the subject. Hall (1977)
reviews the literature on this topic and suggests 'that it might be possible
to find more detailed correlations between the dreams of an individual
patient and changes in his physical condition (Hall, 1977, p. 194). He
provides dramatic anecdotal reports, such as a dream of '"something
exploding inside" prior to the diagnosis of an aortic aneurysm'. Welman
and Faber's (1992) research into dreams of patients who were dying was
aimed at drawing attention to the psychotherapeutic needs of such
patients. Their point, with which I concur, is that depression is too easily
accepted as a normal part of the process of dying. Quoting Jung, they
suggest that dying is part of the individuation process and that depression
may well indicate unfinished business that would benefit from the attention provided by analysis.

Welman and Faber observe that animals are often present in the dreams
of the dying, and they quote Jung's view that animals in dreams may 'indicate an organic condition' (Jung, 1935). However animals are often present
in the dreams of perfectly healthy people, so a certain scepticism is again
required. However Welman and Faber give a notable example of a series of
dreams in which animals that were at first sedentary became active. The
therapist was concerned that this might indicate an organic disease so
the patient was advised to have a physical examination. This revealed the
presence of a cancer. Hence detection of the disease was the direct result of
the analyst paying attention to the dreams, and the subsequent treatment
was successful because of the early diagnosis (Welman and Faber, 1992,
p. 66). Consequently this is an area that merits continued research.

Different types of dream

Freud observed that in the transition from waking to sleeping there is a
change in thought-activity from concepts to images. 'As voluntary activity
gives way to sleep involuntary ideas arise and take form in images' (Freud,
1900, p. 49). It is this borderline area between waking and dreaming that
is the source of much creativity. Writers and artists often report that ideas
emerge just before falling asleep. Psychoanalysis attempts to emulate this

state through the free association method, which could be regarded as a creative venture. The patient is encouraged to lie on the couch and to observe any involuntary thoughts, in an attempt to reproduce the state between waking and dreaming within the analytic frame (ibid., p. 102).

Both Freud and Jung made a distinction between different types of dream. Freud distinguished simple from complex dreams. Simple dreams are those in which the residues of the day are processed, whilst complex dreams can be wish-fulfilling, hallucinatory or regressive. Jung, when discussing cultures in which dreams were an accepted means of making decisions, points out that there are two distinct kinds of dream and these merit different kinds of attention: the 'great vision, big, meaningful, and of collective importance; and . . . the ordinary small dream' (Jung, 1928, p. 4). It is similar in analysis with big dreams. Even when the action of the dream cannot be recalled upon waking, a residual trace remains as an embodied feeling, and the dream may be remembered at a later time when its significance enters consciousness. Thus the sense impression of a big dream may last into the next day or the days that follow, and some big dreams have such a powerful impact that they are always remembered. Whilst complex or big dreams are compelling and demand the dreamer's attention, simple or small dreams are noted in passing and are often forgotten.

Transference

Dreams have differing significance with regard to the transference. The content of some dreams reveals the transference whilst the transference implications of other dreams is less clear. For example if a dream figure resembles the analyst or the dream is set in a room with similar features to the consulting room, it is likely that the transference is active. Many dreams do not incorporate the analyst at all, but the impact of the therapeutic relationship may nonetheless be detected in the manner of their presentation. Let us consider this.

In the context of a therapeutic relationship the dreamer is affected by the presence of the analyst. It may be unusual but exciting to have someone who is interested in understanding dreams. However this is not always simple; when a dream is being discussed, and the analyst senses that the analysand's heart is not in the account, the manner of presentation demands attention. There may be an assumption that the analyst expects dreams and so the dream is recounted, not because it is puzzling or interesting, but because the patient thinks that is what she or he is supposed to do. Alternatively the analysand may not know what to talk about in a session, so recounts a dream to fill the space. In both cases the analyst is likely to detect that the report is almost mechanical. Furthermore to report some dreams may feel like unacceptable self-exposure; it may cause shame to recount a dream involving bodily functions or sexual acts, so shameful or sexual dreams are sometimes 'forgotten'. If the analyst is alert she or he may sense that something is being left out. Numerous other affects are evoked by the telling of a dream and sometimes an erotic or fearsome aspect of a dream may become live in the room. Again the transference is centrally involved, but this time in the telling rather than in the dreaming. Attention to the presentation may bring relief and enable further exploration of the dream, therefore the manner of its presentation is highly significant.

Whether conscious or not, dreams, like pictures, have an aesthetic impact within the analytic setting. The account of a dream may be seductive, in that it can be like listening to a short story or a poem that encapsulates the essence of something that could have no other form of articulation. Some dreams may fascinate, weaving the analyst and the dreamer into the narrative; they can be labyrinthine in their symbolic complexity. Others reveal their purpose in a barely disguised form, simply presenting the facts of the unconscious for the conscious mind to view.

A brief detour into the world of art and pictorial imagery may clarify the approach that follows. My interest in dreams follows from my analysis of several series of pictures that explore the influence on the transference– countertransference dynamic of art objects made within the therapeutic setting (Schaverien, 1991, 1995, 1997, 1999b). Viewed sequentially dreams, like pictures, reveal much about the psyche and therefore a similar approach is taken to a sequence of dreams. However the difference between dreams and pictures needs to be stated. A dream, recounted, is different from a picture, shown, and amplification of this difference may help when considering the dreams that follow. Elsewhere, using a term borrowed from Cassirer, I have suggested that a picture presented in therapy 'may "uncloak" an image of which the artist was previously unconscious' (Schaverien, 1991, p. 7). The idea is that the picture reveals rather than tells. Dreams too may be considered to 'uncloak the image', and they too reveal rather than tell. Both might be seen as examples of that which Cassirer (1957, p. 93) calls 'the pure phenomenon of expression'. However there are significant differences. In some cases pictures come to embody affect that might otherwise have no other mode of expression. Pictures are physical objects and the embodiment can take place in a very concrete sense; a picture can be seen, held and stored in a way that dreams cannot. Nonetheless dream images too offer a mode of articulation for otherwise inexpressible affect, but in a more fleeting and transient form.

When viewing a picture in a therapeutic context both of those present regard the same image. Although their perceptions of it may differ, the image itself is unchanging; it is a concrete object with a physical presence. Similarly when I write about pictures made by patients it is possible to present them as illustrations in the text. The reader can then view the image, so there is some common ground. An aspect of the actual material from the session can be viewed in an unchanged form. Dreams are different from this; it is in their nature that some distortion is bound to take place.

A dream is essentially a mental image which is either recounted verbally or depicted visually and, in the process, it is inevitably changed. The dreamer has a mind picture of a series of events or images that have been experienced in a sensate form. These are transient and cannot be conveyed in their original state. When they are translated into words subtle changes occur because the dreamer may not be able to find the right words to convey the images in their mind. The analyst forms her own set of images and associations in response to the description. The account of a dream is treated like other material through attention to her/his own responses. As the analyst listens and monitors her own sensory experiences she is also aware of the atmosphere of the session. Whatever the situation, dreams are mediated within the transference–countertransference dynamic. Thus the depth and progress of therapy may be both revealed and influenced by the presentation of dreams.

We shall return now to James's story and his dreams. The notes I made after each session form the basis of this account, along with the original description of the dreams. However, even during the session there was no way that I could see the same images that James saw in his mind's eye as he recounted his dreams. Similarly you will see an image or chain of images and form your own mind pictures. It is always thus; when a dream is recounted each person forms her or his own mental images in response. In the telling the dream is removed from its original context and therefore some form of distortion is inevitable. That is the reason why awareness of the transference is so important – it gives a new context in which to relate the dream. This is especially important when the content is of an archetypal nature as this can take the patient, and sometimes the therapist, into an imaginal world that bears little relation to everyday life. Thus analysis needs to be rooted in the present context, in the here and now of the therapeutic relationship.

In the first month of analysis (the period described in Chapter 2.) James brought a 'big dream' from his past. He had been 24 years old when he had dreamed this dream and it had remained important to him ever since. According to Freud (1900, p. 43), whilst many dreams are forgotten upon waking, certain dreams remain significant for many years, and he recalls one of his own dreams that was 'separated by thirty seven years from today and yet as fresh as ever in my memory'. James's was such a dream.

Dream 1: January, year 1

> *I was at home, at the house of my parents. [The same house where he was now living and to which he was so attached.] I was walking on one of the paths there and saw before me a huge Golden Egg surrounded by many animals. There were reptiles, a castle and a dragon.*

The response to a dream from so long ago needs to be measured. The content is clearly important but to attend to that immediately without first questioning its presentation in the current context would be to miss much of the analytic potential. Now in his mid forties, James had been a young man on the threshold of adult life when he had had this dream. Jung (1931) observed psychological differences at different stages of life. Some people seek analysis during the middle years of life (around 35–40) in order to liberate some underdeveloped psychological potential. The fact that this dream was presented at the beginning of analysis seems to indicate such a motivation. Emotionally and psychologically James was much younger than his chronological age. He recalled this dream very soon after recounting his early experiences. It was as though he had already brought to analysis parts of himself from different developmental stages that needed attention. Along with the baby, who had been sent away at four months, and the boy of eight who was sent to boarding school, it seemed he needed to bring into the light the young man he had been in his twenties. At that time he had been on the threshold of adult life and contemplating his future. Now, at the beginning of analysis, his anticipation was renewed. Hence this first dream revealed the hope with which the analysis was already invested.

James said that he had considered the dream to be archetypal and had been so impressed by it at the time that he had confided it to his closest friend. He had been devastated when his friend made fun of it and laughed at him, and ever since he had been suspicious of 'amateur psychology'. It seemed to me that he was expressing concern about the safety of the analysis. He was evidently anxious about how I would receive his dream, so I suggested that he might be worried that I too might be an 'amateur psychologist' and laugh if he told me his dreams. Sometimes the effect of an interpretation is immediate. James's relief was evident and he recounted another incident, this time with a teacher who had ridiculed him. Thus one aspect of the presentation of this dream was that it was a way for James to test how I would respond if he brought vulnerable aspects of himself into analysis.

Having negotiated the presentation of the dream the pathway to the symbolic significance of the various aspects of its imagery was opened up. Let us first consider the place. The location of this dream was his parents' house, which as we know held enormous symbolic significance in his inner world. The path on which the dream took place was outside the house and was reminiscent of the lane he had looked down at the age of four, a lane that had seemed to go on forever. Therefore this house was much more than just a house; his destiny and aspirations had been tied up in it. It was the place from which he had started and for which he had yearned in his absence. The boarding school experience had left him with an intense longing for his mother and so the house symbolised home for him in a very deep and profound sense. Furthermore it was there he returned at times of crisis. The dream place was the background for the archetypal imagery and led to a castle – an archetypal image of the house – and a dragon. As the colloquial saying goes, 'a man's home is his castle', and in fairy tales castles are very often defended by dragons, which have to be overcome by the hero in order to rescue an imprisoned maiden or obtain treasure. We already know from Chapter 2 that James had learned not to cry; he had been given the message that girls cried but boys did not. Thus the vulnerable, receptive aspect of James's nature had been split off and hidden, even from himself. In classical Jungian terms, the castle might be considered to be an image of the archetypal feminine. The castle, viewed in this light, could be seen as holding the split-off feminine aspect of James's psyche; the undervalued aspect of James's personality that was hidden and defended by the fierce and unapproachable 'castle' exterior. This interpretation of this dream was complemented by a later dream in which he enters a fortress (dream 6, Chapter 6).

The reptiles, with their primordial nature also heralded, creatures he was to encounter later in his analytic journey. The imagery is certainly compelling and archetypal, and the central image – the huge golden egg – is very special. The egg is often considered to symbolise the world and wholeness, and the fact that this one was huge and golden added to its power. An egg carries the potential of new life, and when we recall that James had earlier said that he had been 'looking for "this" all his life' we may understand this as presenting a new, as yet unborn, part of the self. It was as if aspects of the self that needed attention had been held in thrall, waiting for the conditions that would permit them to be released. Therefore the dream was complex, revealing diverse aspects of the psyche that James wanted to bring into the light.

None of the above was said out loud; to analyse the dream in great detail at that stage might have stifled it with too much cognitive understanding. Rather the facts of psyche, as presented by the dream, were brought into the open. Interpretations of the context, the transference and James's anxiety about bringing something so special into analysis were made. The arche typal nature of the dream was now out in the light and the image was 'uncloaked'.

The dream was presented in the first month of therapy, when James also informed me, with some sense of achievement, that he had stopped taking the antidepressants. The following week he found out that he would not be prosecuted for the drink-driving charge and so he began to commit himself to the process. However this was by no means straightforward. His depression and sense of hopelessness still dominated and he often said he wanted to die. What was the point in it all; he could not continue to live with his parents and he would soon be unable to afford to continue analysis so he might as well give up. He knew that the solution was to get a job, but it all felt too much. This negative attitude was a veiled attack on the analysis and it eventually gave way to the fury described in Chapter 2. Thus at the same time that the psyche was 'set in motion' in a positive sense, another part of him was resisting fiercely. It seemed that depression and helplessness were masking James's anger that no one was going to rescue him, that he would have to find his own way out of the impasse.

Any discussion of dreams in analysis is necessarily tentative because they are multifaceted, elusive and essentially ambiguous. It is an area of investigation that leads into metaphysics, religion, mysticism and spirituality. Therefore it could be dismissed as too ephemeral for empirical study. However Jung suggests that dreams present 'the facts of the unconscious' to the dreamer. They present what is known at some preconscious level but which is yet unknown to the conscious mind. It is in this spirit that, in the following chapters, I present the dreams of James.

5 Dreams and Diagnosis

As already stated it is questionable whether dreams can be regarded as pre-dictive. Nonetheless in this chapter two of James's dreams will be discussed in relation to the diagnosis of a life-threatening illness. The first could, in retrospect, be seen as revealing an unconscious awareness that all was not well. The second, a 'waking' dream, demonstrates how the psyche can produce the images it needs in times of crisis.

Whilst James was becoming increasingly involved in the psychological processes evoked by analysis, concern about his physical state began to dawn. During February he began to suspect that there was something organically wrong with him. At first he dismissed his symptoms as psycho-somatic and attributed them to the overwhelming sense of depression he was experiencing. However when he mentioned them to his GP she referred him for a physical investigation. Then James had a dream that seemed to indicate that something was amiss. While it was a simple dream rather than the 'big dream' described in the previous chapter, it implied much more than its simple theme suggests.

Dream 2: 7 March, year 1

'*All my teeth were falling out.*' James could remember no more. When prompted, his associations were of a time when his mother had a toothache and he had developed an ache in the same tooth. Then he recalled another time when she thought she had cancer, but it had turned out to be a false alarm. Considering this, he thought it would be similar with the tests he was having, that they too would be a false alarm. With the benefit of hindsight it seems that, as well as revealing his strong identification with his mother through his associations, this dream suggested a preconscious awareness that something was physically wrong.

I was uneasy that the dream might indicate that he was more ill than any-one realised. However neither of us knew this yet, so it was important not to treat the dream as prophetic as it might unnecessarily frighten the dreamer. 'Teeth falling out' is among those dreams that Freud considers as 'typical' (Freud, 1900, p. 37), but it does not always indicate ill-health. Moreover there is rarely a single meaning to any dream so it was important to stay with not knowing. When the dreamer is ready the realisation will dawn with very lit-tle help from the analyst. At times like this the analyst may refrain from speculation and let the dream and its potential meaning rest in the space between the dreamer and the analyst. The phenomenon is 'bared', and when the time is right the meaning will become clear. If, in the associations, the dreamer appears anxious that the dream might indicate illness, it needs to be spoken about. Therefore James's identification with his mother's situation was acknowledged; it indicated his anxiety about the tests. I did not make explicit what I perceived as the disintegration aspect of the dream. Research by Hall (1977) and Welman and Faber (1992) suggests that a dream might lead to diagnosis but I am sceptical about this. Even in a case where tests are not underway I would be reticent to suggest that a dream might indicate physical illness because dreams can have so many other meanings.

For example James's dream of his teeth falling out could have indicated a form of psychological disintegration as his initial defences were breaking down in the analysis. It could also have referred to regression; reverting to a toothless infant state. However in the context of James's fury with me in recent sessions it was likely that it was an unconscious reference to his fear of the potentially damaging effects of his anger. Without teeth it is not possible to bite. I suggested this to him and it led to a discussion of his difficulty with being angry, especially with women. The pattern established as a child when he would be in trouble if he made his sisters cry continued to inhibit many of his present interactions. His terror of his anger and its consequent repression were to become increasingly significant. Thus this dream had many possible meanings.

The following week a chest X-ray revealed a shadow on his lung and James was recalled immediately for further investigations. Recognising the potential seriousness of the situation he said, 'Only one thing gets this sort of reaction – they think it is cancer!' Understandably, for the rest of that week the analytic sessions focused on his anxiety. Because he smoked he was worried about what the tests might reveal. The psychological significance of his smoking now came to the fore. James was ashamed of how he imagined his lungs would look. He thought he would be told to stop smoking and said, 'Doctors don't bother with you if you smoke'. He had first started smoking in the company of his grandparents, who had looked after him when he had been a baby. Reflecting on how very fond of them he was, and the fact that the sucking action of the cigarette was an important part of his pleasure, he thought that for him smoking symbolised love. Thus it was that he made the link with his yearning for the breast. In his embarrassment about being found out there was unconscious reference to his secret inner life that he feared would be revealed by the investigations.

There was another aspect to smoking – when he was angry he often sucked deeply on a cigarette. He vividly described the sensation: it was like drawing the anger in, 'like a ball of fire inside'. When he had been furious with me over my break dates he had said that he wanted to bring in his cigarettes. His presumption had been that my room was a no smoking area, thus his impulse to contaminate or to violate the analytic/maternal space was very clear. It revealed one reason why James was so reticent about show-ing his anger: he feared the immense destructiveness of his repressed feel-ings. If he did not suck in his anger he might wreak havoc. In terms of the erotic transference his desire to contaminate could be understood as an attack on the maternal body/room.

This brought his envy of me into the open. The transference was complex. We explored how I was to be envied as a woman. Women had a better deal; they seemed to have the power but were also mysterious to him. On the one hand they were known and very familiar, like his sisters, but to the public school boy in him they were strange and unfamiliar. Then he perceived me has having achieved the things that he could not attain: a place to live and a job. Most of all I was envied for having something he desired and for which he had to pay. Like his mother I appeared to have the power to withhold what he needed. He recalled being told that, when he was a baby, the doctor had advised his mother to use a smaller holed teat on the feeding bottle so that he would have to 'work for it'. Recalling this he was furious. A part of him wished to spoil all he saw me as possessing. This included attacking my health by smoking cigarettes in my room. In his mind he was breaking all the perceived rules.

These angry feelings were tempered by a strong attachment. His increas-ing investment in me became evident as the multi-layered facets of the thera-peutic relationship were revealed. The transference was playing its magical tricks and all manner of aspects of woman and women in his psyche were becoming manifest in the guise of the analyst. At the same time there was a strong therapeutic alliance, which enabled him to trust that there was some-one present who stood outside his confusion and was able to think. It was very important in the present situation for this alliance to hold.

It might seem strange that someone who had periodically contemplated suicide, most recently a few weeks earlier, now wanted passionately to live. James had never actually attempted suicide, although in the past he had neglected himself to the point where he might have faded away. While sui-cidal thoughts can and sometimes do lead to actual suicide, there are times when they express desperation rather than intent. There is a significant distinction between suicide and death by natural causes; between contem-plating taking things into one's own hands, possibly as a result of repressed or unconscious anger, and being faced with the prospect of dying from a disease. It is a question of control: the person who commits suicide may feel in control of their destiny, but with a terminal illness there is a sense of powerlessness; such a death is unpredictable and awesome. As with an unforgiving authority figure or being sent away to school, there is no arguing or pleading with it.

Now that James's anger and destructiveness had been openly admitted and the analysis had survived, his trust in the structure of the setting and in me seemed to deepen. He began to report every detail of his lonely days and nights, his anxieties and fears, patterns of sleeping and waking, and his contact, or lack of contact, with people. He endured several more tests and every aspect – physical and emotional – of his visits to the hospital were recounted. This included the pain and discomfort of the tests and what the doctors said to him. This was very much as a small child might report every detail of its day and its bodily experiences to a parent in an attempt to allay anxiety and process the experience. Thus I was drawn into his world and became intensely concerned and emotionally involved.

Diagnosis

James had first come to see me in December and it was exactly three months later that cancer was diagnosed. Fortuitously James's next analytic session took place immediately after the hospital appointment. It was evident as he walked in the door that he was in a traumatised state. Without pausing to sit down he said: 'It's as bad as it could be – lung cancer – and it is in the lymph system already.' Then, sitting down, he said in a dazed manner: 'I'm probably dying . . . I've only had it a few months.'

Gradually he was able to recount how this devastating news had been conveyed. He had been told not by the consultant with whom he had become familiar, but by a junior doctor. Having delivered the initial blow the doctor had told him it was likely that he had only two to six months to live. The diagnosis and the unceremonious way in which it had been delivered were totally overwhelming and incomprehensible to him. He was clearly in shock.

There is a skill to delivering news of this type, especially to a patient who is unaccompanied. People unconsciously select to hear only aspects of such news because it cannot be assimilated all in one go. James, being the person he was, had probably seemed confident and asked questions. He also seemed to have remembered most of the answers. Perhaps he had even appeared to be someone who could cope with such a diagnosis with ease. However professionals whose unenviable task it is to give such messages to patients need to be alert to the impact that a death sentence can have on even the most apparently self-assured person.

As James became calmer and better able to think he confided that his immediate problem was the family. He could not bear to tell them as it would upset them. He was unused to sharing his troubles and he expected to bear this alone, as he had done with most of the difficulties in his life. When I pointed out that he would not be able to protect his family from the diagnosis for very long he reflected on how he might approach it. He thought that he might phone this one or that one, but the thought of upsetting them made that impossible. He said, 'So Dr X and you will have to do for now.' He fell silent, and then turned and addressed me directly, which was unusual. With a shrug he said: 'Well now you've got a depressive with cancer!' I inquired what that meant to him, and looking embarrassed he said that this was not part of our contract. 'I came here for depression and now I have this too.' He appeared to be worried that I would no longer be prepared to work with him, and it emerged that, just as he could not burden his relatives with this devastating news, he was worried about upsetting me. Once again the issue of contamination was present in the transference; he felt that he was a pariah and would therefore have to bear this alone. The explicit discussion of this seemed to be a relief.

It is relevant to reflect on the countertransference at this point. I was shocked and felt devastated; the very fact of such news challenged the boundaries of the analytic frame. It brought the real relationship to the fore: I was aware of my affection for James and that, quite simply, I did not want to lose him. On the one hand this was countertransference, generated by his openness and dependence, a response to the maternal erotic transference that was clearly operating. However there was the real situation as well, and to understand my response solely in terms of countertransference would have been to take refuge behind the role of analyst. The plain human fact of James's mortality brought awareness of my own transience to the fore. All who work with people who are dying are confronted with their own mortality, and it is no different when it emerges, as in this case, during the course of psychotherapy.

The following evening James phoned a member of his family, who was understandably upset so James terminated the conversation abruptly. It was clear to me that an interpretation was now necessary. Linking several incidents that had revealed his pattern of rejecting those who got close to him, I suggested that he was even more frightened of loving feelings than of angry ones. Reminding him of the session in which he had been angry with me, I suggested that, as well as his distress about the break, he had noticed that I had been touched by his story and that this might have felt even more threatening than the break. Reminding him of the confusion he had felt when his teacher had been moved by his singing, I suggested that while he wanted to touch people, doing so frightened him. Now it was safer to cut off his family than to bear the fact that they were upset because they cared about him. Anger had become a way of escaping from the intimate, loving feelings that he simultaneously desired and feared. I added that it was important that I had survived his angry outburst without getting upset, but sometimes people who care do get upset.

James reflected on this and admitted he had been relieved that the anger had not escalated on that occasion. He feared that emotion would get out of control. It was evident that, whilst he craved an emotional response by others, he was afraid that any form of emotional engagement might escalate. It seemed appropriate to point out that now he was going to need the support of his family, even if at times they might get upset.

Later that week James saw his GP and found out that the results of the lung biopsy were inconclusive and therefore another sample would have to be taken. The GP explained that there were different types of cancer and that they needed to be sure which one it was. During our next session James became angry, saying 'It is so unfair, I have been through all this [the analysis] and at last feel that life may begin to be worth living – and now this – it is as if I have to climb the Empire State Building!' He was convinced that there were psychosomatic reasons for the onset of this disease. Although he was determined to hang on and fight, he realised that at some point he might need to give in to it.

By the time of my two-week spring break James had told his parents about the diagnosis. In the last session before the break James came directly from the hospital where he had been undergoing more tests. They were considering surgery to remove one lobe of his lung, but this would depend on the results of the second biopsy. The fact that something could be done made him feel a bit more optimistic that he might not die in six months. He gave a detailed account of the hospital procedures, the anaesthetic and the bronchoscopy, which had left him with a sore throat. He then recounted a conversation he had overheard in the hospital. 'A 'prison chaplain' was telling a man that he had only three weeks left to live.' James was outraged: 'The bloke was not fit to take it!' It seemed that this offered a channel through which to express his anger with the doctor who had given him his diagnosis. James said that the whole thing had been very insensitively handled; it had been dumped on him and he been left to cope with it alone. He wondered how he would have managed if he had not been coming to see me immediately afterwards.

He was clearly anxious about the medical procedures that were to take place during my break. This was a time of crisis, so I suggested that he could phone me if he needed to. He seemed relieved to be offered this possibility. This was an extension of the boundaries; making the telephone an acceptable means of contact brought it within the analytic frame. Although the break was a distressing time for James he only phoned once. He had been admitted to the hospital but the tumour had proved inoperable. He was understandably upset and phoned immediately to tell me of this new setback.

Treatment

The next time I saw James I noticed that he was thinner. When in hospital he had been told that the prognosis was very poor as the tumour was already blocking the airways, making breathing difficult. In my absence he had seen his GP regularly and she was insisting that he admit to being terminally ill. Although he knew he would have to do so one day, he was not yet ready to take such a bleak view: at present he just wanted to ignore it. He had agreed to participate in a research project, which meant he would receive small doses of radiotherapy daily for two weeks. The first had been administered earlier that day, and during the procedure he had had the following dream.

It is unclear whether he had actually been asleep or if this had been a waking dream.

Dream 3: 18 April, year 1

I entered my flat, which was a basement in Kings Cross. Then I realised that a burglar was in the upstairs. He was a black man and coming in a half-open window. I consciously directed my attention to him, looked directly at him and the burglar turned round and went out.

James associated the burglar with the cancer and thought that it was the power given to him by the radiotherapy that had made the burglar turn and leave. He felt that it was an optimistic dream; but then, referring to the prognosis he had been given, he said: 'but – it isn't working'. According to Von Franz (1984, p. 68), 'the nearness of death is frequently represented in dreams by the image of a burglar, that is by someone unfamiliar which unexpectedly enters one's present life'. It seems this black man was one such intruder, but for now he was being chased out of the flat by the power of the dreamer's attention. A waking dream is not the same as a dream when asleep. It is usually a form of active imagination in which consciousness is deliberately lowered in order to be open to aspects of the psyche which may find expression through visual or lived imaginal experience (Watkins, 1976; Peters, 1990). While it is unclear whether James had been asleep or awake, the psyche had spontaneously produced this image in response to the situation.

The flat (the dreamer's house) seemed to represent the dreamer's body. The King's Cross area of London was familiar to James but this was a very literal way of viewing this chain or images. Less literal was that, in the dream – flat, he was the King and he was on the Cross, that is, pinned down whilst having the radiotherapy. This dream seemed to be fairly transparent to the dreamer; its message did not seem to be disguised or deeply unconscious but it was significant. James felt that his personal power was confirmed and consciously applied through his concentrated attention. It was effective in challenging the intruder and, given the prognosis, his will to live would continue to be effective in keeping the intruder at bay for many months to come.

6 Dreams and the Erotic Transference

Diagnosis of a life-threatening illness has profound effects. We have seen that James, who had felt suicidal for much of his life, now found that he wanted to live. A series of five dreams, from the period after the spring break, reveals how psychoanalysis had set him psychologically 'in motion'. In the previous chapter the focus was on the presentation of the dreams. In this chapter the dream content comes to the fore. These dreams revealed the unfolding of the erotic transference, weaving analyst and patient into a deepening engagement. They also reveal the psychological processes that were set in motion by James's increasing awareness of his reduced life expectancy.

Reported sequentially, dreams indicate the movement of the psyche and the dreamer's developing psychological awareness. Dreams may be particularly memorable in times of crisis when the psyche is mobilised by a big event or during transitions in life.

However, as we have seen, they are transient, elusive and essentially insubstantial and therefore convey their meanings in an oblique manner. The dream is not a puzzle, nor can it be decoded like a sign, which has merely one single meaning. Dreams are multi-faceted and reveal layers of meanings over time.

Therefore when processing a dream the starting place is usually the patient's associations, after which the analyst might offer her or his thoughts, with attention to the manifest content and the relationship to each other of the images, figures and objects that appear in the dream. As well as the state of the inner world of the dreamer, they may reflect aspects of the transference, so the atmosphere evoked when dreaming or recounting a dream is significant.

Considering the question 'Who is the dreamer?' may help differentiate the dream ego from other characters. Asking how it would have been if the feared or desired outcome had been realised can lead to further insights. This is amplification, whereby the patient is, in a manner of speaking, encouraged to 'dream the dream onward' (Hillman, 1977; Hall, 1977; Kast, 1992; Von Franz, 1984). It may lead to waking dream images, such as the burglar described in the previous chapter. As a form of active imagination, amplification brings to the fore those aspects of the psyche that are not fully conscious (Watkins, 1976; Peters, 1990). This may widen the field of consciousness.

Dreams and transference

Early in analysis James's dreams began to reveal the erotic transference that was to become integral to this analysis. As we shall see in Chapter 7, a well-handled erotic transference may contribute depth to the psychological process. This is because the analytic frame permits intense emotions and even passions to be safely experienced. The 'as if' quality means that the transference is a form of rehearsal, a way of experimenting with feelings but removed from the consequences that would follow in life outside the analytic frame. For this reason any disclosure from the analyst needs to be carefully monitored as it may breach the frame and result in actual consequences.

Freud (1900, p. 105) considered that the dream is only meaningful within the context of the whole analysis. Therefore it is important to pay attention to the transference–countertransference dynamic as well as the presentation of the dream. Some would view this as reductive and as inhibiting the natural flow of the unconscious. However in most present-day schools of psychotherapy, dreams are understood within the framework of the transference. There are times when it is evident that the analyst figures in a ream, and to ignore this would be to avoid an important aspect of the material.

The transference–countertransference dynamic is not a dream but at times it may seem rather like one. The analyst is part of the frame, the temporary keeper of the threads of relatedness. When powerful emotions become manifest between patient and analyst their meaning is attended to in terms of their effects on the patient. This is not always easy and there are times when the analyst is moved to respond as a person. In our everyday lives we usually respond to love with love, and to anger with anger, but in this situation the analyst thinks about the impulse to respond. It is then analysed in association with the prevailing material. When the analyst appears in dreams it is clear that transference is active. The less the analyst-as-person is known to the analysand, the more likely it is that this dream figure represents some aspiration of the patient. Therapeutic distance and the boundaried nature of the relationship are part of the analytic attitude that facilitates the emergence of such material.

The erotic transference

We return now to James and the day after the burglar dream. James described in detail his journey to the hospital, for radio-therapy, earlier that day. He had travelled alone and it had been awful. Then he spoke about an ex-girlfriend who was coming to visit him: she was now married and he was aware of the opportunity he had lost. Feeling the lack of one main person to care about him, he said: 'It would be awful if I shuffled off the mortal coil without ever having experienced that.' The atmosphere was very intimate and there was a very strong appeal to me. I acknowledged this, and that we were working towards him forming more fulfilling relationships; this was now in the balance.

I understood that he wanted me to go with him to the hospital. I felt sad that he had to face this alone and my emotional response was that I would have liked to accompany him. However I was also aware that, as his analyst, I needed to maintain a boundaried position so that I could continue to mediate his experiences. The transference at this time was to me as a potential lover/girlfriend. However it was also dependent and regressed and he wanted the mother/analyst to take care of him. Thus my response could be understood as both a real human response to the sadness of the situation and a counter to his transference.

James had noticed a somatic link between his symptoms and psychoanalysis. Earlier that day, when the GP had told him that there was no hope, his breathing had become worse, but now he was in my room he felt completely relaxed and his breathing had improved. Thus he acknowledged a feeling of safety and an increasingly intimate connection between us. The following dream, reported five minutes before the end of the next session, seemed to relate directly to this and was evidently difficult for him to recount. The background was a questionnaire that he had been asked to complete at the hospital. One question asked whether he had lost interest in sex.

Dream 4, part 1: 25 April year 1

> *I thought yes I had – then had a dream where I wondered how I would find out. I thought of you and the way would be if you put your tongue down my throat and breathed into me.*

It was clear that he had not told me about this until the last five minutes because it worried him, but I felt that he needed me to say something before he left. There was little time to reflect on the dream, so I said that perhaps it was about hope, which at present seemed to be invested in me. James responded: 'Well I do pin a lot of hope on you because the doctors have given up on me. They can't do anything.' This appeared to confirm his deepening engagement in the transference.

The next day, the entire session focused on his fury with the doctors, so there was no opportunity for me to comment on the dream. James quoted from the *Ballad of Reading Gaol:* 'The doctor said that death was but a scientific fact' (Wilde, 1896/1996, p. 158). He continued at length with his perception that, for the doctors, death is merely a technical affair. Coming so soon after the dream where such an intimate connection between us was evident, and following his unfulfilled desire for me to go with him to the hospital, it seemed that he was furious with me. Through his complaint that, for the doctors, it was just a technical affair, he was letting me know that he was worried that it was merely a technical 'affair' for me too. The limits of the therapeutic relationship were confusing and painful to him. He talked rapidly, leaving no space for me to convey acknowledgement of how difficult it had been for him to confess his sexual feelings.

It was becoming far from the truth that I did not care about him. I looked forward to his sessions in an unusually intense way. The complex facets of the erotic transference, the combination of mother/lover, was very involving. Moreover this dream had touched me deeply and I was increasingly moved by his investment in his analysis. My reciprocal attachment to him was complex and, at the time, not easy to separate out. It was in part a countertransference response but, because of the reality of his situation, there was also compassion for him as a man. To confess this to him would have been seductive and would probably have frightened him away. However, the purpose of the erotic transference is its deepening of relatedness. Firstly between the client and analyst, and then gradually, as a result of this, a change is wrought in the client's inner world. So whether the emotions aroused in the analyst are love or hate, they are observed but not acted upon. Nonetheless there are times when it is far from easy to maintain the analytic attitude and this was one such time.

Freud observed that if he asked a person about a dream as a whole the person's mind would go blank but, if he selected just part of the dream for discussion, associations were forthcoming and new material emerged. He therefore developed a method of representing the dream to the dreamer in which the dream was 'cut up into pieces' (Freud, 1900, p. 103). In this case it was James who presented his dream cut up into pieces and he returned to it in the next session. Having totally avoided it in the previous session James returned to the dream and explained that it had been difficult to talk about the rest of it because:

Dream 4, Part 2: 2 May, year 1

'. . . *it was when your hand was on my penis that I woke up.*'

Thus it was that the dream had brought his sexual feelings for me to the fore. He said that the dream was important to him; it felt like regeneration. The tongue I had put down his throat was long and penis-like. The first association was that he had always been worried that he might be homosexual, but now he thought that perhaps he just wanted a 'phallic woman' (his words). The activated transference was evident in both the dream and his associations. The long, penis-like tongue also seemed like a breast. This connected on a psychological level with the earlier observation that he was able to breathe more freely when he was in my room. It seemed that when my interpretations penetrated him it was as though the air he needed was getting through. However, as well as his desire for intimacy – represented by this maternal penetration – the second part of the dream revealed his anxiety that intimacy implied a demand. Something was expected of him: perhaps he felt that he would be expected to perform, to penetrate me, and it was this that had awoken him. This echoed his history of feeling that before he could perform sexually, he needed something but he did not know what that something was. The infantile desire for maternal nourishment was confused with being expected to perform as a sexual man.

Towards the end of this session James expressed his gratitude and said, in a more direct manner than usual, that he felt a great deal had changed since he first came for analysis. It seemed that this was both an acknowledgment of the loving feelings aroused by this understanding, and reparation for his attack on the doctors/me.

The next dream came at the beginning of May when James had had his last radiotherapy treatment. He talked at length and with great speed about the details of it and the inhumanity of the doctors. By now I was beginning to realise that this was a pattern when he was worried about intimacy between us, so after a while I stopped him and pointed this out. It then emerged that he was avoiding presenting another dream, which he had had the previous night.

Dream 5, Part 1: 3 May, year 1

> *I was beating a table tennis ball against the wall – looking in a house that was at school. A couple were in the way and she sent a ball over and it stuck in my hair like a sweet or something sticky. I was trying to find a bag in which to keep things and couldn't. Then there was a handbag and I knew that I might get mugged for it. Some yobs were taunting me.*

Once again there was no time to process the dream immediately, but he said that he felt very hurt and disturbed by it. My subsequent thoughts about its latent content were as follows.

I was beating a table tennis ball against the wall – looking in a house that was at school. This seemed to be about masturbation. He was beating the ball against a wall so there was no recipient, no one else involved, so it was not intercourse. The house at school was a place where there was no one with whom to have any kind of intercourse. *A couple were in the way and she sent a ball over and it stuck in my hair like a sweet or something sticky.* This appeared to relate to the possibility of two-person relatedness – intercourse. In the context of the previous dream it was likely that, in the transference, I had got in his hair and he could not get me out. He was perhaps 'sweet' on me. When he was in a relationship with the girl he had met at the school dance he had been told they were sweet together. There again was a reference to two-person relatedness. *I was trying to find a bag in which to keep things and couldn't. Then there was a handbag and I knew that I might get mugged for it.* Perhaps, in the traditional Freudian sense this handbag related to a womb – a woman with whom to have intercourse. For him it would be dangerous to want such a thing, as in Oedipal terms he might be mugged for it (his father would intervene and keep him in the child position). He might be made to feel stupid by *some yobs taunting him.*

There was a second part to this dream too.

Dream 5, Part 2

> *Then, after all action, I lay down under a big tree, which was an elm. But, in my dream, I heard the words that it was actually a pine not an elm – it was spiralling away to the sky and very peaceful.*

I wondered about death and the types of wood that coffins were made from, but did not say this aloud. In the dream the tree was peaceful, in touch with the earth and spiralling towards the sky. It is sometimes helpful to consider traditional understandings of the symbolism of images. These are not viewed as translations of the imagery but rather their implications contribute to insight. The tree is a common dream or pictorial image and among its multiple meanings I found the following:

'The . . . tree . . . stands for inexhaustible life, and is therefore equivalent to a symbol of immortality . . . . A tree with its roots in the ground and its branches reaching to the sky, symbolises an upward trend.' And 'The volute in ancient cultures was a spiral form symbolising the breath and the spirit' (Circlot, 1962, pp. 347, 306). The spiral and the breath seem to link this dream to the previous one, where I was breathing into James. After he left that day I wrote a note to myself about my sense of loss – I had wanted him to stay longer. I think that the dream was about loss and perhaps about death. This was indicated by James dreaming of lying down under a tree and by my unspoken association with coffins. The word pine could also refer pining – a sense of loss.

The next dream, at the end of May, was preceded by a session that included the following themes. During the treatment he had had various physical symptoms that had made him feel tired and ill. This week he had been feeling dizzy all week, but was feeling better now. However there was a problem, he could no longer stay with his parents, he could not accept their food and could not bear them looking after him. He had been invited to stay as long as he wanted with his brother, who lived in France, but if he accepted, coming to see me would be impossible. I noted that the atmosphere had a flirtatious feel to it that belied what he was saying; it seemed that he was trying to find out how I would react if he were to leave.

As already noted, in recent sessions a pattern had emerged where James would report a dream or complain about a situation without allowing space for me to speak. I drew his attention to this and asked how he felt when I spoke. He said that he wanted to hear what I had to say but was afraid that it might hurt. It seemed that he wanted me to penetrate him emotionally, but was fearful of it. He then said that the consultant had asked him what the cancer meant to him. He had considered this question, and although he had not been able to reply at the time he thought that the answer was 'A life of depression – now psychotherapy – and beginning to come through and then there is this hurdle.' He added: 'If I die I will be a very disappointed man.'

Dream 6, Part 1: 30 May, year 1

> *I am in a fortress and this woman – who is not known to me – comes to me for help. She is being pursued and I take her with me to safety. We climb down some steps into the bowels of the earth. Then I think that we need some contact with the outside world and an electronic device.*

The pattern of not leaving space to process the dream resumed, with James talking rapidly to prevent me making comments. I shall again outline my retrospective thoughts, some of which come from the sense that he and I made of it together in later sessions.

I am in a fortress. A fortress is a bit like a castle, a building that is very strong and protects those within it. James had been defended all his life; perhaps that was a little like living in a fortress. There had been a castle in his very first dream, and that had seemed to relate to the split-off feminine aspect of his personality. *[T]his woman – who is not known to me – comes to me for help.* Jung (1928, p. 9) makes a distinction between known figures in a dream, which he suggests should be taken as a tangible reality, and those who are unknown and are therefore treated as symbolic. This unknown woman could be viewed as primarily symbolic, as a vulnerable aspect of himself to which he was now able to attend (it is quite common for the vulnerable aspect of a man to be characterised in dreams by a female figure). In the past James had ignored this part of himself, but now, perhaps as a result of the psychotherapy, it was able to ask for help. *She is being pursued and I take her with me to safety.* Here he is offering protection to this vulnerable part of himself. *We climb down some steps into the bowels of the earth.* The bowels of the earth could symbolise the earth mother or a womb. All the images in this dream are traditional representations of the psychological feminine – the castle/fortress, the female figure and now the earth. Thus we might consider that the dream revealed psychological movement in relation to the feminine aspect of the psyche. *Then I think that we need some contact with the outside world and an electronic device.* Deep underground, contact with the outside world is necessary and an electronic device could provide the necessary link. Alternatively the electronic device might relate to the radiotherapy treatment that could help save his life. It was only later that these thoughts could be offered to James.

Welman and Faber (1992, p. 70) write of a terminally ill man who dreamed that he was entering a house via the chimney and ended up in a dark tunnel from which he was unable to escape – he found himself descending deeper and deeper. They refer to Von Franz (1986), who writes that 'images of descent are typically reported in the dreams of the dying and are clear death allegories' (quoted in Welman and Faber, 1992, p. 72). They also suggest, again following Von Franz, that it is often the contrasexual archetype, the figure of the opposite sex to the dreamer, who appears in dream images as the 'messenger of death' (ibid., p. 73). The woman would then be a representation of death, accompanying him into the bowels of the earth. However it became evident that, following the transference dreams, this dream woman was an aspect of James's own psyche. This seemed to indicate, alongside the deepening of the transference, an unconscious deepening of the relationship to himself.

There was a second part to this dream too. It seemed that potentially rich material was often being lost, so I decided that, if the opportunity presented itself, I would try to bring James back to this dream. However he was controlling me by filling the sessions to such an extent that I could not respond or interpret. In the next session he was very excited: he had had an X-ray that showed that, as a result of the radiotherapy, the tumour had reduced and there was now little trace of it. He had been told that the prognosis was now very good and he had been proclaimed fit to work. He was euphoric; he knew that his condition could deteriorate at any time but for now things looked very bright. It seemed to him that the burglar had been driven from his house.

After attending to his thoughts about the burglar dream I suggested that the dream he had reported last time merited some attention. At first he did not know which dream I meant. Then he remembered and said, 'Oh I had that one again'.

Dream 6, Part 2: 6 June, year 1

> *Every time I descended 100 yards it was by the square root of 2 – don't know fully what it means but it makes me feel very good when I wake up.*

James had the feeling that the number had magical significance. Then he asked me, 'What did you mean about the dream?' I told him that I thought it was like a rebirth – descending into the bowels of the earth to be reborn. The fact that he was in a fortress said something of how he had been defended for years against anyone who might touch him emotionally. Then I suggested that the woman who came to him for help was perhaps a part of himself to which he was at last able to give attention.

There seemed to be a link between this dream and part 2, of dream 5, where the dreamer lay down under a tree. In that one he rested on the surface of the earth and in this one, he descended into the bowels of the earth, perhaps like the roots (square root) of the tree. However I did not know what to make of the 100 yards or the square root of 2. Furthermore, root in this context could also be read as route. Thus there were multiple possible meanings, including origins, paths and journeys.

Perhaps the square root had something to do with the self and two parts of him that were descending into a deeper relationship. It might also reflect the transference, with two people – him and me – descending into the realms of the underworld/unconscious. However at that point my thoughts were too unformulated to offer them to him. Instead I asked what the woman was running away from. His immediate response was 'Men with spears, a macho image of men. I hate that but I feel I was sent away to become like that. When I was at school I read a story of a pageboy who was sent away to become a knight. I identified with him then. But I know I should never have been sent away. I am not a knight.'

This was a touching admission of his vulnerability. The simple acknowledgement that he should never have been sent away also indicated acceptance of his own suffering. It need not have been this way. This was an important indication that a more realistic self-image was emerging. James said that the dream had made him feel good. It seemed that he was beginning to accept that it was all right to be him, even if he did not achieve great things. Thus in amplifying this aspect of the dream the theme was expanded and James realised more than had been apparent at first.

James was still thinking of moving to France as he felt he had to move – he could not go on living in his parents' house until they died. Optimism was evident here as he seemed to be contemplating outliving them. He then reflected on how he could find another analyst if he moved but that he might not like 'the way they interpreted him'. He said that things would have been different if he had come to me as a cancer patient, so it was important that he had come before his diagnosis. I suggested that perhaps part of what he was saying was that the cancer was a symptom of the wider problem and not the reason he had come for analysis in the first place. It was also important that I saw him as a person, and not merely his physical condition. This may have been one reason why the analysis continued until the very end of his life. There was work to do and the analysis was essential, irrespective of how long he had left to live.

Then he addressed me directly: 'You have not said that moving would be avoidance.' I pointed out that he had said it himself and then asked what he might be avoiding. He replied: 'I don't know but there are some nasty things in there.' Then he said that he had found my interpretation of his dream as rebirth was too much because it confirmed his own view, but he added, 'the hope is too much'.

Reflecting on his own gender identity and the male-female conflict engendered by the dream, he said: "I am a man, I identify as a man and yet I also identify as a woman.' Then after a thoughtful pause, 'but I wouldn't want to have babies. You [women in general – me included] are very different because you can have babies . . . . Women have hurt me often.' Then he reflected, 'I don't think I am homosexual. I want something from women but I just can't make it happen. I feel I have been rejected by someone I love and I don't understand why.' Then he went on to recall his first love as a school boy. He remembered the macho boys laughing at them and calling them sweet, so he had dropped her immediately. Thus it is that the same themes emerge at different times in an analysis as their significance alters and clarifies.

His reflections on the differences between women's bodies, with their reproductive function, and his male body had an innocence about it that was much younger than his years. I tentatively suggested that it was his mother whom he had loved and lost. When he had been sent away to school he had felt as though she had rejected him and this major loss was still haunting him now. He agreed, saying that this was the reason why he needed to move away from his parents' house; it was a constant reminder of that hurt. Then I referred to the dream where he had been going underground, and suggested that it related to his need to be earthed, to put down roots, before he could form relationships.

During another session it became clear that he had responded to the idea of being earthed. He had been going for long walks in the gardens around his home and appreciating how lovely they were at present. When a path he had been following emerged from the trees he had stood on the earth and looked at the sunrise (as he spoke I had a sense that he was in love with this place). I told him that I was reminded of his dream about the pine or elm because, as in that dream, he was finding peace under the trees. He was amazed that I mentioned it today because earlier in that week he had discovered, in a book about trees that pine trees used to be called aulm. This had 'blown his mind' because in the dream 5, he had heard the words that the tree was a pine not an elm. During his walks he had also noticed that, because of a drought, the stream that ran through the gardens had dried up for the first time in his memory. He saw this as a sign that was time for him to move on. I thought that it reflected the maternal source and that there was no longer any hope he would get the nourishment, he had needed as a boy.

This theme continued the following day when he discussed how living with his parents was causing him to feel like a little boy. He had been destined to become the boss one day and had not been able to reframe his identity. He felt really angry – he had been betrayed, sent away to school to become an industrialist, but when he was nearly old enough he had been deprived of his intended future. What struck him forcefully now was that no one had discussed it with him or acknowledged his loss. Then reflectively referring to the house he said, 'I don't know who I am without this place'. I pointed out that it sounded as though he was in love with his home but his description of the stream drying up appeared to indicate that there was no longer anything there for him. It seemed to me that the house was symbolic of the mother and the garden the soil from whence he came. It was no longer moist and nourishing – like the stream it had dried up, the life force was no longer located there.

Later in that session he said he might write about his experiences. He thought that he could find an angle – 'I beat cancer with a psychotherapist and Mars bars'. He laughed and explained that it would have a 'do it your own way' message to people. As I write this some years later, I know that this book is his legacy.

At the end of June and the beginning of July he had more check-ups. He discussed his anxiety before these appointments and how he now faced a choice: to live or to die. If he lived he would be confronted with the old problem of what to do with the rest of his life. This presented him with the life-long problem of finding a job and a place to live. The check-ups evoked more stories about the incompetence of doctors, some of which were probably justified. This set of tests revealed that things were OK for now, but the doctor had warned James that the cancer could recur any time. James then reported the dream he had had the night before the appointment.

Dream 7: 4 July, year 1

> I was carrying eggs. I had decided that they were probably bad and so threw them all away. Then panicked, as there were none left. I returned to the main depot and a man gave me half a dozen. These were all he had left. I opened the box and they were dark at the top, like commas.

I asked, 'Like . . . ?' He completed the sentence – 'foetuses'. He seemed pleased and surprised at the realisation. I think that we were probably both avoiding the other thought that they were all contaminated with something dark, like a cancer growing within them.

My retrospective thoughts about this dream were as follows. *I was carrying eggs. I had decided that they were probably bad and so threw them all away.* Perhaps this was like his life, much of which had been spent depressed and with suicidal thoughts – he had thrown it away. Then came the diagnosis and he had realised there might be none left, so he had panicked and wanted to live. *I returned to the main depot and a man gave me half a dozen. These were all he had left.* The man at the main depot might be the doctor at the hospital who had given him, not six eggs, but six months to live. *[T]hey were dark at the top, like commas.* They were perhaps foetuses, indicating potential, but they could also have been contaminated by cancer.

The Impending Break

When a patient is seriously ill the breaks in analysis can have a detrimental effect. This was the case with James as the summer break brought his depression to the fore. The period since April had been a relatively positive time, with psychological progress indicated by the dreams. However as the break approached James started to feel depressed and took to spending a great deal of time in bed. At first I did not connect this with the impending break, but it became evident from his appearance that he was not taking care of himself. He reverted to depression as a form of attack. He complained about his inability to get a job and to pay for the sessions after August. When he had been asked at the hospital about his support system he had realised that he had none, only the consultant and me. Thus the sense of pointlessness that he expressed seemed to mask his anxiety about my absence.

James reflected that he and his mother had both been heartbroken when he had gone to school but he could not forgive her. As he said this he was unexpectedly overwhelmed by grief. It seemed that the impending break reminded him of being sent away to school; each new term had been a renewed rejection. James recalled how he used to get ill in an attempt to attract his parents' attention, and said wryly that the cancer was working where other illnesses had not. Then he remembered a dream.

Dream 8 July, year 1

I woke up last night having a major row with my mother.

This dream heralded the themes of the next phase, where James's furious rage and destructiveness nearly put paid to the analysis. It seems that it was not only his mother with whom he was angry, as demonstrated by the attacks on the analysis that preceded the break.

The fee became the focus of these attacks. It presented a real problem but was also a convenient means of attacking the analysis/me. James was running out of money and was very depressed. He refused any interpretations I offered about his anxiety about the break and his anger. He was not interested in insight; it was merely that he was at 'rock bottom'. If he came in August he would not be able to pay. In another session, when he was less angry, he said that even if his funds ran out he would find a way. He was testing the boundaries. I offered to see him for a percentage of his income. Some days he was unmovable, saying that that would put things on a different footing, that he would then owe me and he did not like 'bumming off' anyone but his parents. Then he considered owing me until he could pay me, saying how much he valued the sessions – even when it was just for a chat! This was yet another way of attempting to devalue the psychotherapy: it was merely a chat. Unconsciously James was attempting to find a way to leave me to avoid the pain of separation.

During this angry phase he thought that the cancer had returned and questioned the point of fighting it. It seemed that he was unconsciously showing me how he used to attempt to stay at home by getting ill. Then, having checked with the doctor that he was all right, he thought that it was psychosomatic; not because of my impending absence, as I suggested, but because he was feeling better and therefore was faced with getting a job. In the last session before the break he said that this had to be the final one as he had run out of money. The previous night he had phoned the Samaritans. I realised that he needed to be reassured that the Samaritans would be there in my absence. I interpreted his anxiety, as well as his fury with me, as fuelled by his wish to find a reason to leave to avoid the pain of separation. I refused to accept that this was the final session. James said that he was fed up with Dr X (the GP) as she was never there when he needed her. I suggested that he found it easier to be fed up with her than to admit he was fed up with me. He was dismissive, saying that ours was merely a commercial transaction. He then added, very convincingly, 'I am thinking of suicide. This time it really does look hopeless – that is why I phoned the Samaritans.' When I commented on him phoning them rather than me, he said 'What is the point in phoning you? You won't let me go if I want to end the sessions and I really want to kill myself.' I acknowledged that the break was making him anxious, that he was feeling trapped by his need for me. Then I reminded him that we had agreed to meet until the end of September and that he would pay only what he could afford.

So it was at the end of a period of psychological movement, as revealed by his dreams, that the analysis hit the major obstacle of the break. James's dependency needs, evoked by this period of positive transference, now became unbearable. His creative impulses were often overwhelmed by the immensity of the destructive ones. This is often the case with regression. It leads to the emergence of infantile dependency that can be confusing and immensely painful, especially around the time of breaks in analysis.

7 The Erotic Transference and Countertransference

In the previous chapter we saw how James's engagement in analysis intensified as the erotic transference deepened. Revealed first in dreams, it began to draw analysand and analyst into an intimate form of relating. In this chapter the theory that informs my understanding of this process is discussed.

In 1995 I published an extensive review of the literature on the transference and countertransference between the male patient and the female analyst. The aim was to investigate the nature of the engagement that I had experienced with men, like James, with whom a deeply erotic transference dominated from the very beginning of the analysis. At that time it was frequently noted that, despite the extensive literature on the erotic transferences of female patients working with male analysts, there were relatively few reports of long-term erotic transferences of male patients. It had even been suggested that male patients did not form erotic transferences. This was contrary to my own experience so I reviewed the literature. This revealed a number of women writers who had observed this same lack, and each had proceeded to contribute to the topic of women analysts working with men (Tower, 1956; Karme, 1979; Kulish, 1984; Guttman, 1984; Chasseguet-Smirgel, 1984; Goldberger and Evans, 1985; Spector Person, 1985). Since then a small but signifcant body of work on this topic has evolved including (Schaverien, 1995, 1996; Covington, 1996). However it remains the case there are still relatively few reports of long-term erotic transferences of male patients. Neither male nor female analysts have explored the psychology of men as extensively as they have that of women. Although some writers have begun to address this matter (for example Jukes, 1993; Mitchell, 2000), specific psychological and transference issues that confront men continue to merit attention. Thus in concert with the effects on the therapeutic relationship of the diagnosis of a serious illness, it is my intention to present here common themes that emerge in the treatment of men in analysis with women. I will not repeat my review of the literature (Schaverien, 1995, 1996) but will recap and update some of the material that is pertinent to the story of my journey with James. First we shall look briefly at the history of the erotic transference.

Transference

It is well known that Freud's understanding of transference stemmed from his observation that female patients, in particular, tended to fall in love with their male analysts. Although at first this was regarded as a problem, Freud soon realised that this was regression to an earlier state, which revealed the origin of the neurosis. He wrote that the pattern for conducting erotic life, laid down in the early years, influences the aims and objects of love in later life. 'If the need for love has not been satisfied the person is bound to approach every new person he meets with libidinal anticipatory ideas' (Freud, 1912, p. 100). Thus Freud came to view 'transference love' as the main pivot of the treatment (Freud, 1915). He emphasised the importance of abstinence and recommended that the patient's desires should be allowed to persist, rather than being gratified. It is the struggle that this engenders which brings the unconscious impulses to consciousness. The task of transference analysis is to understand rather than to act (Freud, 1912, p. 100). Gratification of the desire would merely repeat 'what ought to be remembered' (Freud, 1915, p. 166). Thus at this early stage Freud was making a strong plea against acting out. It was the analyst's task to maintain an objective stance despite the demands of the patient.

Following Freud, Greenson (1967) divided the therapeutic relationship into three, artificially linear, component parts: The Real Relationship, The Therapeutic Alliance and The Transference. Of course these are not fixed, but they do offer an imaginal framework for understanding the therapeutic relationship.

The real relationship is the real relationship between the patient and analyst. It is the baseline that permits real transactions such as negotiation of the frame, the fee, the duration of sessions and the limits of therapy. Initially this is a meeting between two people who both recognise the separateness of the other. Certain real things are inevitably noticed about the other person, such as gender, age and style of being. When the analysand become seriously ill the real relationship inevitably takes a more prominent place than usual.

The therapeutic alliance is the alliance made during the initial meeting and built on in subsequent encounters. There is an implicit agreement that a part of the analysand will be in alliance with the analyst to reflect on the behaviours and emotions that emerge. A psychological split is necessary which permits the analysand to observe, at the same time as engaging in the transference.

The transference is present in all therapeutic interactions. It is typified by ambivalence, and therefore whatever emotion dominates, its opposite is likely to be present but unconscious. If, for example, there is an extreme positive transference, the negative will be present but unconscious. Similarly a negative transference will mask an unconscious positive transference. The setting and the undivided attention of the analyst engender regression. Experiences from early life that have been internalised, and therefore continue to influence patterns of relating, are reactivated in the transference. Affect, associated with the original experience, becomes 'live' and hence is again experienced as external. This is confusing, and the analysand experiences 'anxiety, tension, pain and the need for love' (Racker, 1974, p. 73). But there is another side to the psychoanalytic process: 'it unites what is separate, connects what is disconnected and is thus essentially an expression of eros' (ibid.)

Problems may arise if the real relationship becomes obscured by the transference. This may be a temporary state that is amenable to interpretation, but at its most extreme a delusional transference may develop, with an associated loss of the therapeutic alliance. This is a failure of the symbolic function which permits the 'as if' nature of the therapeutic relationship to be understood. When that fails the learning potential of the transference is lost (Blum, 1973). The erotic transference may then become eroticised, the patient is no longer open to interpretation and there is an insistent demand for reciprocation. In the 1960s Greenson observed that all the cases of eroticised transference of which he knew were women in analysis with men (Greenson, 1967, p. 339), but since then it has become clear that such transferences occur in all gender combinations (see Goldberger and Evans, 1985; Spector Person, 1985; Lester, 1990). Although some writers do not make a distinction between erotic and eroticised transference (for example Wrye and Welles, 1994, p. 45), I consider the distinction significant because in eroticisation the demand for gratification can become insistent and intrusive, and overwhelm the mediating function of the therapeutic alliance. The erotic transference may be a defence against becoming conscious, but that is different from the extreme of eroticisation, which can lead to an intractable situation or a psychotic breakdown. The distinction is relevant because, with James, an intense erotic transference developed but it was always amenable to interpretation.

The erotic transference

Freud and Jung's divergence over the developmental role of sexuality has been well documented. For Freud the significance of eros in the transference was that it led back to actual childhood and to the incestuous desires of the Oedipal stage. Jung related eros to the wider cultural context; he considered that incestuous desires in the transference indicated a need to return to an earlier psychological state from which to grow forward anew (Jung, 1956). Regression in the transference therefore had a 'meaning and purpose' (Jung, 1959a, p. 74). The very nature of the unconscious means that it is not accessible without the help of an 'other', and it is the analyst who holds the conscious attitude that the patient seeks. It is this which temporarily binds the analysand to the analyst and therefore sexual desire in the transference is a symbol for patterns of relatedness. The apparently infantile erotic connection is motivated by a desire for individuation, for a state of consciousness (Jung, 1956, pp. 7–16).

Jung's (1946) understanding of the transference–countertransference dynamic was informed by alchemy. Despite its apparently arcane origins it offers a useful means of understanding the affinity that emerges in cases such as that of James. Jung realised that the spiritual parallel to the alchemist's quest – to transform base metals into gold – was similar to the transference–countertransference engagement. In the alchemist's alembic, chemical elements were drawn together by a powerful chemical affinity that bound them together and transformed them both in the process. A similar attraction of opposites takes place in the transference. Although this is primarily a heterosexual metaphor it applies in all gender combinations. Unconscious elements from the psyche of the patient unite with unconscious elements from the psyche of the analyst, and so the pair are drawn into an intimate form of relatedness. (For more detailed discussion see Schaverien, 1998; Young-Eisendrath, 1997, 1999.) The resulting unconscious mix may be irresistible. This does not happen in every case, but when it does the analyst may be temporarily affected by the patient's material and drawn into an unconscious incestuous dynamic. The process is then profoundly engaging for both people.

Child development and the self

Transference regression evokes the earliest and most intimate relationships of life and therefore the mother–infant dyad has become the dominant metaphor in psychoanalysis. This is the earliest erotic attachment and the first relational bond, which has been described in various ways by different psychoanalysts. Each has contributed to the understanding of the path of development from the complete dependency of infancy, through the various stages of interest in the world, to an autonomous adult identity (Freud, A., 1965; Klein, 1975a,b, 1980; Bowlby, 1974, 1980a,b; Fordham, 1976; Mahler *et al.*, 1975; Winnicott, 1971, 1965, 1958). In analysis, when something in this early developmental pattern has gone amiss it is revealed in the pattern replayed in the transference.

Jung did not posit a theory of child development; his interest was in childhood states of consciousness in adult patients, rather than in actual children (Jung, 1930., p. 392). However Fordham developed a Jungian approach that takes account of the 'self' as a core sense of being, distinguished from the ego-based 'Self' by the use of a lower case 's' (Astor, 1995). The prevailing attitude of his time was that the infant experienced a mass of undifferentiated sensations, and until these were organised by the mother or primary carer the baby did not begin to develop a sense of self. Fordham (1976) placed the infant in a more active position by proposing that if a core and pre-existing self is present in the adult it will have been there from the start. In a reversal of the predominant view, Fordham observed that it is the baby who engenders the mother's response. The baby is an integrated being who deintegrates from its self, stimulating the environment to provide what it needs. When sufficient stimulation has been obtained the infant withdraws into sleep; in this way it integrates, returning to its self to assimilate the waking experiences (Fordham, 1985).

Like Winnicott (1971), Fordham considered that the baby is attuned to adapt to the mother's moods, so if what is needed is not freely given, for example when the mother is depressed or otherwise preoccupied, the baby adapts and tries to please the mother. Thus Fordham's infant is a full participant in the mother–child interaction, rather than a passive recipient. This was a radical contribution to developmental theory and a major innovation in analytic thought. It has some commonality with the work of Winnicott and Klein, but it is also a distinctly Jungian view. Recent studies of mothers and babies have produced very similar findings. The theory of intersubjectivity accepts the mother and baby as two people who participate in a relationship from the beginning (Stern, 1985; Benjamin, 1988). This is relevant to James's case because in his early years, living with what had probably been a depressed mother, he had learned to adapt rather than to express his own needs. This behavioural pattern had affected his relationships with women throughout his life.

Regression and the male patient

The power imbalance of the therapeutic relationship evokes the memory of past relationships, especially those of early childhood. When the analyst is a woman and the patient a man there is an apparent paradox. Women, as mothers, are powerful in the early years of a child's life. It is the mother or primary carer, usually female, who is the first object of desire. She is the focus of all the ambivalent emotions associated with dependence. It may have been a struggle for a man to establish himself as separate from his mother, so when he enters therapy with a woman, conflicted feelings associated with gender and power may surface. Whilst unconsciously awed by the perceived power of the analyst, he may defend fiercely against any form of dependent transference. Thus the return of affect attached to the mother of infancy may evoke eros but, in the adult, this generates confusion.

With a male patient whose erotic transference evokes a regressed desire for his mother there is a paradox. The early maternal – infant bond may evoke a desire for an idealised state of at-oneness with the fantasised, nurturing 'good mother'. At the same time the complex mix of attraction and repulsion of the adult towards this image may engender a train of negative emotions. This may be perplexing and humiliating. Sexual themes may become mixed up with pre-Oedipal material. Images that are apparently maternal often have a sexual element, whilst overtly sexual images may be related to the maternal (Guttman, 1984). Neumann's (1955) research revealed the 'Great Mother' as an archetypal constellation of terrifying proportions which may be evoked by the regressed transference.

The idealisation often experienced in the transference of the male patient working with a female analyst may be a defence against this mix. It was Horney (1932) who first drew attention to this in her paper 'The dread of woman'. Challenging the Freudian view that the main fear experienced by the male patient is castration anxiety, Horney proposed that, particularly in analysis with a woman, idealisation of the feminine conceals an unconscious fear of women, specifically the vagina. The little boy's terror that the woman 'possesses an organ which allows access to her body' evokes an unconscious fear that he might be sucked back into the womb and thus annihilated. Hence the 'desire for the mother is associated with a fear of death' (Chasseguet-Smirgel, 1984b, p. 171). Aspects of this occur with women patients, but it is usually less terrifying for them because the feminine is not 'other' as it is for men (Chodorow, 1978, p. 182). The development of a separate masculine identity is problematic for the boy and there is a period in adolescence when the feminine is repudiated, with a consequent denial of relationship and connectedness (ibid., p. 174). In their development of some of these ideas Wrye and Welles (1994) analyse the 'maternal erotic transference', in all its horrifying as well as seductive guises. They vividly show how maternal transferences can be libidinal and aggressive, as well as making a contribution to genital sexuality (ibid., p. 35).

In traditional theory it is the father who facilitates the transition to masculine identity. In analysis this paternal function is facilitated by the boundary-setting nature of the enterprise. The female therapist, by maintaining the limits and structure of the analytic frame, may evoke a paternal transference. Thus it is important that the analyst's view of her own gender and sexuality is not too fixed. Too rigid a self-image may limit interpretations to the maternal realm, maintaining the analysand in a dependent position. If eros has been blocked it may emerge with tremendous force. Unleashed in the analytic context, in all its multitude of guises, it may evoke all sorts of apparently inappropriate arousals that transgress the perceived limits of gender and sexuality. This may be very disturbing for the analysand.

Whilst demands on the analyst are often related to early experience, I consider that limiting interpretations solely to the maternal means that adult sexuality may be denied. At the same time as the infantile transference there may be awareness of the real relationship, and of the fact that the analysing couple are an adult man and woman. Therefore, whilst seeking the gratification of pregenital desires the analysand may have adult sexual feelings and bodily sensations. The intimate pattern that originated in infancy is experienced as a desire in the present. Images of the analyst as tantalising and sexually powerful may emerge, and this may lead the male patient to fear the potential rapist in him. He demands, but also fears, his analyst's reciprocation of his sexual wishes and his potential to lose control. Therefore acknowledgement of the adult who desires sexual intimacy needs to be made at the same time as enabling the expression of the regression.

Countertransference and sexuality

When such powerful material is activated both analyst, and patient need to have a way of distancing themselves from the feelings evoked, but without cutting them off. Understanding the symbolic nature of the transference may be a relief; it helps the patient if his interest in the analyst's body is understood as connected to early developmental phases. Such understanding can also help the analyst, but problems arise when this is used as avoidance. If there is too speedy recourse to conceptual understanding, without permitting the full expression of the reality of the relational implications in the present, the patient may feel that the emotions are taboo. This is compounded if the female analyst finds it more acceptable to remain within the frame of the maternal, rather than to confront the overtly sexual.

Moreover sexuality and violence may be denied by both patient and analyst (Guttman, 1984). This material may be particularly difficult for the female analyst as it brings her body into the subject matter of the sessions, so she may unconsciously resist its recognition. The analyst who feels embarrassed or intimidated may be reticent to open up such material for discussion. She may feel uncomfortable with being seen as seductive and therefore unconsciously deny her own sexual interest or arousal. The idealisation, described earlier, may seem preferable to confronting images of women as sexually powerful or denigrated. These may be subtly masked, and at first only evident in asides or the occasional derogatory comment about women outside the analysis. It is only through close attention to the countertransference that this material becomes conscious. The task is then to interpret it so that the negative erotic transference can be expressed.

Originally countertransference was considered to be the analyst's unresolved transference to the analysand, that needed to be eliminated by further analysis of the analyst. Countertransference is now more generally considered to be the analyst's response to the whole of the analytic situation. It was mainly (but not exclusively) women, (for example Heimann, 1949; Little, 1950) who wrote about the countertransference as a total response. Considering this, Guttman (1984) has suggested that female analysts are more likely to admit openly to their countertransferences, while men focus more readily on the transference. Whilst this might have been true in an earlier period, it is no longer strictly the case as in recent years a number of men have openly admitted to their own erotic countertransference experiences (for example Samuels, 1985a; Rutter, 1989; Sedgwick, 1994; Mann, 1997; Bonasia, 2001).

The erotic is not merely about love, as we shall see, and love is not merely one thing. Lambert (1981) distinguishes between platonic love, affection and sexual love, all of which may be evoked by and experienced within analysis. In social interactions it is usual for love to evoke love and hate to evoke hate. It is similar in analysis, but here the task is to observe rather than to act on the feelings. This 'talion law' means that a positive transference will evoke a positive countertransference, whilst a negative transference will evoke a negative response (Racker, 1974, p. 137). The unconscious attitude is, in the transference, attributed to the analyst and so the conscious attitude may mask the unconscious one. In the extreme this manifests as projective identification, whereby the feelings of the patient are so effectively split off and projected that the analyst experiences them as her own (Klein, 1946).

Even so there are times when there is genuine affection between analyst and analysand. Tower (1956) has observed that this seems to facilitate a positive outcome. Linking this to developmental theory, Searles (1959) points out that during the Oedipal stage the parent experiences an appreciation of the child as a potential partner. It is similar in analysis, and the analyst, like the parent, renounces his incestuous desires (ibid., p. 289). Samuels (2001) has developed this point, suggesting that a healthy form of erotic playback between parent and child, particularly a child of the opposite sex, is vital to their sense of themselves as desirable.

There are occasions in analysis when a genuine sexual attraction exists, and we have seen the complexity of the origins of such material. Even so it may be of positive benefit for the analysand to feel that he could be attractive to his analyst. Therefore a consciously considered attraction to the patient may facilitate his feelings of self-worth and enable him to express feelings he might otherwise not easily share (Guttman, 1984). If these are not consciously admitted they will be communicated non-verbally in gestures and body language. Thus, just as with other material, the analyst needs to be alert to the effects of such a countertransference, irrespective of the perceived limits of gender or sexual orientation. It may be defensive, or even an abuse of power, by female analysts to reduce all the desires experienced by the patient to the residues of infancy; this may be an affront to the adult.

Conclusion

This chapter has concentrated on just one gender dyad, but no form of transference is gender specific. Clinically as well as culturally, the old gender certainties no longer dominate and the predominantly heterosexual model of transference is giving way to a more fluid approach. It is now accepted that homoerotic elements are played out in same-or cross-gender pairs, irrespective of the dominant sexual orientation of the participants. Nonetheless it remains the case that few men have written explicitly about homoerotic arousal with their male patients (Mann, 1997, p. 116). It is possible that awareness of such arousal may be blocked by heterosexual and homosexual men alike as unacceptable to the prevailing – heterosexual – masculine identity. Although neither Bosnak (1989) nor Lee (1996), referred to in Chapter 1, theorise it as such, both describe long-term erotic transferences with their terminally ill male patients.

Transference demands an imaginative capacity on the part of the analyst. If the constantly changing nature of the transference is to be observed, a fluid view of gender identity and sexuality is required. Thus what Samuels (2001) refers to as a healthy form of gender confusion, rather than gender certainty, can be usefully applied in clinical practice. In the chapters that follow, as the clinical narrative unfolds it will become clear how the analyst may be viewed in many different guises. There are many manifestations of eros, which far from remaining fixed, alter during the course of an analysis. The challenge, as will become clear in the next chapter, is for the analysis to survive so that understanding of its multi-facetted meanings can gradually develop. This process may be hastened and intensified by the onset of a terminal illness.

8 Sexual Attraction and Erotic Violence: Men Who Leave Too Soon Revisited

As already stated, one of the central aims of this book is to analyse the sustained erotic transference of a male patient working with a female analyst. We have seen that, in contrast to the large body of reports on the erotic transferences of female patients towards their male analysts, reports on the long-term erotic transferences of male patients are rare. In *Desire and the Female Therapist* (1995) I questioned why relatively little has been written on erotic transferences by female therapists working with male patients and proposed that:

> It is possible that male patients terminate before, or when, the erotic transference begins. It also seems that female therapists may find it more acceptable to remain within the frame of the maternal rather than to confront the sexual transference (ibid., p. 24).

In a paper entitled 'Men who leave too soon' (1997) I further developed this idea and suggested that among the reasons why male patients might leave therapy too soon, is confusion between the different manifestations of the erotic. In all erotic transferences the infantile and adult aspects of sexuality become mixed up. This can cause a man to feel confused about what feels like an inappropriate arousal in relation to a female authority figure, and he may leave to avoid the pain that this evokes.

Feminist writers have convincingly argued that, as a result of social and cultural pressure, boys and girls generally develop psychologically in different ways. In order to establish their difference, boys have to sever their primary identification with their mother and develop a separate masculine identity. Therefore intimacy may be seen as threatening their masculinity and drawing them back into the maternal realm. Girls, too, have to separate from the primary identification with their mother, but then come to terms with it again. Their sameness means that they are more likely to fear separation (Chodorow, 1978; Gilligan, 1982; Eichenbaum and Orbach, 1983; Olivier 1989).

As intimated above, to avoid intimacy some male patients terminate their therapy with female analysts before the erotic transference has fully developed or at the point at which it intensifies. During the phase of his analysis, after the return from the summer break, James very nearly became one of those 'men who leave too soon' (Schaverien, 1997).

As the shock of the initial diagnosis lessened, the focus of our work shifted away from cancer and back to the presenting problem. In the weeks following the first summer break the conflict between the opposing forces in James's psyche became more evident. Love and hate, as well as creative and destructive aspects of his personality, were powerfully activated within the analytic frame. His desire to love and be loved – the pressure to engage in life – was often crushed by the impulse for revenge and the associated wish to die. The swings between these came to the fore as they were replayed, enacted and acted out within the transference. A pattern emerged in which, if James felt good in one session, he felt awful in the following one. If he acknowledged love he soon became consumed with hate. His need for revenge frequently led to thoughts of suicide, partly generated by the imagined effect it would have on his parents, or on me. Eventually the pattern became so obvious that James could no longer ignore it, so very gradually conscious awareness began to replace unconscious acting out. His desire to punish others through his suicide was at odds with his growing investment in the analysis, and therefore in himself.

It became increasingly evident that the depression and lack of connection to other people that had first brought James into analysis had been with him since his childhood. The intense transference that characterised this case reveals the purpose of eros in analysis – it establishes a connection. It also led to an extreme crisis that nearly ended the analysis. Without the strong erotic bond established before the break, James would almost certainly have left. Paradoxically it was this that led to the crisis. The unconscious impulse to continue his customary pattern, of abandoning every project he attempted in life was strongly evoked within the therapeutic relationship. However, perhaps because the therapeutic relationship was already well-established, this phase was overcome and the analysis survived. The unusually strong countertransference engagement meant that I held fast when it might have been easier to let James leave. In order to convey the way in which this pattern became manifest and eventually led to a deepening of the transference, I shall report, sometimes verbatim, from the sessions after the first summer break.

At the beginning of September James was in total despair. His holiday, spent with members of his family, had been really good, but on his return he had been confronted by the loneliness of his situation. This highlighted the contrast between his enjoyment in the company of others, and the state of futility and depression he experienced when he was alone. It seemed, as he expanded on this theme, that he was letting me know how useless the analysis was. I reminded him that he had been very angry with me prior to the break and suggested that perhaps he was still feeling something of this. His immediate response was that he had been really shocked by the violence of his anger; it had seemed 'almost primitive'.

This comment indicated that he was ready for, and in need of, an interpretation to help him make sense of his confusing feelings. I said that the intensity of the anger and the fact that he called it primitive suggested it might be a repetition of feelings from an earlier time in his life. Using the term transference, I explained that sometimes emotions emerge within analysis that echo feelings experienced in the past. The impending break had made him feel as though I was abandoning him, and it had evoked feelings associated with earlier separations. James seemed relieved when he considered this, and appeared to relax.

He discussed the fee and explained that it was still difficult for him to pay. As he was not working his financial situation was precarious, and it would remain so until his entitlement to sickness benefit was agreed. Prior to this session I had already considered the concession I was prepared to make. Therefore, after some discussion about the situation, I offered to see him for half the fee until the end of the month, when we would review his financial situation.

At our next meeting he said, 'I've been thinking since the last session – she certainly earned her money then. Something really shifted and I wonder if I can afford not to come.' Two things had impressed him. Firstly, he had confessed to the degree of his anger with me and labelled it primitive. Secondly, my explanation of the transference repetition had brought relief because it had helped him to make sense of his confusion. He had all these feelings about me, and yet somehow he knew they were for his mother. This realisation had been so powerful that it had had a physical impact and when he left he had felt really shaky; it was as if the ground had shifted.

Later that evening he had watched a TV news report from a war zone. He had not been able to get the scenes out of his mind, and that night and the following two nights he had dreamed violent dreams. He could not remember them in detail, but in one a building was exploding and collapsing onto him. He associated these dreams with his anger with his mother; it was his relationship with her that had shifted. He was angry because he could not remember her cuddling him and, when he was four months old, she had sent him away for about three weeks. He realised that he had always been unconsciously searching for somewhere to place his feelings about his mother. This led to a recollection of his feelings for a particular girlfriend in the past; somehow he had always known that the way he felt about her belonged to his mother, but he had never before been able to understand that. I embellished this further by pointing out that when he was with a woman the little boy who wanted cuddles seemed to get in the way of the man who felt sexual. This was why he experienced love as a demand: it felt as though he had to perform in order to be loved.

There was a brief pause, and then out of the silence he said: 'What do you do when you fancy your analyst? This is the most intimate relationship I have had in my life – ever.' He confessed that the reason for his despair about the money running out was that he was afraid of losing me. He said, 'I am used to being rejected and people not being there for me – but you were there when I got the cancer – and then the money – and still you would not let me go.'

I was deeply touched. Furthermore it was reciprocal: I was attracted to him. However I did not say so as it would have been seductive to do so, offering the hope of a relationship that could not be. His loving and sexual feelings were mixed up, as he himself had indicated. The love and attraction I felt for James was genuine, but it was also an aspect of a complex countertransference. This is the privileged position of the analyst – temporarily to love and be loved. Kristeva (1983, p. 13) expresses this when she writes:

> The analyst is within love from the start, and if he forgets it he dooms himself not to perform an analysis. . . . the analyst occupies that place of the Other; he is a subject who is supposed to know – and know how to love – and as a consequence he will, in the cure, become the supreme loved one and the first class victim.

At this point I had become central in James's life. It is rare that the love our patients feel for us is returned in the way that it was in this case, but when it is, it might be considered as one of the privileges of the work. However it was very complicated. The feelings James expressed for me also belonged to his history; they were one aspect of the transference. The analytic setting operates as a laboratory in which the patient's ways of being in intimate relationships can manifest themselves. The analyst lends herself as a partner in this enterprise, and so it is that these patterns begin to become conscious.

In this regard it is possible to understand how the cases of sexual abuse which occur within therapeutic relationships can happen. In the outer world it is likely that my feelings for James would have very quickly dissipated; in reality we would not have been partners, but this did not make the demand any less intense. When feelings are reciprocal the analyst has to be firm, and needs a strong support network in order to resist the powerful attraction that draws her into the world of the patient. Jung writes of this attraction in the *Psychology of the Transference*:

> The transference . . . alters the psychological stature of the doctor, though this is at first imperceptible to him. He too becomes affected, and has much difficulty in distinguishing between the patient and what has taken possession of him as has the patient himself. This leads both of them to a direct confrontation with the daemonic forces lurking in the darkness (Jung, 1946; p. 18).

James's admission of the intensity of his loving feelings led to the emergence of its opposite and a confrontation (as described above by Jung) with the shadow aspects of his personality. In retrospect it is possible to see that it was the terror evoked by the growing awareness of his violence that nearly led to the breakdown of the analysis.

By describing the sessions that followed this disclosure I hope to show that this is one of the reasons why sexual acting out in therapy can be so damaging. The transference is a repetition of previously repressed and unfulfilled desires and their re-emergence in the present is painful. In order to make a difference the repetition has to be understood rather than re-enacted. Acting on these delicate feelings dispels the erotic tension, and while it might be briefly gratifying the developing consciousness is destroyed in the process. Acting on the loving feelings evoked in analysis is an evasion of the pain of the original loss. It is also an avoidance of the shadow; the opposite of love is hate, and this too is smothered, prevented from coming to the surface. By acting on one set of feelings its opposite is ignored. Thus the abuse of the analyst's power compounds the pain and leads back to depression and unconsciousness.

It is for this reason that the potential for a relationship outside the bounds of analysis is relinquished. Abstention is the sacrifice made by both partners in this enterprise in the service of consciousness. The analyst who respects the fragile nature of the gradually emerging awareness is rather like a parent who delights in the beauty of her or his child, not to possess it, but for itself. Ultimately, like the parent the analyst relinquishes the patient, taking pleasure in his or her capacity to develop relationships outside analysis. The maintenance of analytic boundaries, even when there is a strong pressure to act out, is essential to this process. Only then can analysis become truly creative and transformative. Kristeva (1983, p. 30) puts it well: 'During treatment the analyst interprets his desire and his love, and that sets him apart from the perverse position of the seducer.'

The themes of love and hate and problems related to money were threaded through the next months of the work. A pattern of alternating highs and lows began immediately after the rather positive beginning of this phase. James again became very depressed. He could not or would not eat in his parents' house and therefore was not eating at all, spending all his time in bed. He imagined that if this continued his parents would give up on him, and then social workers would come and take him to a psychiatric hospital. Some evenings he would drink a bottle of wine and then phone friends. This temporarily made him feel better but he would wake up the following day feeling awful. He said that he was confronted with the old problem from his life before cancer, of whether to live or die.

This behaviour seemed to be an expression of his fury with his parents. He wanted them to look after him, as if he was a little boy, but they could not offer what he needed. I pointed out that he was similarly angry with me – I was not offering what he felt he needed and so I too was witness to his self-destructive behaviour. His response was, 'Well, we only have three Thursdays and two Mondays left.' It seemed that he was counting the days until the time we had agreed to reassess his financial situation. He was assuming that it would have to end, he could not conceive of the possibility that we could negotiate an agreement that would be acceptable to us both. This led to the crisis that could have finished the analysis.

James was still attending twice a week when he phoned two hours before an appointment to say that he wanted to end his therapy and that he would not be coming that day. I refused to discuss it over the phone and suggested that he keep the appointment so that we could address the matter in person. James was adamant; he had decided 'to jettison things' and this was one thing that had to go – there were only five sessions left anyway. I felt powerless to argue with him, but reiterated our agreement and told him that I would hold his sessions open for him until the end of September. He said that if I sent him the bill he would do his best to pay it. Then tantalisingly (even seductively) he said, 'How do you say goodbye to your therapist?' I pointed out that that was why he needed to come and discuss it in person, and reminded him that it was only a short time since he had said he could 'not afford not to come'. He was definite and ended the conversation.

I felt dreadful – abandoned. This was a complex countertransference response; it was my own loss, fuelled by the genuine attachment I felt for him, but it was also, I suspect, a reflection of the loss he was feeling. He was cutting himself off despite the importance of the analysis to him. I was seriously concerned about the possibility of suicide, and I wondered how far he might take this attempt to kill off the bond that was growing between us. In his past relationships, whenever the potential arose for a loving relationship he had left. It had happened repeatedly; there had been no negotiation and the women had been left wondering why this romantic soul had abandoned them. Clearly it was this that was replaying in the transference. James had admitted his loving feelings, and as a result felt vulnerable. The dependency this engendered meant that I had the power to hurt him, to reject him, so he was rejecting me first. He was furious and it seemed that he was trying to kill his feelings by smashing the emotional connection.

In retrospect it seems that his financial uncertainty was putting him in a difficult position. If I had demanded the full fee he would not have been able to pay, and this emphasised the power imbalance. The alternative, another reduction in the fee, would make him feel powerless. He resorted to the only way he knew of retaining some power: he cut himself off. It is also possible that he was afraid of my tenacity and that I would not let him go. The fear of being trapped in the world of the feminine – the archetypal world of the Great Mother, in all her terrifying as well as seductive aspects – was perhaps part of this too. He desired but also feared a connection with that part of his psyche, which I had come to represent. He could not bear it either way, and therefore had to 'jettison' me. I wrote him my standard brief note acknowledging the missed session and confirming the time of his next session two days later.

James left a message on my answer machine: 'Thank you for your letter – I won't be coming at "5.30 as usual". And please don't phone back.' His voice sounded thin and wobbly, but paradoxically his tone, and the fact that he asked me not to phone back, seemed like a cry for help. At the appointed time I waited in the consulting room for ten minutes, but when he did not come I gave up and went into an adjacent room – patients knew they could ring a bell if I was not in the consulting room. Again I sent the standard brief letter reminding him of his next appointment.

There was no message and he did not keep his appointment. He had now missed three sessions and I decided that he needed help if he was to return. I wrote him a more substantial letter, reminding him that his sessions were available until the end of September and acknowledging his financial difficulties. I indicated that it would not be impossible to continue after the end of September but this could only be discussed if he made contact. It seemed appropriate to offer some psychological understanding, so I wrote that he seemed to be in the grip of some very intense emotions: 'I cannot make interpretations in a letter but perhaps you can see the transference pattern in what you are experiencing'. The letter concluded with confirmation of the time of his next appointment. Interpretations are made in person so that their impact can be monitored and so refraining from making interpretations in a letter maintains the boundaries.

Two weeks had now passed and, when he did not come for the fourth session, I sat in the room thinking about his telephone message. He had commanded me not to return his call, but it had sounded like a plea to do just the opposite. Eventually, after a quarter of an hour, I decided to phone him. When I got through I told him that I accepted he had a right to leave but that first we both needed to understand what it was about. He said 'I can't come near you – you were safe and now you are not safe.' I queried this and he said sarcastically 'To use your gambit I can't say it over the phone.'

I asked 'Am I unsafe on the phone?' His response was 'No', and then after a silence, 'You are just too much.'

'I think I understand', I said, 'You feel too much and you are frightened of what you feel.'

'Something like that; the last letter you wrote helped [grudgingly] it was short – but it helped a bit.'

I acknowledged the difficulty and explained that this was part of the process. If he could face these feelings with me, in a situation that had clear boundaries, then perhaps he could break this pattern in other relationships.

'Can you just give me time?' He asked.
'Yes I can give you time – but I am concerned about you.'
'I am concerned about myself.'
'Will you come on Monday?'
'I don't know – just please give me time.'
'OK – you know you can contact me when you want to.'
'OK – bye for now.'

After the call I realised that I was very touched by his predicament.

This phone call highlights another aspect of the boundaries in psychotherapy. In strictly technical terms I knew I should wait for him to come to me, but I doubted that he could do it without some help. I hesitated before phoning him because this was relinquishing the strictly analytic stance. To initiate phone contact in such a situation is to risk either being experienced as intrusive or being manipulated by the patient. However the analysis was in danger of breaking down completely so there was little to lose. I trusted my intuition, based on my knowledge of this patient; James needed warmth and I genuinely felt it for him. He had been abandoned in the past and needed help to alter the pattern in which he would reject and then feel rejected. If we consider this in terms of the pattern identified earlier, there may be a general point that with the 'men who leave too soon' a different approach is sometimes needed. Perhaps it is important to reach out. What remains essential is that any intervention needs to be understood in the context of the particular analytic relationship.

Any relinquishing of the usual boundaries needs to be analysed firstly by the analyst, so that she can understand the meaning of it, and then, at an appropriate time, with the patient. As in all aspects of analysis a distinction needs to be made between the impulse and the act. This is important in terms of potential sexual acting out; to have the desire is unavoidable, but there is a difference between admitting it to consciousness and acting on it. The patient is unable to make this distinction and that is why the analyst needs to be clear about the limits of the relationship. The boundaried approach enables feelings to be expressed without a demand being placed on the patient.

Just before his next appointment James phoned to say that he was in France. He explained that a member of his family was unwell so he gone to visit. He said, 'I think I would have come otherwise.' It seemed that he was still anxious about returning and was now running away. I commented on this and reminded him that, at the beginning of the analysis, he had told me that he had never completed anything in his life. It seemed that now he was attempting not to complete the analysis. He said that he realised it could go on for years but could not see how that would be possible, and therefore it would be best to stop now. He said that money was a problem, it always had been, but there was another, probably more significant, problem.

'When I come what I really want is a cuddle and there is no way I am going to get that, and that is unbearable.' He was clearly angry when he said 'It is a purely technical affair that you call transference.' Then he observed that he always used to sleep curled up but now he was sleeping between two pillows. 'I have read about infantile sexuality and I think something went wrong. Maybe I was lying on my mother and got an erection and she rejected it – I don't know.' Then he said, 'The other thing is that – I did come that time when I said I wasn't coming. And you weren't there. I drove up at 5.30 but couldn't park and drove away then came back ten minutes later. I could go on and flail you with it but I know that I arranged it that way.' He continued, 'It was exactly ten months from the day when I first came to see you. I felt that I was coming out of the foetus and into the infant stage. I came for my first feed and you weren't there.'

I was very moved by this image and his admission of the depth of his feelings. The image of the erection rejected by his mother seemed to resonate with all the other negations of potency he had experienced over the years. This included his disappointment that I had not been there for him.

He said, 'When you phoned the other day it was 5.45 – so I know it was how long you waited. I don't know what I'd have done if you had been there that day anyway.' There was silence, and then 'I can't afford to come.'

'Well I see your capacity to earn as linked with the rest of this so why not come and discuss it.'

'It means you are taking a gamble on me . . . yes – OK – I'll come on Thursday.'

Thus it was the second week in October when James finally returned. He was unshaven and looked as if he had put on a little weight. He began speaking immediately, telling me that he had been furious that I would not let him go, and this had intensified when he received the first letter. He knew that he had unconsciously set things up so that I would not be there for him that day in September, but even so it had been a great shock to find that I was not waiting for him. He thought that he had been replaying something that had happened in his early childhood. The link I had made between his inability to pay and his difficulty getting a job had infuriated him; it had reminded him of girlfriends who had wanted him to get a job when he felt incapable of doing so. The offer I had made before the break to reduce the fee or delay payment, had made him feel ashamed and embarassed. The fact that I was prepared to shift my boundaries to enable him to continue to attend had pleased him, but it had also made him feel compromised.

The destructive aspect of his personality then came to the fore. He complained that he was doing nothing – just staying at home, sitting in a chair and feeling dreadful. He was unable to get a job and had started smoking again – 'so that the cancer will get me anyway'. I interpreted this to mean, 'If you care about me I will destroy myself to hurt you.' This pattern was becoming increasingly evident. He would contact some positive feeling or accept something that was offered, and then almost immediately set out to destroy it. Making a link with his own assessment of his emotional age, I suggested that his description of his state of being at home made it seem as though he was trapped, stuck in the womb. He said 'Yes and I am a 47-year-old man – I have to do something about it. It feels like you are being my mother and you are not my mother.'

Again it is Jung who helps my thinking in such a case. Here he writes of the purpose of regression such as James was experiencing:

> The incest motif is bound to arise because when the regressing libido is introverted . . . it always activates the parental imagos and thus

apparently re-establishes the infantile relationship. But this relationship cannot be re-established because the libido is an adult libido which is already bound to sexuality . . . . It is this sexual character which now gives rise to the incest symbolism. Since incest must be avoided at all costs, the result is either the death of the son–lover or his self-castration as a punishment for the incest he has committed, or else the sacrifice of instinctuality, and especially of sexuality, as a means of preventing or expiating the incestuous longing (Jung, 1956, p. 204)

The purpose of the regression to incestuous desires in the transference, according to Jung, is less a desire for actual incest than a desire to return to the maternal shelter, and from there to grow forward again. 'The forward striving libido which rules the conscious mind of the son demands separation from the mother, but his childish longing for her prevents this by setting up a psychic resistance that manifests itself in all kinds of neurotic fears – that is to say a general fear of life' (ibid., p. 297). Jung also describes the excruciating embarrassment caused by the replaying, in the transference, of infantile incestuous material such as James was experiencing:

The existence of the incest element involves not only an intellectual difficulty but, worst of all, an emotional complication of the therapeutic situation. It is the hiding place for all the most secret, painful, intense, delicate, shamefaced, timorous, grotesque, unmoral, and at the same time the most sacred feelings which go to make up the indescribable and inexplicable wealth of human relationships and give them their compelling power (Jung, 1946, p. 15).

Recognising that these are the most sacred feelings is extremely important for the analyst when working with someone in this state because, of course, it is also the gift of analysis to relate at such a deeply intimate level with another human being.

The next day James did not have an appointment, but he phoned in the evening:

Last time I phoned the Samaritans you said that I should phone you. I have had it – I can't take it any more. I want to ask questions about you. Who are you? Why are you doing this? I don't understand how you do the work you do. Have you been through difficult times? I want you close – I want to push you away. I know it is transference and when I'm adult I can think and relate to you but when I'm infantile I can't. I don't know what to make of you. When I first came I thought you were about 30 – then I thought you must be about 60 to deal with all this. I thought you are somewhere between 30 and 80. Then I looked at you and I thought you were 47, which shows I want you to be my age. I know you won't answer these questions. I hate you – I want to kill you – I want to strangle you – no I don't.

It was important that he was beginning to express his aggression and his sexuality so I did not cut him off immediately. I commented on how he seemed to find it easier to say these things on the phone:

> Yes I even had to cover my face when I was with you last time. I want to hurt you – to find your weak spots and go for them – I thought I'd kill myself but then I would not be around to see the effect. I started smoking after I spoke to you on Monday. I've only smoked 10 and won't take any more. [In a different tone] I have fantasies about sorting myself out and then coming back to you in 10 years time and saying – here I am!

Much later I learned that this tirade had been fuelled by a bottle of wine. It had fortified him and permitted him to say things that otherwise would probably have remained unsaid. Jung vividly expresses the complexity of the process in which we were engaged:

> The man who recognises his shadow knows very well that he is not harmless, for it brings the archaic psyche, the whole world of the archetypes, into direct contact with the conscious mind and saturates it with archaic influence. This naturally adds to the dangers of 'affinity' with its deceptive projections and its urge to assimilate the object in terms of the projection, to draw it into the family circle in order to actualize the hidden incest situation, which seems all the more attractive and fascinating the less it is understood. The advantage of the situation, despite all its dangers, is that once the naked truth has been revealed the discussion can get down to essentials; ego and shadow are no longer divided but are brought together in an – admittedly precarious – unity (Jung, 1946, pp. 77–8).

In a rather paradoxical manner James was expressing his love for me, but it was all mixed up with curiosity, hatred and sexual aggression. He was in the shadow:

> This is a great step forward but at the same time it shows up the 'differentness' of one's partner all the more clearly, and the unconscious usually tries to close the gap by increasing the attraction, so as to bring about the desired union (ibid.)

Thus the process was engaging us both in its intensity. James had initially described himself as auto-erotic, but this no longer seemed to be the case. His confusion about my age is an example of how the anima operates in the psyche of a man. In the transference the analyst may be attributed every part in the patient's psyche. The mind plays tricks, so sometimes I was a young woman for him and sometimes an old one.

During the rest of the phone call I said very little, but told him that we needed to discuss this in person. He told me he had picked up the *Art of Psychotherapy* by Anthony Storr (1999), who is very clear about the importance of paying. I said, 'Then we will discuss it but not on the phone.' I found it hard to cut him off but eventually did so and he said he would see me on Monday.

On the one hand it was positive that he had phoned me rather than the Samaritans, thus keeping this conversation roughly within the analytic frame. He was clearly troubled by his complicated engagement with me and it was preferable that he discussed it with me rather than strangers. However it is important to take expressions of violence very seriously. The analyst needs to monitor her own response; if she is frightened for her safety the work cannot proceed and some other solution has to be found, for example the patient might be referred on to a colleague. There may be good reason for the fear so it is important not to override it without giving it due attention. Patients do attack their therapists so the therapist's safety is a priority – we cannot work if we do not feel safe. Supervision is essential for monitoring such a situation. Having made this point it may seem strange that I was not particularly frightened by James's expressions of violence. I understood this as being rather like a parent who is not frightened by expressions of rage by their child. Such a child may momentarily intensely hate the frustrating parents, who is also loved. James's love and ability to understand the symbolic aspects of the transference meant that he was able to experience the intensity of his feelings without there being any real danger of him acting them out. Thus we were together in the alchemical vessel and feelings were being exchanged between us with some intensity. However such a conversation cannot be ignored for long.

In the next session James was again unshaven and looked generally uncared for and unwell. He said: 'Sorry about Friday. I thought I would be on the phone for about 5 minutes but it was like getting an extra session.' I agreed and wondered how he felt about that. He said 'I feel that I am manipulating like mad at the moment.' He then went on to talk of his extreme feelings about his parents – not just anger, but also contempt, fury and even hatred. It seemed that when he was with me his anger with his parents was easier to address than his anger with me. He said that if I had not phoned him on that earlier occasion he would never have got going. It mattered because he had experienced my concern as personal and not just professional. (That was probably true, although it is hard to draw a line between the two.) He had left because he had understood me to have said, 'If you want to keep coming you could find a way of paying.' With one of his girlfriends he had thought 'Even if I do fancy you something rotten I'm going to leave because you want me to get a job.' Likewise he had felt that he was obliged to get a job in order to keep me. Thus in the transference many different aspects of the psychological patterns of his life were simultaneously being replayed.

James reviewed the analysis so far. When he had first come there had been an immediate sense of relief in being able to discuss his emotional state without being judged to be mad. Then had come the break, which had been followed by recognition of his anger with his mother; he was aware that he had only scraped the surface of this. This had been followed by the shock of the diagnosis of cancer and at that point he had felt that I had become the friend he had not had but badly needed. After the summer holiday had come transference, and the realisation that it was not just the money but losing me that had sent him into despair.

As the session progressed the time came to remind him that on the phone he had said he wanted to kill me. Without hesitation he connected this to his reluctance to use the couch. 'How do I deal with wanting to kill you and loving you at the same time? It might get out of control.' Referring to the time I had not been there when he came, he said 'I think that I was prepared to risk the couch and see what happened – really I just wanted to be cuddled.' It was the end of the session and I told him so. He said, 'Yes that too – how do I cope with 50 minutes if I am in the middle of those feelings and the session ends?'

The realisation that he could not have the cuddles he so desired had led to a feeling of hopelessness and destructive fury with the analysis. However he had returned and was able to acknowledge the sexuality and violence from which he was trying to escape. I suspect that many of the 'men who leave too soon' are running away from just such complex emotions, but they leave rather than confronting them. The admission of his need for the analysis, and me, seemed to mean that the relative trust that had been established had permitted his depression and despair to become manifest in a more conscious manner. Thus if 'the men who leave too soon' do stay there is evidently much to be gained, although it is usually a rough as well as a rewarding passage.

9 The Inner-World Parents: The Paternal Function and the Maternal Realm

It is the psychological project of the young adult to leave the maternal shelter. In traditional psychoanalytic theory the transition from childhood into the adult world is understood to be facilitated by the father (Winnicott, 1971; Lacan, 1977). Feminist discourse has questioned whether it is the actual father or the paternal function that is significant in this regard (Irigaray, 1974; Wright, 1992; Samuels 1993, 2001). The boundaries and framed nature of the analytic setting establish the paternal function irrespective of the gender of the analyst. This contributes to the emergence of material relating to the father. It is important to remember that in psychoanalysis and psychotherapy it is not the actual parents that are in question but their imagos; the residual traces of the original parents. In the adult patient these inner-world representations continue to transpose out-of-date patterns into present relationships. It is the analytic task to bring these patterns to consciousness. This takes place firstly through the transference, where the roles attributed to the analyst may alter from day to day and week to week, indicating the presence of different developmental stages. Once again I turn to James's story to illustrate this pattern. The three dreams that will be described in this chapter reveal the changing nature of the inner-world parental imagos, as the movement from the archetypally charged maternal realm is facilitated by the paternal function.

During the events, described in the previous chapter the nature and limits of the boundaries of the therapeutic relationship were thoroughly and painfully tested. Analysis now settled into a phase in which it became increasingly evident how closely James's depression was linked to his anger. This was revealed in a cycle of episodes in which whenever something positive happened to him it was followed almost immediately by destructive behaviour. This brought to the fore the connection between James's inability to work and his long-standing, unconscious anger with his parents.

We saw in Chapter 2 that James's relationship with his parents had been problematic since the time he had been sent away to school. Although parents who make such decisions may be well meaning and following a long-standing British tradition, the effect is very often traumatic for the child (Meltzer, 1992; Duffell, 2000). James's childhood state had been shattered by this experience of banishment from home. A further blow to his self-esteem and sense of his position in the world had occurred when he was 16, when the decision had been taken to sell the family business. The assumption that James had had no interest in it had devastated him; his one consolation during his exile at school had been the understanding that he had been sent away to prepare for his role in the company. Deprived of this role he had felt lost, and the sense of hopeless rejection was compounded. It was 30 years since this had taken place but it still haunted James and fuelled his resentment. He had been an exceptionally bright student and therefore was presented with many opportunities over the years, but although he had started a university course and secured a number of jobs he had given up all of them. He had never understood the reason for this catalogue of failures, but the meaning of this now began to emerge.

The Paternal Function

In psychotherapy many of the roles the patient lacks psychologically, or those that are unresolved from the past, are attributed to the analyst. When these become manifest in the transference they can be worked through and a new attitude attained. In order to understand the multiple projections that may occur, the analyst needs to relinquish too fixed an idea of the reality of her self-perception. This is the case with gender and sexual orientation, as well as other aspects of the reality of the situation. The intense erotic foundation that was established from the beginning of James's analysis was based in the reality of gender – the man–woman pairing influenced the material that emerged first. However if understanding had rested at that point the analysis would soon have ended. The transference is an imaginative enterprise as well as a very real one, and to identify with any one facet of it is to be misled. Eros is fire and so demands immediate attention, but its seductive power may mask the complexity of the underlying distress. Refraining from acting on any one aspect of the transference leads to a deepening of the patient's relationship to himself, and then to others. It was the pain caused to James by the denial, rather than gratification, of the desires described in the previous chapter that led to the emergence of deeper material relating to the parental imagos.

For James, alongside continuing attention to the maternal erotic bond, a phase was now entered where the paternal transference demanded attention. Paternal erotic material very often first emerges in association with the boundaries. Established with compassion, these too have an erotic, but not necesssarily sexual, dimension. Successfully negotiated this leads to psychological separation, the ability to speak with authority (Gilligan, 1982) and to play a part in the adult world. It is less the actual father than this function that is important. The gender of the analyst is less significant than the law-giving, boundary-setting function. In this therapeutic relationship the boundaries, which had been tested in the previous period, had implicitly established the presence of the paternal function in the female therapist. This now became explicit, as the meaning of James's inability to work came to the fore.

Work

As James struggled with his difficulty paying for psychotherapy he recalled various work-associated incidents from different times in his life. An incident that had taken place when he was 11 seemed to have particular significance. At the time school had been very difficult for him. He had been beaten on successive occasions for trivial misdemeanours and he knew that the punishments had been unjust. The school holidays had been eagerly awaited, but on his return home he had been unable to confide his problems to anyone. Miserable, he had gone to bed and had been unable to get up. His parents had misunderstood the nature of the problem and interpreted his behaviour as laziness. They had decided that the solution would be for him to have a holiday job. One was arranged in the family business, but this compounded the problem as he was teased mercilessly for being the boss's son. There had been no refuge and he had felt alienated at home as well as at school.

Immediately after recounting this James became unwell and spent the whole weekend lying on his bed with cold/flu symptoms. He reported that he had been avoiding his father because he was unable to look him in the eye. He imagined his father wondering, 'Why can't you get a job after all I've done for you?' His mother, troubled about him, was bolder and would come into his room, which made him feel like screaming 'Don't touch me – go away'. It seemed that he had regressed to feeling and behaving like the little boy he had described, who had needed comfort and understanding but had been sent to work. The origins of his despair and lifelong fury were becoming conscious and affecting his present relationship with his parents. Even now the only way he had of expressing his vengeful anger was through non-compliance with their expectations. This contributed to his inability, or unconscious refusal, to work, and hence to his depression. It also masked the fact that he still craved his parents' affection and approval.

James's fury with his parents was now conscious, but less conscious was the underlying sense of loss. We saw in Chapter 7 that whatever emotion dominates in the transference at any particular time its opposite is nearly always unconsciously present (Jung, 1946; Racker, 1974). It had become clear over the past few months that James's fury with me was fuelled by his need for love. This seemed to be the basis of his anger with his parents, so an interpretation was needed that would draw his attention to it.

I pointed out that his thoughts about what his father might think of him lying in bed rather than going to work indicated that his anger stemmed from being sent to work at the age of 11. James had an investment in keeping his father wondering. His rejection of his mother's solicitous concern was because it had come too late – he was no longer the little boy who longed for her affection. Conversely, part of the reason why he hated his parents and rejected their overtures was that he still yearned for their love. The little boy he had once been was still craving their approval.

A long silence followed this interpretation. The atmosphere was of overwhelming sadness and I sensed that James was very close to tears. The immense sense of sorrow that pervaded the room was affecting me, so I was shocked when he abruptly started talking very rapidly about something else. Rather than moving with him, in my mind, onto the next topic I continued to hold the sense of his sadness within myself and waited. When he paused I pointed out that he had seemed very sad when I suggested that he wanted his parents' love, and that I wondered whether this was why he had changed the subject. He sat quietly reflecting on this and the weight of sorrow returned; we remained with it, in silence, until the end of the session. It is the task of the analyst to hold to the depth of the emotion when the patient is avoiding it. This enabled the first layer of the meaning of his stubborn refusal to work to give way to his underlying sense of loss. The immense sadness associated with this had haunted him ever since he was first sent away, but until now its origins had been masked.

Crying

A train of memories related to crying now emerged as James realised that, when he was a child, crying had never made any difference. It seemed that he had received few of the usual parental responses that children evoke when they are upset. Again he recalled an incident from when he was about five (described in Chapter 2). He had awoken in the night with the terrifying realisation that one day his parents would die. He remembered crying out but no one had heard, no one had come to comfort him, and he had cried alone until he found consolation in sleep. Now, recounting this, he struggled with his emotions. Other similar memories were revisited. When he had arrived at school, aged eight, he had cried in secret under the bedclothes, but the situation had been hopeless, he said sadly, 'crying would never restore me to hearth and home'. As he recalled this, his distress and tremendous sense of hopelessness became very present in the room. Although these incidents had been related before, his recognition of their emotional impact on his life was deeper now. When material is repeated during an analysis it is very often because the patient's relationship to the psychological impact of the event is deepening. James now realised that crying had never brought him solace. Over time other related memories emerged.

He recalled that, after one particularly humiliating incident, he had vowed never again to cry. Even if he felt like crying now he was unable to do so, he felt paralysed.

James's relationships with women had followed a similar pattern. James had ended most of them abruptly and without really understanding his motives. He recalled an occasion when, in the midst of a passionate embrace with a girlfriend, he had suddenly withdrawn. She had asked him what was the matter, but he had been unable to answer. Now he said, 'I was stuck inside my head – this huge empty space – I was terrified. I don't know what it was but I know that I could not answer.' It appeared that he had been overwhelmed by the emotional impact of their mutual affection. It was what he had desired all his life and so it had brought his emotional vulnerability and the tears associated with it to the surface. He had frozen. Soon after that he had left her without explanation and without comprehending why, despite the fact that she was the only person who had ever tried to get to know that bit of him. Then he paused and said reflectively, 'Now I guess you do.'

Thus he acknowledged another dimension of the transference. James's recognition of this pattern of self-destructive behaviour became more evident when he came to realise that he cut himself off because he did not know how to be in a relationship. He recalled how a woman with whom there had been a mutual attraction had invited him to stay at her place overnight. He had refused 'rather than risk it'. He said, 'I would not know what to do. How do you tell an adult woman that you want a boy–girl relationship with them?' It seemed that his unexpressed sorrow had atrophied into stubborn non-compliance. This had become chronic and entered every aspect of his life: he was unable to work, relate sexually, maintain close relationships or even eat. Despite this he had a number of friends from different times in his life who responded if he contacted them. Most were ex-girlfriends, usually married, with whom he kept in touch periodically by telephone. It seemed that he could cope if they lived a distance away and were in other relationships so that no demands would be placed on him.

Trapped in the maternal realm

The self-destructive aspect of this behaviour continued to replay in the transference. As the pattern of alternating highs and lows became more obvious they revealed just how trapped James felt. If he was feeling all right in one session the following one was often a total contrast; he would smash the small gains he had made with the magnitude of his losses. His inability to express his distress and anger meant that these emotions turned inward, leading to depression or acting out such as smoking. His creativity was completely blocked. He reflected on how he had lived in other people's houses until they had become fed up and 'chucked' him out. By overstaying his welcome he had forced them to take action, whereupon he gave in and left, but with unspoken resentment. It now seemed that the unconscious aim of his negativity was to get me to 'chuck him out' of the analysis or his parents to chuck him out of their house. Perhaps this was an unconscious compulsion to repeat the original trauma of having been sent away from home too young.

When he was down, James would complain that analysis was no use, that what he needed was practical help. On more than one occasion he said he needed a social worker to take him by the hand and lift him out of this space. He confessed, 'I feel OK after I leave you for half an hour but it doesn't last; I just sit crumpled in a chair the rest of the time.' The sessions continued in this vein of despair, depression, hopelessness and devaluing of psychotherapy. Then eventually he admitted that part of the problem was that he felt humiliated by his need. I was the only person he talked to and he wanted me to give up on him but dreaded that I would. My seeing him for a reduced fee made him deeply ashamed. It seemed that what I was offering was both too much and too little. The fantasy social worker would be less intense; this was an image of a combined parental figure who would do something practical. As well as a nurturing maternal image, it was a kindly paternal figure who would take him by the hand and show him how to be in the world. This was far from his experience of me at that time – I was resisting his appeals and attempts at manipulation, and that made him furious with me. The negative transference to the combined boarding school/father barring his way into the world of men emerged more strongly as I was experienced as, withholding what he felt he needed.

An interpretation was needed that would make conscious the unconscious meaning of his behaviour. I suggested that he was psychologically trapped in the maternal realm. His apparent helplessness indicated regression to the inside of the mother's body, as though he was still unborn. It seemed that he was unconsciously yearning for the return of the mother of his early childhood and the close bond of infancy. At the same time he was waiting to be rescued by a strong social worker/father, who would take him by the hand and show him how to move out into the world of men.

There are a number of ways to test whether a particular interpretation has been effective, for example by monitoring the immediate response produced during the session or the material in sessions that follow. A 'big' dream immediately followed this interpretation and set a train of associations in motion. At the beginning of the next session James kept his coat on and, holding himself, reported that he had a funny sensation, a pain and a cough. This was a reminder to both of us of his health problems. As soon as he experienced any physical symptoms cancer would come immediately to his mind. It was also in my mind and, knowing that he had a hospital appointment the following week, I mentioned that. He was surprised that I had remembered. Then he recounted the dream from the previous night.

Dream 9: 31 October, year 1

I was underground again but this time in a place like Harrods. It had a marble floor, oak pillars and beams. It was a male environment. I asked a man 'Why are humbugs so expensive?' The man went off to find out. Meanwhile at the checkout there was a woman in front of me with two tubs of ice cream – one white and one red. The saleswoman at the checkout counter said 'that is not an acceptable combination'. I realised that I had the same colours and looked round to see if I could change them. Then decided that no one is going to dictate to me! I was very angry and woke thinking how could I tell you how angry I am.

His first association was to the male environment; he thought that this was evoked by the interpretation of his need for a positive father to help him leave the 'maternal realm': the underground location. He remembered that there had been something in this dream about a leather handbag and a jewellery case. Then, as he was talking, he recalled a TV programme the previous evening in which there had been a description of Freud's linking of handbags with female genitals. He recalled that he had previously dreamed of a handbag for which he might get mugged (dream 5, part 1 Chapter 6). As James considered the expensive humbugs he realised that they cost the same as a therapy session. In the dream he had asked, 'Why are humbugs so expensive?' and the man had gone to find out. It seemed that this too related to the interpretation from the previous session: was it just humbug, or could he trust it? This first part of the dream had taken place in a masculine environment but the second part had clearly been much more to do with the feminine: there had been a saleswoman at the checkout and another woman had been holding two tubs of ice cream, one white and one red. James associated the contents with milk and menstrual blood. Following this line of associations I suggested that the ice cream tubs might be like two breasts. It seemed significant that he had been holding the same combination but wanted to exchange them. His own interpretation of this was that he was too identified with the feminine.

Then, in the dream, his anger had taken over – he was not going to be dictated to and told what combination was acceptable. The anger that he had experienced when he awoke evoked a tirade directed against his mother for unjust punishments in childhood. Then a frighteningly puzzling memory came to mind with regard to the mystery of the female body. He had been watching his mother breast-feed his younger sibling and her cleavage had terrified him because it reminded him of his clockwork toy that he could take apart. He had worried that his mother's body would come apart in a similar way. His fear of the insides of the female body and its mysterious products were evident. His awe of it now emerged in place of the former identification; it was its difference that terrified him. In Chapter 7 we saw how, for a little boy, the mother's body is particularly mysterious and fearsome. Wrye and Welles (1994) use the term 'erotic terror' to describe this extreme fear of the insides of the mother's body that emerges in the 'maternal erotic transference'. This is the realm that the latest dream revealed.

In practical terms, James was still so angry and regressed that he could barely eat, although significantly he was drinking a little milk and eating a few digestive biscuits. I pointed out that this was remarkably like baby food and that the two tubs of ice cream and the association with breast-feeding seemed to be connected to the present regression. This dream seemed to be helpful in deepening our understanding of his psychological state and it was followed closely by two more. The psyche had, in Bachelard's words, been 'set in motion' and insights were rapidly emerging. The next dream seemed to take him into the masculine world and to confront him with the basis of his fear of it. However, whilst the psychological momentum was evident in the dreams from this period, they began to relate more strongly to the dawning awareness of death.

Dream 10: 4 November, year 1

> I was in a park and there was some line connecting one side with another. I had to walk uphill carrying a board on which was a glutinous mess with two frogs, a mouse and some other undefined animal. I had to keep them on but they were in danger of falling off. The frogs kept jumping and the mouse running towards me. Then I was walking along a ledge on top of a cliff. Then suddenly I was up in the sky being pulled in a chariot by two bulls. I looked below about 1000 feet and there were hundreds of bulls running amok in the park and tossing all the people. One bull even got tossed in the air. The chariot crashed and the bulls fell to the ground but I was left in the sky looking down on the whole thing.

It is rare for the full meaning of a dream to emerge immediately; it is more likely that the processing of it will resonate over several sessions and be returned to again later. It was so with this dream and the others in the sequence. The meanings seemed to be linked and emerged in a number of indirect associations over time. James's first associations were with death – the chariot reminded him of heaven. The line connecting one side of the park with another might be a link between opposites – heaven and earth. In the context of the previous dream the line might also be between the feminine and the masculine. James felt that both these dreams were preparing him for death. He then wondered if the checkout girl (from the previous dream) had been seeing if he was OK to go to heaven. At the beginning of that session he had been worried about his health and so the 'checkout' could be a metaphor for the forthcoming hospital check-up. He wondered whether he would have the acceptable combination to pass that test.

Dictionaries of symbols are only helpful when the meanings they present are viewed as suggestions rather than concrete facts. Furthermore they only make sense in the context of the life and current state of the dreamer, and most importantly in conjunction with his or her associations. When all this is taken into account they can indicate potential meanings that were latent in the first impressions of a dream. In this regard it is relevant to consider traditional views of the symbolism of some of the animals in James's dream. In Cooper's (1978, p. 72) view 'The Great Frog represents the undifferentiated *prima materia*, the primordial slime, the basis of created matter.' On the board in the dream there had been a glutinous mess, which might be understood as the 'primordial slime'. There had also been two frogs, a mouse and 'some other undefined animal'. According to Cooper the frog is often thought to symbolise fertility, fecundity and eroticism. It is a lunar symbol and is therfore linked to the feminine and the earth. 'As rising from the waters it is renewal of life and resurrection; it is life as opposed to the dryness of death' (ibid., p. 7.). In the dream they had kept jumping – they had been lively, so perhaps were an image of life or rebirth. Psychotherapy was certainly fertile and erotic and the earlier associations with the inside of the maternal body gave weight to this interpretation. It seemed that the frogs were optimistic elements and connected with the earth. However this was 'in the balance' as they had been balanced precariously on the board and carried uphill.

The mouse has more sinister implications. According to Cooper it symbolises the 'chthonic; the powers of darkness; incessant movement; senseless agitation; turbulence' (ibid., p. 110). This mouse had been running towards the dreamer, so perhaps it represented the danger from cancer. This accords with the Jungian view (see Chapter 4) that dreams of animals moving may indicate physical disease. Moreover in Christian symbolism 'the mouse is depicted as gnawing at the root of the Tree of Life (ibid., p. 110). The dreamer had then changed location, first walking along a cliff edge, which had made the whole thing even more precarious, and then suddenly he had been up in the sky in a chariot pulled by two bulls.

The image of bulls pulling a chariot is archetypal. Cooper writes that 'Bulls drawing a chariot is . . . a solar-warrior attribute connected with sky, storm and solar gods' (ibid., p. 26). The bull is a profoundly masculine image: 'the masculine principle in nature; the solar generative force sacred to all sky gods; fecundity; male procreative strength; royalty; the king; but it also symbolises the earth and the humid power of nature' (ibid., p. 26). Therefore this seems to be a potent symbol of instinctual masculinity. In the dream there had been hundreds of bulls running amok in the park and tossing all the people. They had been out of place: a park is a relatively domestic environment and no place for bulls; they were where they should not have been. They too might represent the cancer. The dreamer had been separated from this danger by his position in the sky. The chariot had then crashed and the bulls pulling it had fallen to the ground. The dreamer had been left in the sky beyond the reach of the worldly violence. The carrier (the chariot) and the motivating energy (bulls) had fallen away as his life was beginning to fall away. Perhaps it was this that led to James's association with heaven. It was reminiscent of the separation of the spirit from the body upon death.

If we consider this dream in relation to other recent dreams we can see that James's relationship to the masculine in his psyche was altering. In dream 6 (Chapter 6) the dreamer had been hiding deep underground, accompanied by a woman who had needed his help to escape from unspecified male pursuers. Here the masculine represented something terrifying and unknown. In dream 9 James had been in an underground shop that he had identified as a male environment. He had not had the right combination because he had too much of the feminine. The fact that it had taken place under one roof might indicate that these elements were now more integrated.

The latest dream was in contrast to both of these. One thousand feet up in the sky the dreamer had observed a scene of bullish violence; the aggression had come out into the open. Its powerful impact and the symbolic imagery indicate its archetypal nature. It seems that the psyche was in transition. Psychologically James was coming to life, but at the same time he was beginning to confront his death. As the multiple layers of these dreams were unveiled James became quite exhilarated; he was interested and liberated by the sense it was beginning to make. Then after some silent reflection he said wistfully, 'It feels so awful to die when everything is falling into place like this.'

The check-up

After his hospital check-up James phoned to let me know that the news was good: there were no signs of change so his next appointment would not take place until three months' time. Despite his evident relief he found it confusing, and explained in the next session that he had expected to die but was now confronted with his old problem: he had to deal with living. He had told the hospital doctor that that he was spending 16 hours a day in bed and that he wanted to die. He had said, 'You are told you should have a positive attitude to combat cancer – well I am trying a negative one.' It seemed to me that this was a reflection of how anxious James had been about the outcome of the check-up. But rather than acknowledging the gravity of the situation, as well as his relief at the positive result, he had made light of it. This defensive, attention-seeking behaviour masked his vulnerability. As most of the doctor's patients would have been delighted with this news she had become concerned, and inquired what he was doing about his depression. When he told her that he was in psychotherapy her response had been unequivocal: psychotherapy was no good and what he needed was a psychiatrist. Unconsciously she may have been retaliating for what she perceived as an attack on the success of her treatment. Even though James had offered her the ammunition he had been shocked by her vehemence and felt aggrieved.

We could understand James as being in the grip of the archetype and acting out of it. This means that the archetypal atmosphere overwhelms thinking and drives action that is based on an unconscious impulse rather than rational thinking. Linking this to his latest dream, I suggested that James had got the doctor to be the bull on his behalf and then observed from a distance while she used the ammunition he had given her to toss me aside. His self-destructive actions had come into play because he had been confronted with good news.

The paternal

A similar pattern became evident in James's relationship with his father. In the next session James looked well. He had been cooking for the family, his father had been encouraging and they had all eaten together. His pleasure at his father's approval seemed to indicate the beginning of a positive masculine identification. He had felt useful and had enjoyed cooking and eating with them. This positive experience was soon dashed. The following day he had been ready to repeat the whole thing but then saw that his father had taken over and was doing it himself. This had spoiled his pleasure and evoked the pattern in which if he attempted anything creative he perceived it to be ruined. He had been so furious that he had gone to bed in a rage. He asked, 'What can I do with the anger?' It seemed that he was at last recognising that it was his anger that was fuelling his depression.

To help him think about it I referred again to the bull dream. In that dream he had been at a great height above the violence, watching from 1000 feet in the sky while the bulls below had run amok and tossed the people. I suggested that his retreating upstairs to his bedroom represented a similar situation. Up there he was safe from a bullish confrontation with his father downstairs. Thus as well as analysing the symbolic aspects of the dream material, this rather more pragmatic approach helped him to think about his behaviour. Perhaps it was this that enabled him to begin to relate to the feminine as separate and therefore as having something to offer him.

Relating to the psychological feminine

Having attended to the inner-world parental figures James began to relate to me differently. In inner-world terms, consciousness – and therefore separation from maternal identification – was beginning. At the same time his admission of his need for paternal approval and his rage at its thwarting had combined to liberate him. The beginning of a more mature relationship to the psychological feminine now emerged. This became evident in a later session when James again reflected on the hospital visit. He had thought about the doctor's suggestion and was glad that he had not gone to a psychiatrist. He realised that a psychiatrist or a social worker might have been able to help him out of his predicament, but then he would not have done it for himself. He confessed that the reason he had been so upset was not only because the doctor had undermined my authority but also – and this was more difficult to say – because she had attacked someone he loved.

Immediately after this session he became worried about his health. He reported that when he had left my room he had felt a constriction in his throat. I listened as he described the physical symptoms. Then I reminded him that, at the end of that session, he had been talking about love. He had been telling me how his bull impulse had set in motion the attack by the critical doctor, and that this had evoked an impulse in him to defend me. Perhaps the lump in his throat had something to do with that. James responded that he had not been going to mention that again because he thought it had upset me. Abruptly he changed the subject, but after a while he stopped and said 'I don't know how I got onto that.' 'Possibly avoidance?' I suggested. He responded angrily: 'I resent that, just because we were talking about love.' Then I pointed out that he was now resorting to anger rather than confronting his anxiety about upsetting me. He stopped and considered this, and after a pause said, with an element of humour, 'Yes I am probably angry and so I won't come back!' This observation of his own processes is important to note because it reveals that he was becoming conscious of his patterns of relating. This is how psychotherapy works: as the experiences gained from the process begin to be internalised the patient starts to take over the analyst's function.

It was similar with his feelings about me, which were now openly discussed. It was November, and reflecting on the time in September when he had gone to my consulting room and I had not been there he remarked 'What is so amazing is that we were dancing to the same tune; you waited 10 minutes and then went into the other room and I waited 10 minutes before I came.' This comment seemed to acknowledge the rhythm of the intercourse between us: we were 'dancing to the same tune'. Then, referring to the ice cream dream, he said he had been considering the implications of the interpretation of milk and menstrual blood. It made sense to him that he was too identified with the feminine and that the bull dream represented the masculine. Thus it now seemed that he was taking in what I had offered, digesting it and then returning to it. After all the struggles and denial, these comments seemed to acknowledge that we were two separate people but that there was a relationship. This admission of the relationship was an indication that psychological separation was taking place in his inner world.

Winnicott (1971) discusses the developmental process whereby, at the age of a few months the infant makes a transition from 'object relating' to 'object use'. In the earliest months the breast is experienced as under its omnipotent control. Then at some stage the infant is frustrated, becomes angry and makes an attack on the breast. This is an extreme attack, for which the baby musters all its energy. If the mother survives the attack she is seen by the baby as a separate person – someone who can be loved and hated and can survive. This is followed by love and gratitude. This was the phase into which the analysis with James now moved. James had had another dream 'full of animals', and before discussing the content of the dream he said that he wondered if he might be dreaming about animals again in the hope of getting more interpretations from me. (He had probably noticed my interest in the dreams from this period. The immensity of what they seemed to reveal at both the archetypal and personal level had engaged me. It is likely that this had been conveyed in my response to them.)

Dream 11: 14 November, year 1

> There were giraffes with long necks reaching the sky, which was very blue – the biggest one's head was in the sky. Its mouth was like a horse's eating – reaching for food but it was eating a hare, which was itself eating a rabbit. The rabbit dropped to the ground at my left side. It was a bit chewed and its mother licked it better. Hair was missing from its left side. Later I was carrying it around in my arms and it was female. I put it down so that I could go into the men's room and another rabbit was biting my legs. Then there were two horses with water up to their chest and they were harnessed together.

In association he talked first of his desire; he wanted something physical from me but was not sure exactly what. He knew that he would not get what he wanted and it made him angry that I could not be his personal woman. The temporary reduction of the fee was like an act of love that enmeshed him. It reminded him of how his ex-wife had stuck by him when his financial and emotional resources had reached rock bottom; he had felt that he could get through it because she was supporting him. I thought that it also seemed reminiscent of dream 5 (Chapter 6), in which a woman had sent him a tennis ball and something had stuck in his hair and he could not get it out. I was in his hair.

When linked to his previous dream, in which James had been in the sky but disconnected from the earth, the giraffes in this dream took on a particular significance. With their feet on the ground and their long necks reaching into the blue sky it was as though they were mediating between earth and heaven. Like the tree in part 2 of dream 5 they were in contact with both the earth and the sky. The circular movement is notable; a giraffe, with a mouth like a horse, was eating a hare, which in turn was eating a rabbit – in real life all these animals are vegetarian. Both the hare and the rabbit are usually associated with the feminine (Circlot, 1962). The hare is connected with the moon and may represent rebirth, rejuvenation, resurrection, intuition and light in darkness. It also acts as an intermediary between god and man (Cooper 1978), so like the giraffe it mediates between heaven and earth.

The rabbit had dropped to the ground on James's left side. In the Classical Jungian tradition the left is the unconscious or the feminine side. The rabbit had also lost hair on its left side after being chewed by the hare. James associated this with the fact that hair was missing from the left side of his chest as a result of the radiotherapy. The mother who had licked it better might have been the analyst. Then the dreamer had carried the rabbit around in his arms; it was female. Following on from his comment in the previous session that he had too much of the feminine in him, perhaps here he was becoming sufficiently distanced from the wounded female side of the psyche to be able to care for it himself. In order to go into the men's room he had had to put the injured female rabbit down, and then another rabbit had been biting his legs. The implication seemed to be that, it was not safe to go into the men's room.

According to Cooper (1978) the rabbit and the hare are both lunar animals and are associated with Moon goddesses and Earth Mothers. The hare symbolises fecundity and lust. This might make some sense of the fact that James's first association after recounting the dream was that he wanted something physical from me. There had been much oral contact in this dream, from the devouring aspect of all these animals eating each other to the rabbit's mother licking it better. These images seemed to represent the instinctual devouring, engulfing aspect of the feminine as well as its nurturing potential, all of which were elements of the complex erotic transference.

The horses with water up to their chests could represent the instinctual power of the masculine and feminine combined, different from the bulls but a development of that image. Harnessed together, the horses could refer to the dreamer and the analyst being together in the waters of the unconscious or submerged in the analytic vessel. (For an example of rather similar imagery see Schaverien, 1991, plates 5 and 13, in which a couple are portrayed in water up to their chests. They represent both the analytic couple and aspects of that patient's psyche.) The mother that licked the rabbit's wounds might be the analyst; this is reminiscent of the analyst's tongue breathing life into the dreamer in dream 4 (Chapter 6). However the dreamer too took care of the injured rabbit and so it could be viewed, like analysis, as a joint project. These dreams seemed to reveal the way that the masculine and feminine elements in the psyche were beginning to move from their previously fixed positions.

However these opposites were in conflict. This became evident when James became aware of the connection between his lack of motivation and his sense of not being loved. Referring to forms that needed to be filled in, he said 'I just can't do it.' Then reviewing his considerable abilities he realised that when he was with me he felt inspired and believed he could motivate himself, but when alone he sank into despair. He needed me to understand the impossibility of it, explaining that it was now as it had been with his wife: without her, and now me, he was unable to sustain his creative energy. It seemed that he was no longer auto-erotic – he was unable to perform without a relationship and lacked the internal resources to motivate himself. Just as when there had been no one to watch him win the race at school, it seemed pointless to achieve anything in the world without a parent or a partner to celebrate with him.

Observing this alternating pattern of highs and lows James recounted how, after the previous session, he had made a list of all the things there were to do, but there had been too many so he had given up. It often seemed as though his will for life was beginning to override his need for revenge, only to be dashed again. This revealed his thought processes. He would see a path, but before embarking on it he saw the problems that might arise and therefore stayed where he was. This could be understood as evidence of the missing internalisation of the paternal function in the psyche. However this became more sinister when it related to his health. James described how he was unable get around his room without puffing (the example he used was trying to find my bill in order to pay it). He said that it might be the cancer as he was coughing very badly at night and found it hard to sleep. He was sleeping all day, getting up at 9.00 pm, and eating only the stale bread his parents kept for their dogs. He admitted that he had found himself thinking, 'This is an awful way to end my life.'

Responding to this catalogue of symptoms of his depression, and having made progress on the underlying symbolic aspects of his behaviour, it seemed that a reality-based intervention was appropriate. I told him that I thought he was angry with me and that was why it had been difficult to find my bill. I also said that I found it hard to sit and watch him starving himself to death, and it must be even harder for his parents; but probably this was his intention. The strong father/analyst was getting tired of watching this chain of destruction. Intuitively I felt that he was sufficiently aware of what he was doing and a real response was called for.

In this chapter it has been my intention to convey the ways in which the erotic aspects of the transference are not limited by outer-world realities. As the field of consciousness widens, the inner-world parental imagos alter in relationship to each other. Relationships in the external world begin to follow.

10   Talking about Love, Sex and Death

Sex used to be the main taboo topic, in Western society, but today the subject of death is more proscribed. Both of these central human concerns feature at some point in all analyses. When patients become seriously ill it is inevitable that their attitude towards death and dying will be considered. Because the British boarding school system creates a culture where children learn that displays of emotion are unacceptable, those educated in this system may find it especially difficult to discuss their feelings about such emotive and socially taboo topics. We have already seen from James's story how this can continue to affect people into their adult lives. In this chapter we look at how the transference opens up these areas for discussion. In analysis with someone whose life expectancy has been severely reduced it is common for psychological progress to intensify alongside physical decline. This was the tragedy of this analysis: as a renewed appetite for life developed, James was relentlessly confronted with the deterioration of his health. His genuine physical problems made it difficult to distinguish between the psychological and physical meanings of the symptoms. Their connection became evident as the link between his breathing difficulty and his anger was gradually made. In one session near the end of the first year, after expounding at length on his fury with others he challenged me directly, asking angrily why I continued to see him: 'You might as well give up; I am dying anyway and you won't get me better.' After a pause he added, 'It is difficult – you are the only person I talk to.'

I sensed the underlying meaning of this and acknowledged that the impending break in therapy was a painful reminder that I was not his personal woman. This was a cue for the tirade to continue: 'Yes that's right you are just someone who sits in a chair. Anyway why do you see me? Is it a personal interest – or professional – is it the cancer? What do you get out of it?' This led on to more anger and to how he wanted to die. Then he stopped, and after a silence said very seriously, 'But one day I'll wake up and realise what I've done.'

In the silence that followed we both sat quietly, assimilating the implication of what he had just said. Before the session ended I broke the silence confirming that, although he was angry, this was why he needed to come. Even when it felt useless he knew that I was on the side of the part of him that wanted to live. It was evident that this awesome realisation continued to exercise him, because the following evening he phoned, sounding desperate. The reason he felt so bad was because he was waking up to what he had done; the cancer!

Consistent with the now predictable pattern, by the next session James was feeling fine. This was a direct result of an expression of love from a member of his family who had phoned to ask how he was. Instead of his usual non-communication James had confessed just how bad he was feeling. This was a major breakthrough, as normally he would not say a word about how he felt, so no one could reach out to him. Now it seemed that, outside the psychotherapy too, he was beginning to be able to articulate a little of how he was feeling. The response had been immediate, and as soon as he had permitted his relative to care for him, she had done just that. Moreover she had told him that she loved him. He was elated, but then he said, 'I can't handle it.' It emerged that he felt something was expected of him; thus love freely given felt to him like a demand.

It was only when I noted my own sense of relief after this session that I became aware of the weight of responsibility of this therapeutic relationship. It was a relief to know that someone from James's life outside analysis was being permitted to care about him, and so the responsibility was now shared. This could be framed as countertransference, but even so, when someone is facing the end of life the analyst-as-person becomes involved. This is especially so with a patient like James, who had been socially isolated for much of his life.

The psychological and physical aspects of the illness continued to interact and attention to both was always necessary. Whilst James was making psychological gains, the disease was also progressing and at times his breathing became laboured. This was exacerbated when he became ill with a cold. He coughed excessively, which was exhausting and he genuinely thought he was dying. But when he recovered from the cold his prospects did not seem so bleak. The next dream took him underground again.

Dream 12: 16 December, year 1

> *I was deep underground 500–600 feet. There had been a nuclear explosion and I was alone down there with a woman. I realised it was my mother and I was going to have to talk to her about this – having sex with her.*

This had been followed by a second dream.

Dream 13

> *I was carrying a dead rabbit around with me. I had shot it. Other shooters were around and so it was dangerous. There was a bull held behind an electric fence which I felt was inadequate.*

The second dream took James's attention first. It reminded him of the danger from the bull, which we now understood as representing his instinctual nature. In this dream the bull had been held behind an inadequate electric fence, possibly a metaphor for the boundaries of the analytic relationship. The dead rabbit may have represented the frightened, vulnerable part of himself, which he had tried to kill off. James's unconscious concern, revealed in this dream, was that if his instinctual nature broke free the fence would not hold and he might damage his vulnerable rabbit/self or commit murder. The latter was evident when he associated the dream with a newspaper report of a man who had strangled his girl friend. He had understood this because it reminded him of how he had been worried that he might strangle me (Chapter 8). Describing violent fantasies that he had had before falling asleep, he said 'Some count sheep but I count bodies. I was shooting people with nuclear bombs; that helped me to get to sleep a couple of weeks ago when I was depressed.' Thus his previously unacceptable murderous impulses were now becoming conscious.

Turning to the first dream, he admitted that he found the dream about sex with his mother really embarrassing; he was not conscious of a desire for her. When I suggested that this dream might be understood through his feelings about me he was greatly relieved. Developing this, I explained that these feelings were rooted in a childhood desire for his mother, of which he had been unconscious. This made sense and freed him to confess that, when he had been angry with me, it was because he had wanted me to say that the reason I saw him was because I was attracted to him. When he had asked if my interest was personal or professional it was because he had thought that it had to be both.

Countertransference

Reflecting on this I realised that, given the special circumstances of James's illness, it was difficult to draw a line between the personal and the professional. It would have been possible to interpret his comment opaquely, but it was true that I did care about him. Therefore I acknowledged that it was probably both. However, just to let him know that the metaphorical fence was still in place I reiterated that this was a professional relationship and would remain within the bounds of the analytic frame. James thought for a while and then said, 'It's because of the way you are and the way I am – I am attracted to you – but it has to stay that way. I can't think of anything else.' Thus the reinstating of the boundaries seemed to have made him feel safe. This led to acceptance of the limits of what he could have, which freed him to reflect on the meaning of his desire.

I was attracted to James, drawn to him as a result of a complex transference; the 'affinity' described by Jung (1946, p. 77) was at work. The attraction of opposites was drawing both of us into an intimate form of relating. The alternatives at that point were either to pull back from the force field that characterises such a powerful erotic transference, or to succumb to the attractions of the 'domains of intimacy' (Bachelard, 1969b). There was a strong inclination to give up the analytic stance and to stop thinking and act. However the point about transference is that it is transient and perpetually changing, so to act on one aspect would be to ignore the rest. Disclosure from me would have been seductive; it would have fixed the meaning of the attraction between us and therefore limited its imaginal scope. As Guttman (1984) suggests, attraction is communicated in all sorts of unconscious and subtle ways, through unspoken messages and body language. Therefore, whilst I did not deny the attraction, I tried to stay with what it meant to him.

If I had moved towards James he probably would have retreated, replaying the old pattern of leaving when someone cared. This was confirmed when in the same session he moved on to discuss a woman with whom there had been a mutual attraction – the one who had invited him to stay overnight but he had chosen to walk home. (His reference to this incident seemed to confirm his recognition that there was a mutual attraction between us.) Then he told of a younger woman friend. He felt nearer to her age than his own but he did not have sex with her because she had been abused in the past. I understood this as his recognition that if I acquiesced to his demands, it would be abusive. James was vulnerable and any sexual contact between us would have shattered the fragile progress he was making. However I did intuitively move towards him, as I shall now describe.

Talking of love

It was the last session before the winter break and the atmosphere was very intimate. After talking at length about his health and the break, James sat in thoughtful silence. Eventually he said sadly: 'I am a nice sort of a chap and all this is wasted [he indicated himself]. Someone could have had what I have to give – and now it will all go into the crematorium – to nothing' I was profoundly moved by this and we sat in silence for a while. There were tears in my eyes, and I spoke from the heart when I said 'Yes – I think you are a nice chap.' James was silent for the rest of the session and it was unclear what he was feeling.

After this intervention I questioned myself. I felt that I had broken some taboo, that I had lost the analytic attitude, that my comment had been damaging. I feared that it had been seductive and that perhaps I had missed his aggression in the moment. It was not until after the break that I was able to understand the effect that my spontaneous comment had had on him.

The new year

When he returned after the winter break James was looking particularly well. He began by telling me of his holiday with his family: he had eaten well and had had lots of energy. However on his return to his parents' house the depression had descended on him. Then he stopped himself and said, 'This is the surface level . . . . It's the transference I need to address – I never know, when I come in that door, what you will be. Sometimes you are just the psychotherapist who sits in that chair – at other times it is just so powerful.'

Then referring to the session before the break and his comment 'I'm a nice sort of a chap really', he said 'You know that was not me now – it was the little boy of 40 years ago. That isn't how I talk now; but it is how I talked then. It was as if from a distance that I heard you say, "I think you are a nice sort of a chap too", and it was like the ground went out from under my feet.' Then he paused and said reflectively, 'But then they would have said "You are a horrible little rubbish." You were my mother then; and that is what should have been said to me then; that childhood voice.'

In relation to this he reflected on the words from the dream: 'I must talk to my mother about sex.' This did not make sense if it was his mother, but 'it does make sense if it is you'. He realised that he did need to talk about sex, 'but that is scary – it is like jumping in the pool'. It seemed that my words had penetrated his defences and reached the boy who had been psychologically imprisoned for so long. In conjunction with his dream, this had been psychologically liberating. The psyche was now becoming ready to relinquish its defences against talking about the taboo topic of sex.

My agreement that he was a nice sort of a chap had caused him to think that I could be attracted to him. This thought had made a big difference and he considered that this was why he felt so well. He said 'It is like being reborn – like a butterfly emerging from a chrysalis.' Just as he had permitted his relative's statement of love, he had been ready to hear what I had said. Previously neither of these affirmations would have been possible because he would have blocked them. Now both had contributed to a more positive sense of self. In Chapter 7 I discussed how a well-handled, positive attraction to the patient might promote in him a feeling of self-worth (Tower, 1956; Guttman, 1984). My genuine affection for James had communicated itself to him and enabled him to internalise an image of himself as lovable.

An intervention such as this cannot be faked; at that moment I had been in touch with him, and instead of withdrawing or running away he had stayed with the grief and permitted me to care. Nor had he rejected me in the following session, which would have been his usual pattern. Thus something positive had emerged from this intuitive and genuine response to the immense sadness of the situation. It was clear that intuitively I had offered him the affirmation he had so desperately needed all his life. It was as if for years he had been in involuntary exile. The grief of this recognition had been fully present in the last session before the break. It seemed to have released him from the cycle of anger and depression. He was at last beginning to mourn the immense losses of the past and to stand on firmer ground from which to contemplate his future.

James said he had been thinking that if I could possibly like him, then, someone else might too. Then after a pause he said wryly, 'But I don't know whom. It would have to be someone who wanted a short-term relationship.' Although we both smiled at his wry humour, I pointed out that it was extremely sad that, whilst his engagement with life was offering hope of a more positive future, he was also confronting death. The past pattern of engaging and then withdrawing was replaying, but now in more sinister guise.

Facing death

By the start of the second year of analysis the erotic element of the therapeutic relationship was relatively easily discussed and so the power of the archetypal transference began to diminish. As a consequence James's narcissistic defences gradually gave way and he became increasingly open to interpersonal interaction. This had repercussions in his other relationships and he began to permit closer relations with some of his family members. There was still a strong appeal to me to relinquish boundaries and befriend him, and as he began to confront the increasing likelihood of an early death, as well as the immensity of his impending losses, this became more complicated.

Journeys and the loss of possessions are common themes in the dreams of the dying (Gordon, 1971; Hall, 1977; Von Franz, 1984) and these began to feature in James's dreams. He said 'I awoke in the night from an awful dream.'

Dream 14: 13 January, year 2

> There were three men. I was going on a journey with two others. One was the leader and he had money. The other was a shadowy figure. One went over as if to fight with me but pointed out that I had a wounded chest. Then I had no chest at all, just a rib cage, like a fish. There was a noise that continued throughout and then I realised that it was me – the noise was my own breathing.

James was feeling so much better that he was shocked that this dream was so clearly about the deterioration of his health. We considered the three men as aspects of himself. The leader, who had money, was possibly a paternal presence – a capable, coping aspect of himself. The shadowy figure was its opposite, the non-coping part. This could also be seen as death stalking him, threatening to fight him. The third figure was the dream ego, a part of the action, but also the observer. What struck James most forcibly was that in the dream he had not been up to the fight because of his wounded chest. This, the empty ribcage and the sound of his breathing had starkly confronted him with the reality of the disease in his body, and had woken him up with a shock. James was clearly anxious about his health.

He then announced that he was considering asking the GP to refer him to a cancer counsellor. I wondered aloud why he would need a cancer counsellor when he already had a psychotherapist. He adopted a dismissive air, saying that it would probably be a woman anyway and he had had enough of women! This seemed to be a negation of the positive transference that had recently dominated the material; a safeguard, making sure that he did not invest too much in me. I speculated to myself that there were a number of other possible reasons for the idea of consulting a cancer counsellor. He might be worried that the cancer was too much or too distressing for me. Perhaps he feared that I would give up on him. Seeing a cancer counsellor would protect me from contamination by keeping the cancer outside the analysis. This and a multitude of other reasons fitted in with his now well-known pattern of feeling that he was potentially damaging in relationships.

Paying the fee

In the next session James paid his bill. He noted that in the past there had always been a problem when he tried to pay me: either he had not been able to find his cheque book or something else had got in the way. Now something had shifted emotionally and there was no longer a problem. A dream recounted on the same day reflected this change in attitude.

Dream 15: 23 January year 2

I was doing an audit for my company. There was a woman sitting behind me with her hand on mine. It felt comforting. Then she said 'I have to ask you something really difficult now.' It was about something that had been paid that should not have been accepted. I was very angry with my boss. Then I realised that I could sort it out and that felt great.

We discussed how the dream woman might have been the analyst, sitting behind him with a symbolic hand on his; he was now able to accept comfort. The dream woman also seemed to represent an internalisation of this function and so a supportive aspect of himself. The 'something that had been paid' might have been the cheque, which he would have preferred me not to accept. The anger with his boss was similar: he was still on sick pay and accepted the money but felt that he should have refused it. However the most important part of this dream had been the realisation that he could sort it out himself. He now felt freed from the usual blocks and able to bring the cheque.

In the depths of winter

James's feeling that he could now sort things out was reflected in his ability to relate. He realised that he had run away from women because he did not know what to do. Now he felt differently. Someone who knew a little about psychotherapy had asked him whether he had fallen in love with me. He had experienced the question as intrusive and anyway, he said, 'It is not that simple.' Then, 'It feels very odd to be sitting here talking with you about fancying you. You wouldn't do that with someone in a pub.' I asked, 'Why not?" He answered, 'It's taboo.' Later it was to emerge that my simple query had had a powerful impact.

James came for his next session carrying a bunch of snowdrops in a little vase, which he placed on the table between us. My immediate, but unvoiced, impression was that the vase looked like a tiny urn. He confessed that he had wanted to bring snowdrops the previous year, but 'I thought you might suspect my motives – this time I know my motives'. It seemed that, whilst aware of the limits of the frame, he was courting me within the analytic vessel. He had had two more dreams.

Dream 16: 27 January, year 2

> *I was fighting in a battle. It was in the mountains and it was a dispute over territory. There were three women tied to stakes: two known women and another who had her back to me. [He admitted that he thought it was me.] And they were all shot. I thought that if they had to die then I would have liked to do it myself.*

The number three was reminiscent of dream 14, in which three men had been going on a journey. This time it was three women. James thought of some territory disputes that he had had to negotiate in his last job. Then considering the fact that the women had all been shot, he described at some length many possible causes for his anger with these known women. The one with her back to him had been his analyst; a known but also unknown woman. I commented on the sexual aggression implied in the thought that, if they had to be shot, he would have liked to have done it.

Dream 17

> *I was setting traps for rabbits – the crops were very small – and then I found a tiny baby in the station, which I would have to look after. Then the crops were cauliflowers that had grown bigger and were now enormous.*

Setting traps for rabbits could perhaps be understood as setting traps for the cancer. The baby seemed to indicate a new born part of himself that he would have to look after. James commented that cauliflowers were the sex organs of cabbages. Then he suggested that they looked like lungs with bits missing, like his own – but these cauliflowers were doing OK. Neither of us remarked that this seemed to imply that the cancer was growing. Hence this dream seemed to reveal the painful fact that his psychological development was accompanied by the relentless progress of the disease.

The impending check-up

James was very anxious about the hospital check-up in two weeks time. It took him great courage to do so but this time he asked me directly if I would accompany him. He said it was because 'You are the only person I have to phone at that time." He explained that he imagined telling me if the news was good, 'That at least it is making slow progress and that I have some time left.' However he realised that if the news were good he would want physical contact. If it was bad he could not imagine what he would do; he could not imagine telling me or even phoning. Then he said that if I came with him he would want me to come in the room and not wait outside. He reflected, 'Of course it couldn't be, because I would want you there as my girlfriend/lover and not as my psychotherapist.'

    This was a very moving request and one that I took very seriously. I could hardly bear to refuse because it seemed so inhuman, given the situation. I told James that I could imagine going with him but would not do so. I would maintain the boundaries in order to protect the therapeutic relationship. James said that a part of him knew that it would not really work, but at least he was expressing what he felt, and this was very different from usual. Then sounding rather amazed he said, 'And it's alright.' This was a marked change because previously he would have run away rather than discuss such intimate desires. 'I am starting to feel that I would not run away. I can show you anything – there is nothing to hide.' When he had said, in the previous session, that he would not talk like this to someone in a pub he had been surprised when I had responded by asking 'Why not?' He said that this had made him realise 'that perhaps it is OK'. Thus my simple query had the effect of releasing the boarding school boy from something he had unconsciously assumed to be taboo.

Transference, countertransference and boundaries

We shall pause here to reflect again on the transference and countertrans-ference. James was now secure enough to know that I would want to share the news if it were good. His inability to share the bad news revealed the old pattern: bad news was to be borne alone for fear of upsetting others. This is like a baby whose mother gets upset if the baby gets upset. As we saw in

Chapter 7, such a baby learns to adapt to its mother's moods and not to express emotions that will upset her. In terms of the countertransference, the snowdrops and the invitation to travel with James had a powerful effect on me. I was deeply touched and, at a level, seduced by him. However the key to understanding these responses was the admission that he wanted me with him as his girl friend/lover. The invitation and the snowdrops were intended for a girlfriend/lover rather than his analyst. At present he did not have one, and although it sometimes felt as if I was his woman, this was not my relationship to him. I saw him twice a week, and this permitted me to be the many different aspects of woman that he needed me to be. The term girlfriend, rather than woman-friend, was itself revealing of the developmental stage this image represented.

In James's mind I was temporarily his girlfriend, and at times I shared this fantasy. But if I had acted upon it, the individuation process would have been arrested, because this was only one of the roles he attributed to me. At other times I was, in his mind, his ideal mother and even at times the strong father. The intimacy of the erotic transference is sometimes very appealing, but had I acted on it, it would have been shattered. It is when the analyst believes too concretely in the shared dream that is the transference–countertransference engagement that boundary violations take place. To act on such delicate feelings is destructive of the emergent sense of self. Like the butterfly that James described as emerging from the chrysalis, such fragile gains are easily crushed by too strong an identification with any one aspect of the projection.

Analysis can sometimes be a form of rehearsal for life. In the transference the analyst is like an understudy, a temporary stand-in for the real partner of the future, a symbolic representation of the desired lover. The analyst is also like a parent who by positive affirmation gives the small child the sense that one day they will grow up to have a real lover. This developing potential is killed off if the parent abuses that trust. The analyst makes few demands and is therefore available, like the parent of early childhood. This evokes the idealised image of the perfect mother/lover. If the analytic frame is breached the analyst-as-person enters the frame. Then, like any other woman or man, she or he makes demands and the illusion is destroyed. Although at one level James desperately wanted me to go with him to the hospital, I was fairly sure that if I had agreed he would have been profoundly confused. Thus it is that understanding the nature of the countertransference is crucial. The appeal to befriend is also an appeal to betray the nature of the original contract.

Confronting anger

Things did not continue in this positive vein. During the next session James looked at the snowdrops and commented 'They are still alive – just.' They were actually very much alive but he had been feeling really bad since he last saw me; he had crashed right down. He had wanted to speak to someone on the phone but felt unable to phone me 'because of boundaries'. He was very angry and complained about everyone. He presented a catalogue of reasons for his anger and despair, but it was when he spoke of his anger with caring, holistic therapies and the GP who did not help him to claim his benefits that I realised he was angry with me. I pointed this out, saying that it was because I had declined his invitation to travel with him to the hospital. I recognised that this had compounded his despair because he felt that it was too late for him to form a new relationship, but there was another level to this too. The way he had wanted me to be at the hospital put me in mind of a mother who would go in with him and speak to the doctors on his behalf. This evoked a memory of when he was very small and had his tonsils out. He had been 'left to get on with it'. Then he described the elaborate game that he now played in his mind. He pretended that he was not living with his parents. In a rather magical way he seemed able to convince himself that, if he did not eat their food or talk to them, then he was not there. Throughout the session he continued to be evidently furious with his parents and with me. The two dreams he described in this session confirmed the self-destructive nature of his anger.

Dream 18: 30 January, year 2

> *I was driving a car up a mountain. Then it went over the edge and dropped down in flames. The scene was repeated, each time adding more detail. I shot myself on the way down. My head was out so the gun would disappear. Then I noticed that the car had no number plates.*

The repeated self-destructive violence of this dream was striking. So was the oddness of the image. Shooting himself on the way down and then it repeating seemed to indicate his agency in the drama. The car with no number plates – not registered, did not belong anywhere – seemed to suggest death, the unknown.

Dream 19

> *I was stuffing a man into a pit and he just would not go in. So I had stirrups on my feet so these were sticking in me. I decided that as I could not get him in the pit I would have to take care of him and did so.*

James associated both these dreams with his self-destructive attitude. He realised that, as he could neither kill nor stuff himself into a pit, he would just have to take care of himself. This would be an uphill struggle, as driving the car up the mountain seemed to indicate. It also meant that he had to begin to confront the immense grief that was just below the surface.

Facing death

This session was immediately prior to the hospital check-up and James was in a very serious frame of mind. He talked sadly about dying and about his children, and wondered how he would tell them if the news were bad. He discussed my refusal to accompany him to the hospital and said that he had known I would refuse, but he had had to ask because he needed to test the limits. Then, looking at the snowdrops and seeing that they were still alive, he said in a pleased voice, 'That is amazing'. (Symbolically, to me they seemed to represent James and I started to feel responsible for keeping them alive.) It appeared that he was coming to terms with the limits of the relationship, and although that was sad and frustrating for him it was also an acknowledgement that life did exist within the bounds.

I would be away from home on the day of his appointment so I gave him another phone number to call. If the news were good he wanted to tell me about it, but if not he did not think he could do so. I knew this was a real problem so I agreed to phone if I had not heard from him by 6.00 pm. He speculated that he might be told that he had 3–6 weeks to live, or maybe two years. As he left I said, 'I'll be thinking of you.' It seemed important to let him know that he would be in my mind. I could travel that far with him.

This time the news was not good. James called immediately after the appointment to tell me that the tumour had grown and was now the size of an apple. It could be slowed by chemotherapy, but not cured. They had given him a maximum of a year to live. During the following session he was very distressed. He had not told his family: 'I can't cope with that.' He just wanted to go away alone. His grief about his children was very present and he struggled on the verge of tears throughout the session. He speculated about a hospice and told me that Wittgenstein had died of cancer when he was 51. It had been diagnosed when Wittgenstein was 49 and he too had been a loner and had no close people, but his doctor and the doctor's wife had taken him in. I acknowledged James's wish for me to take him into my home and that he was sad because he knew that could not happen. He coughed during the session, perhaps because of the pressure of keeping his tears in check. I too felt the pressure of sadness and tears near the surface, but I recognised that it was he, not I, who needed to cry.

Considering the problem of where to die, he said that it would be nice if it happened in his own place, but he had no place, no people, no one and nothing. He said, 'As I have lived so I shall die.' Then reminding me that he had previously wondered whether or not his dreams were portents of death, he said 'Well now they are.'

Dream 20: 10 February, year 2

I am driving a car up a hill. It conks out. The engine breaks down.

Dream 21

My children were coming to see me but they couldn't get to me because of ice on the roads. I woke up shouting at them 'You can't take me for granted. I won't be here forever!'

In association to these dreams, James talked at length and very movingly about his children. He was very close to them. He explained his concerns about them and how it would be for them to lose their father when they were so young. He worried about how they would be after he had died. Throughout the session he was again close to tears.

I too felt very close to tears – the pain and grief were almost unbearable. After the session I recognised that my feelings were a reflection of James's unexpressed feelings, but whilst I was with him it felt powerfully as though it was my own deep sorrow. My impulse was to touch him, to hold his hand, to facilitate expression of his grief. However I held back, in part constrained by the sexual tension that was so often present between us. I was uncertain how he would read such a move towards him. Afterwards I regretted it and thought I should have offered him that physical contact.

This was typical of the conflict an analyst is confronted with at times. The taboo on touch in therapy exists for a number of important reasons. It is there first of all to preserve the personal space of the client and to reduce the possibility of sexual contact. Contact initiated by a therapist who is unable to bear the pain the patient is experiencing may have the effect of infantilising the patient. It may be an unconscious attempt to repair what cannot be mended and in the process the emotion is stifled. Even so I sensed that, on this occasion, a touch of the hand might have facilitated expression of James's grief.

The snowdrops were now dead and again I became aware of the symbolism and the urn-like appearance of the empty vase. James commented on the fact that they were dead. There was a poignant silence between us, during which we both recognised its symbolic significance. After a while I said that perhaps he wondered how I would cope with his dying. He admitted that this was the reason he had thought of seeing a cancer counsellor. He assumed that 'psychotherapists aren't really trained to deal with this. Two things are taboo – cancer and dying. It means you have to face your own mortality and it isn't fair.' Then talking of his family he said, 'I don't want people crying all over me, I want to die in peace.' I realised that he had probably noticed that I had been touched by his sadness in the previous session, and perhaps thought that I was not 'really trained to deal with this'. He did not want me crying all over him. With this in mind, and treating my sadness as a reflection of his unexpressed distress, I commented that I had noticed he had been near to tears both today and last time. He admitted this but said he was determined not to express it: the thought had occurred to him, I won't cry – not with her. He said: 'I don't know you well enough. I don't trust you enough. It would probably take another two years.' He was pretty sure that he would not live that long. This paralleled his attitude towards sex: crying was a form of intercourse where he might lose control in the company of someone else.

He returned to this topic in the next session. Without hope that he would live, there was no point in contacting these emotions. 'The grief feels too much – it's like a time bomb waiting to go off.' He feared crying because there was an actual lump in his throat; he might cough and splutter and he did not know what would come out. It seemed evident that the time bomb was also the cancer – that too was a lump in his throat. I told him I had sensed that if I had touched him last time he would have cried. He responded, 'That is right – it would have gone off.' It was thinking about his children that had upset him so much. He had always vowed that he would never leave them. Then after some reflection he said, 'But of course I was only eight.' In the next session he brought the following dream.

Dream 22: 14 February, Year 2

> *I was in a tunnel going deeper underground than ever, and there was a fire and it was extremely hot. Then I went sideways and there was a path away from the fire. And I was coming out of the tunnel onto a hillside. My head and shoulders were just out when a big boulder crashed down and crushed me to death.*

This seemed to summarise James's situation vividly. He had escaped the danger posed by the fire, only to die as he was about to emerge to safety. The head and shoulders emerging from the side of a mountain made me think of birth. I suggested that it seemed as if he had been about to be born but then had been crushed. This reminded him of a thought he had had: 'Why are we born only to die?' He could not answer it, but if he could he would feel better about dying.

The profoundly sad meaning of this dream resonated with the feeling tone of the session. It encapsulated the tragedy of analysing whilst living with the diagnosis of a terminal illness. James had been travelling into the underground, deep into the earth where there was fire and heat. It seemed that this was a metaphor for the analysis. The transference regression had led back into the psychological womb of the mother/earth, the source of vibrant life, the libido; this was the fire that had so long been buried as if underground. He had found a path, like the birth canal, that led away from this danger. Then he had emerged, head and shoulders first, onto a hillside – this was like a birth image, perhaps a psychological rebirth. Then a big boulder had crashed down onto him and crushed him to death. Thus this dream had encapsulated the whole situation in a few succinct images. There was little that either of us could say, all we could do was accept its evident meaning and remain in touch with the depth of the tragedy it conveyed.

The next dream, which came a couple of weeks later, again reflected James's awareness of death.

Dream 23: 27 February, year 2

> *I was in a fight, boxing with Frank Tyson. I hit Tyson, who fell down. Then we were chasing each other round corridors, shadow boxing. Then Tyson disappeared.*

James felt that this was an optimistic dream; it reminded him of the one in which he had chased a burglar out of his house (dream 3, Chapter 5). Tyson, is a well-known boxer, who, following the association to the previous dream, might represent the invasive disease. Earlier the tumour had reduced in size, and this could be why James had dreamed that Tyson had fallen down. The subsequent chasing each other round corridors – shadow boxing – seemed to be a reference to the disease being active again. It was also reminiscent of dream 14, in which there had been three men, one of them shadowy. In that dream one of the men had tried to fight with James but had then pointed out his wounded chest. In the latest dream James had fought back and hit the Tyson figure, who had fallen down. However they had resumed pursuit of each other; shadow boxing. 'The shadow' is often used as a term for the unconscious, and here it seemed to represent death as well. Then Tyson, the disease or death, had disappeared, leaving James feeling optimistic. Thus the dream may well have been revealing the realisation that, although the threat to his life might temporarily have disappeared, it had not gone away.

Part Three

Mourning and Moving

11 Boundaries and the Bereavement of Dying

In the psychotherapy literature on bereavement the focus is usually on bereaved relatives. Far less attention has been paid to the bereavement experienced by those facing death. This is odd because a person who is preparing to die is on the verge of losing everything. Whilst relatives lose their loved one, they still have their own lives, even when it feels as though life is not worth living without the lost person. For the person who is facing death, everyone and everything is about to be lost. Those with spiritual faith may be consoled a little, but nonetheless the sense of loss is immense. The psychological tasks of dying need to be given a similar degree of attention as other transitional life events. The process of individuation continues throughout life, so the bereavement experienced by the dying person is significant. If the person wishes, it is important for analysis or psychotherapy to continue until the end of life. Therefore even when there is a strong inclination to relinquish the analytic boundaries, maintaining them is essential.

Individuation and the stages of life

Jung considered that no one was too old for analysis because, whether consciously or unconsciously, individuation continues to the end of life. However he distinguished between the psychological tasks of different stages. He wrote that people's aims in life, and therefore in analysis, are different in youth, middle age and old age. In youth, which extends from puberty to the middle years, life's task is to leave the childhood state, to make relationships and develop a career. 'If the individual is sufficiently prepared, the transition to a profession or a career can take place smoothly' (Jung, 1930: p. 392.). Problems arise if there is a reluctance to grasp the tasks of adult life and a desire to cling to childhood ways of being.

In middle life, which begins between 35 and 40, 'An important change occurs in the human psyche. At first it is not a conscious and striking change. . . rather a matter of indirect signs of a change which seems to rise in the unconscious' (ibid., 1930 p. 395). If all has gone well the achievements of the earlier years are now consolidated. However if, as with James, there is a sense of having failed to negotiate the earlier stages then depression will ensue, engendering a 'feeling of inferiority which springs from an unbearable sensitivity' (ibid., p. 392). This sensitivity may be a result of unfinished business of childhood that leaves the adult troubled and feeling exposed, unable to cope with life. We have seen that this was James's problem: unfinished business from childhood had prevented him from making the appropriate transition into adult life, so in his middle years he was unable to move on to the psychological tasks of middle age. The analytic undertaking is to release the person from the lingering regrets and desires of childhood, which may dominate the psyche and inhibit psychological growth. In the context of James's analytic life, all these phases needed attention. However this was complicated by the prospect of early death. This led him prematurely to the third of Jung's stages.

In Jung's account, if the first two stages have been appropriately negotiated there is gradual acceptance of the transition into the third stage, that of ageing and awareness of mortality. Similar issues apply both to those who are dying relatively young and to those facing death in old age, but there is the added tragedy of aspects of life unlived. The immense undertaking facing James was that, as well as negotiating the earlier stages in his analysis, he had to deal with tasks usually associated with the later stage of life. He was confronted with a speeded up ageing process and increasing awareness of his own mortality. Thus whilst working to liberate the life energy of youth, we both had to confront the prospect of his imminent death. As he made progress he was able to celebrate his achievements, but this was accompanied by sorrow that aspects of his life would now remain unlived. As his analyst, and of a similar age to him, I too had to confront my own mortality in this intense analysis.

The analysis was now in its second year and James had already lived past the time given to him in the initial prognosis. Boundary issues continued to concern him, and now that he was able to talk more freely about sex and death he began to address the immensity of his impending losses. He said 'I desperately need you to be my personal friend now. And yet if you dropped your boundaries I couldn't take it. I'd probably run away.'

The fact that I had maintained the boundaries had permitted him to get close. He told me that when he had thought that I cared, this had fuelled his creative energy, but it had also alarmed him; he had been worried that I might not be up to the task. This confirms the importance of adhering to the analytic frame even when the appeal to relinquish it is very strong.

James now reviewed his experience of analysis, saying that when he had first come I had been 'the psychotherapist', dressed all in black, and he had not been able to see my face. Then I had explained to him about transference and that had made sense of what was happening to him. Now he said, 'This is not psychotherapy; the reduced fee is an issue.' Thus it is evident that the fee is symbolic of the bounds of analysis. James was suspicious of my motives and the meaning of his involvement with me.

When he had first come James had described a large bubble, that kept him at a distance from other people (see Chapter 2). This bubble was evident when he isolated himself in his room in his parents' house. There, cocooned against the reality of his present life, he could indulge in the fantasy that he was living alone in a flat. As a symbolic image this was very much like being insulated from the world in the womb and when I had drawn attention to issues between us, it was symbolically as though I was penetrating his bubble/womb. He had no longer been able to retreat from me, nor had he wished to, but the trade-off was that he had been forced to relate to me. James had been confronted with the fact that he was in a two-person relationship; no longer secure in his lonely bubble. He said that he felt on the brink of some major shift and was worried that he might to lose control and be different afterwards; the problem was that he did not know how.

It seemed important to confirm my confidence in the process by making clear that, despite the concession, the boundaries were still in place. Things had changed a little because of the cancer, but I reiterated that this was indeed psychotherapy. Then James said, sadly, that there was no point in psychotherapy now. Because of the cancer his hope of changing his life had gone. There was a dual implication in this statement of hopelessness. On the one hand it was evidence of his resistance and denigration of the part of himself that was invested in the analytic process. However it was also genuine bereavement; James was mourning the loss of his earlier opportunities and relinquishing his hope of being able to change what had already passed. He was giving up the past, and with that came a sense of mourning and loss.

There are times when the boundaries need to be renegotiated as well as restated when working with someone who is seriously ill. Consideration needs to be given to the possibility of hospital admission, which is different from hospital visits. If the patient cannot travel the analysis will end if a compromise is not reached. So when James said that he was going to see his GP to discuss the possibility of hospice care it provided an opening for me to introduce this topic. I needed to ascertain what he would want from me if he became too ill to get to his sessions. He said that he would phone, but if he could not do so then 'that would be it!' His resistance to discussing this further, and therefore confronting its implications, closed the topic. He acknowledged that one of the reasons he wanted to be in a hospice was that it might make it possible to continue when he was too ill to make the journey. This was a topic we would return to several times, but on this occasion it developed no further.

Talking to the family

James was very lonely and spoke to no one between the sessions. The chemotherapy that he had been offered was worrying him as it was an experiment that might hasten his death. He wished he could discuss this dilemma with his family but was unable to do so; instead he pushed them away. He recognised that he was angry but had also noticed his frequent use of the expression, 'good grief'. This made him realise that behind the fury lay grief. He felt hopeless about it and thought that he would probably die angry rather than with dignity.

To illustrate how bad it had become he described one of his mother's tentative moves towards him. She had come into his room and he had sat with his back to her, ignoring her attempts to make conversation. He had done this as part of the fantasy described earlier. In his mind he was living alone in a flat, and if he did not interact with anyone he could pretend not to be living in his parents' house. If he showed his mother that her caring touched him he might be obliged to admit the depressing reality that he was still living with his parents.

Now the anger was conscious it seemed a good time to plant the seed of a more positive attitude towards his family. I reminded him that much of what he felt with me originated in his family, including the loving feelings. I told him it was evident that his mother cared when she went into his room and tried to engage him in conversation. I added, 'and actually I think that you care about her'. It seemed timely to remind him of the almost romantic love that he had expressed for her when he first came. His response was 'Yes I remember that but I have lost all that and I am furious with her.' A tax form had arrived and he needed help with it but there was no one he would ask. He said 'I feel like a perfectly functioning and healthy middle-aged man watching this wreck dying.'

The illness

Following this discussion James reflected on how he wanted love and friendship but had always resisted it for fear that if people came too close they would see what he was really like. Telling his family how bad things were posed a similar problem. If he were to tell his parents he thought they would take over, placing him in the role of a child and thus depriving him of his autonomy. He would like to have a distant visiting relationship with them, and thought regretfully that it would have been different if he were still married. Then it would have been his wife and children who were the first to know and they would have told his parents.

However James was making moves to confide in other people and had spoken on the phone to a friend. When he had told her how ill he was he could tell that she had been tearful. This had made him feel helpless; he had not known how to respond to her evident emotion. Then he admitted that he felt like that with me too, he feared that I would get too close and see what he was like. Then he acknowledged that he did not trust himself; if he lost control and cried he might not be able to control his sexual aggression, and he might attack or rape me. I suggested that this was because of the confusion between his infantile and adult desires. He concurred but said there was no time to sort them out. The losses associated with death now confronted him with stark reality in a dream.

Dream 24: 13 March, year 2

I was losing everything – my wallet, my cheque card and a box with all my personal belongings in. They were left outside and then they were stolen.

James said that this had been a real nightmare and it had been a relief to wake up and realise it had not really happened. It was clear that this dream had confronted him with the magnitude of the losses he was facing. He was indeed preparing to lose all his personal belongings; as the disease progressed it was as though they were being stolen from him.

The appointment at the main hospital was imminent but he had yet to decide whether to accept chemotherapy. He reflected that although he was not gaining weight he was not losing it either, and as he was feeling quite well at present he had more or less decided that he would not undergo chemotherapy. After the hospital visit he phoned me as usual. While he was relieved that the consultant had told him he could defer the decision until his next visit he had been shocked to learn that the deferment was due to the advanced state of the disease; the situation was now very serious.

The following day James explained that the affected lung had nearly packed up. There was a tumour in the top part of it, which he had not previously known about, and this had spread. The tumour lower down, which he had thought was the problem, was growing slowly. He realised that it would kill him and that there was probably a secondary somewhere, 'but they won't investigate because they can't do anything about it'. James talked rapidly and without a pause, thus ensuring that I could not comment. He had ascertained that the chemotherapy on offer was a stage 1 trial and it might worsen his quality of life. Therefore he had decided he would not take it.

Faced by the hopelessness of the situation, the previous evening he had at last found himself able to speak to his father, but this had only been possible because he had not had to say he was dying imminently. Then he said that he really wanted to find a flat to live in. This too was significant because he was addressing the difference between fantasy and reality. He recognised that, in reality, he was not living in a flat but in his parents' house.

Throughout the session I listened, and formed the impression that the speed at which he was speaking reflected the fact that he was extremely upset. I respected that he needed to keep me at bay whilst he assimilated the news. It had been a death sentence. It is very important for the analyst to know when nothing is needed of them except their attentive presence.

Loss

A great feeling of sadness pervaded the next session. James felt totally stuck and said he had an empty feeling that was kept at bay by worrying about the cancer, and without that there was nothing. 'It is a feeling that I don't exist. I disappear to nothing and I just don't know what to do about it. I realise that there is no meaningful relationship in my life except the children. They are the only people in my life.'

This sense of hopelessness seemed to be associated with his realisation that the hospital could not help him now; the cancer was too advanced. There was silence and an air of hopelessness, and then he looked at me and said 'Where do we go from here?' There was more silence. I suggested that perhaps this was a poor substitute for a meaningful relationship in his life, especially when another break was imminent. After another silence James said 'It was when you put the boundaries back I was left with nothing. This is the most intimate relationship I've ever had in my life, as I have told you before.' Then, as if clarifying it for himself, 'You are my psychotherapist.'

For a while we both silently reflected on what he had said, and then I suggested that because he felt that the hospital had given up on him the forthcoming break in analysis made him feel as though I was doing the same. This was very hard because he wanted and needed so much more. He said hopelessly, 'There is no point then.' It seemed that the break that I was about to have was reminding him of the limits of what he could have with me. This seemed to evoke a very early pattern related to mirroring. Without the reflected gleam of appreciation in the eye of the parent the baby loses the sense that it exists. I had offered warmth, but the forthcoming break was reminding James of the limits of the relationship. He said, ' A friend is someone you can call on when you feel like it.'

This exchange was heartbreaking. James really did need a friend at that difficult time but I could not be a friend as well as his psychotherapist. This conflict confronts many analysts in their daily work, but when someone has a reduced life expectancy the situation is so much more poignant. The temptation at that point for me was to befriend him and relinquish the analysis. However this would have betrayed our work and the contract we had made at the beginning. As his friend I would become like his other friends and he would probably have retreated from the relationship, replaying his past pattern of seduction and rejection. It was only because I was his analyst that I was able to maintain this particular type of friendship.

The following session he began by saying 'I don't want you to think that I am considering leaving – I'm not. I thought that at sometime in the last session and again on my way here today. Well that's that . . . ' He fell silent and looked embarrassed. He then said that he had seen his GP, who had been surprised that he was still alive. After another silence I said that it sounded as though he thought I expected him to leave or, like the GP, to die. James replied, 'Well I did leave before – when I decided to leave it was after a difficult session. I remember thinking at that time, as I got in the car, I haven't thought of not coming any more and then I thought well I can and so I did. But that did not even occur to me this time.'

I pointed out that an improvement was indicated by the fact that he recognised the pattern rather than acting on it. Then I referred to the despair and hopelessness he had communicated in the previous session. It was complicated because as an adult man he wanted me as his friend or partner, but the young part of him wanted me as the mother. Speaking of his childhood desire for his mother, again I reminded him that at one time he did have a close bond with her.

James responded that my words had brought an image to his mind of a time when he was very little when his mother had saved him from falling. This recollection of his mother taking care of him and making him safe was followed by the memory of her often being unavailable from his earliest days. This led on to other memories. James recalled seeing a video of an experiment with two baby monkeys (Harlow, 1959). One was given a soft and cuddly surrogate mother and the other a hard metallic one. The one with the metallic surrogate grew up neurotic while the other one was OK. James said that he had not realised at the time why it had upset him so much see this monkey clinging to the metal thing. Thinking of it even now clearly upset him and tears came to his eyes. Then he abruptly changed the subject and said: 'Still there is nothing I can do about it. I'm not going to get it from my mother – nor am I going to get it from you.' He clapped his hands on the chair in a gesture of finality. As usual I pointed out the violent switch from the emerging grief: 'It seems to me that it touches you deeply – you looked as if you were about to cry and then you cut it off. But the grief that you feel is evident.' James went quiet and looked very sad, and the atmosphere became profoundly distressing.

This led very naturally on to him talking with immense feeling about the expectations he had had as a boy and his love of the houses they had lived in. As this story evolved it became clear why he found it so difficult to move on – he was still attached to this history. I suggested that this went some way towards explaining his inability to house himself. Tremendous grief and loss as well as fury were associated with these expectations.

Very revealingly James described how smoking had enabled him to fantasise and imagine that he would one day live in a big house. Until now there had always been hope, but because of the cancer this hope had gone. Even worse was the fact that he could not enter the fantasy without smoking. I suggested that smoking was like the breast. He could suck on the cigarette, taking something in, and as with breast feeding it enabled him to engage in a form of reverie in which he could comfort himself and fantasise. He said, 'Yes it is very much like that – I can't reproduce it with a pencil or a hollow tube.' As with the monkeys, the hollow tube was a poor substitute for a warm milky breast.

James was truly in touch with the loss of what might have been, and mourning it enabled him to begin to let it go. In Kleinian terms this might be seen as achieving the depressive position. It was in the past and would never come to be, no matter how angry he was. The expectation of a relationship with me seemed to be similarly tantalising. The maintenance of the boundaries enabled him to replay his past hopes and disappointments. Admission of this loss at such a deep level permitted me to feel very touched by him. It seemed that this series of sessions really had begun to make a psychological difference.

The next session took place immediately prior to the spring break. James still thought that I expected him to express grief, and he confessed that he still felt 'Not with her!' But reflecting on this he commented that this was odd, because 'If not with you, with whom?' He thought that it came down to boundaries and this not being a 'proper relationship'. He admitted that he did now cry alone, but that was repeating the old pattern: it was always 'You shouldn't cry', so he used to cry alone under the bedclothes, even before he went to school. I reminded him that when he first came to see me he had described himself as auto-erotic, and I suggested that his crying was the same sort of thing – doing it alone was safer than with someone else. Now he was relating to me and this was a form of intercourse. He responded 'Yes it is safer there is no involvement, you don't have to worry about someone else.' I pointed out that his technique for pushing me away when I got close was to change the subject. He said 'I want to cry but I can't do it; it is the boundary issues.' It seemed that in the transference I had become the hard metallic mother.

Dreams and bereavement

Jung wrote that 'dying has its onset long before actual death' and this shows itself in personality changes and dream series. 'The approach of the end of life is often prefigured by certain symbols, which 'in normal life also proclaim changes of psychological condition – rebirth symbols such as changes of locality, journeys and the like' (Jung, 1935: p. 411). James's dreams began to reflect such changes.

Dream 25: 27 March, year 2

> *I won a holiday for two. I did not know whom I was with but I went. I was in a kitchen in an Arab country. It belonged to a man who was letting me use it. Then I remembered that I had left my wallet and panicked but then I found it. Then I really lost it and it had my return tickets in it so I could not get back.*

James associated the loss of the wallet with losing his life. This was similar to the previous dream, in which he had been losing everything. However it was also a reference to his anxiety about the break. The holiday for two seemed like the analysis – a journey we travelled together. The fact that the kitchen belonged to another man who was letting him use it seemed to relate to his assumption that I was married; he was using 'another man's kitchen' when he was with me. As well as loss of life, the lost wallet seemed to indicate a fear that he would not be able to get back after the break, which could indeed happen if he were not well enough. At the end of the session I reminded him that during the break he could contact me if he needed to.

In this chapter I have attempted to convey the very real sense of bereavement faced by the person who is dying. The end of life is the end of all connections and relationships, and most of all it is the loss of the future. James had been fully in touch with this during the period described. After all the intensity of the previous sessions, he had permitted me to accompany him in mourning these losses.

12 Envy, Contamination and Countertransference

Envy: A feeling of discontented or resentful longing aroused by someone else's possessions, qualities or luck (*The New Oxford Dictionary of English*).

In psychoanalysis it was Melanie Klein who explored this most repudiated of human emotions. She traced envy to its origins in infancy and considered 'primary envy' to be characterised by 'a destructive attack on the good object' (Hinshelwood, 1989, p. 167). In the earliest stages this 'good object' is the breast, which is attacked because it is perceived as belonging to a separate person who has the power to withhold the desired nourishment. Thus envy is very different from ambivalence, frustration and rivalry (ibid., p. 168). The Kleinian emphasis on envy has since been challenged by many writers. Recent research on infants has revealed an early reciprocation in the mother–infant dyad, which renders untenable the emphasis on negative emotions in infancy. Even so there are times, particularly in cases of early deprivation or abandonment, when primary envy is evident in analysis.

Envy is one of those most shameful and therefore repudiated emotions. If it is not analysed it may remain unconscious, and consequently highly destructive. Consciously mediated and ultimately reframed, envy may be viewed as evidence of aspiration and so as a positive motivating force. However it is first essential to analyse its destructive nature. In the transference the analyst may be placed in the position of the unattainable 'good object' and then attacked for the perceived deprivation. This provides an opportunity to work through these barely tolerable feelings and to develop a conscious attitude. This may be problematic because most people hate to be envied and so the countertransference may be extremely challenging. The analyst may find the impulse to retaliate, to defend or deny the patient's experience almost irresistible. This is further complicated when the patient is losing their life as the analyst's health may become the focus of the patient's envy (Wheeler, 1996). This is distressing for both people.

As is clear, the themes of James's analysis are reported here in chronological order. The benefit of recounting vignettes from a single case, rather than disparate parts of different analyses, is that a pattern becomes discernable. As the analysis comes under increasing scrutiny a progression from the conscious acknowledgment of one theme leads to the transition to the next. A similar progression occurs in all analyses but it is sometimes less clear. It may be, as suggested in Chapter 1, that when a person is facing death the analysis accelerates and intensifies.

Now, as James began to struggle with the gap between his aspirations and the depressing reality of his situation, envy came to the fore. This chapter traces the themes between the spring and summer breaks in the second year. For much of this time James felt stuck and the creative energy that had characterised the positive transference now became obscured by a silent resentment. In retrospect it is possible to see that this stasis and the envy that accompanied it formed the necessary prelude to his eventual move.

James's need to move out of his parents' house became increasingly pressing but although he professed a desire to move, obstacles seemed to confront him at every turn. On a practical level his illness and the associated lack of income were major impediments. A sense of futility and of his own inadequacy dominated. James's envy of me, and of people like me who appeared to be doing all right, was at first apparent in verbal asides, followed by increasingly overt attacks on the analysis. Then gradually, whilst denigrating the analysis and complaining of how stuck he felt, things began to change. He started to make forays into the world and to stay for days or weekends with relatives and old friends in different parts of the country. Sometimes he missed sessions in order to do so. This was a positive change and indicated increasing investment in the world outside the analysis, but there were times when his contempt for the process was evident in a 'forgotten' session.

James continued to pay the agreed fee on time each month, but his resources were limited so the need to claim the benefits to which he was entitled became urgent. The psychological block on filling in forms continued to be a major impediment. He was unable to move house because he had no money, and whilst he was increasingly conscious of his psychological investment in maintaining the 'stuck' situation he seemed incapable of making any significant change. He knew that other people did not regard filling in forms as a problem and his envy of others' ability was excruciating. The associated humiliation meant that he could not let anyone help him to claim, and this felt insurmountable. It was similar with moving to a place of his own: he would first have to admit that he wanted to do so, and that would make him vulnerable.

As James discussed where he might live it became clear that part of the problem was that no house he could afford was going to be 'special' like those of his childhood. When he drove by the largest houses in town he would think 'This where I belong'; nowhere else would do. As he put it: 'Houses in this culture symbolise money. At one time they said something about who you were in the world, but now money can buy houses so people can move anywhere up and down the social scale.' His envy was closely linked to the despair that he was not part of that. Then one day, referring to his life and the analysis, he said that since the break he had not known what he was doing: 'This is like a dead end' The analysis came to feel hopeless and for a while he seemed to withdraw some of his emotional investment.

Transference

James had been invited to stay with his family in France. He wanted to go but could not because it would mean missing his analytic sessions. He hated me for his dependence and the fact that I still saw him for a reduced fee. He said angrily, 'This is not psychotherapy it is like going to see a friend for a chat – it is charity.' Then another time, referring to his sense of being stuck, he said that this was so much a part of his life that it was not psychotherapy.

The fact that I had somewhere to live and he did not made him very aware of the gap between us and he became both angry and envious. He said tellingly, 'You are housed. We are not the same. We could never be because we are different. You are housed and I am not.' Later he explained that the fact that I was housed and he was not made him feel separated from me. This applied to his body and how he inhabited it, as well as to real houses, and there were also psychological parallels. James recognised this as the old familiar feeling: 'She is too good for me', which was how he had felt about every woman with whom he had been involved. Thus at the same time as thinking he was special and therefore the world owed him something, he also felt completely the opposite – totally inadequate and unequal to other people. The difference between us, the separation between his desire and the object of it, made the relationship unbearable. He felt that he had nothing to give a woman; he said 'Companionship and sex are not it.'

Reflecting on this I pointed out that we had neither companionship nor sex, so perhaps it was difficult for him to recognise that there might be something he did give to me. He paused and then said he realised that he did give me something, but that it was unequal. He was acutely aware that I gave to him by continuing to see him for a reduced fee. Then he expressed puzzlement, saying that he was supposed to be a man but whatever that was he did not seem to have it. This is typical of the 'boarding school survivor' (Duffell, 2000) who has grown to maturity without growing up.

Bodily countertransference

The countertransference is particularly complex when working with a life-threatening illness. The analyst's emotions reflect the roller coaster of hope and despair that the patient experiences. During this phase there were times when James seemed really well and it was almost possible to forget that he was seriously ill. However there were times when concern about his physical state dominated. Sometimes the maternal function continued to be significant as I was called on to contain the anxiety that James seemed to experience in relation to his body. It was understandable that every bodily change, no matter how small, was immediately taken as a sign of secondary cancer. He would worry about a spot on his leg and show it to me, and if he had a pain inside his body he described it in detail. One time he movingly described how at night he was sometimes aware of his lung physically closing down. This was frightening and made him feel very alone and sad. I was extremely touched by the loneliness of his situation and desperately wished I could do something about it but I was as powerless as he was. This was a human response to the demands of the situation, but it was also a countertransference whereby I was placed in the maternal role as container of his anxiety.

Whilst with James I occasionally had powerful bodily experiences, which I later understood to be an embodied form of countertransference. Very often James was in touch with the seriousness of his illness and the imminence of death. One day he reported feeling ill and that it felt as though things were going on in his body; he felt sick all the time and was unable to think. As he recounted this he was tearful and there were long and painful silences. The emotional tone of the whole session was of great sadness and loss. At one point I experienced a physical reaction of isolation, combined with a sense of loss and loneliness that was so overwhelming there was no way it could be articulated. This was followed by an unfamiliar chill in my spine – this might sound rather dramatic, but it was as though I was in the presence of death. At first I was so struck with the nature of it that I thought it was my own feeling, but as it passed and I recovered, I realised that in some unconscious way I had picked up the isolation and abandonment that James was experiencing. Such bodily countertransference experiences are not uncommon in analysis (see Samuels, 1985a; Field, 1989; Fordham, 1989 see Wiener, 1994). However, because the feelings are so intense it is not always immediately clear that they are a form of countertransference.

Once I had become aware that this was countertransference it became available for me to use and when I spoke to James of his great sense of loneliness it came from a depth of understanding informed by that experience. James responded by saying that he had given up: it was too late for any desire and he felt alone, crushed by the impossibility of it all. At that point I had a strong impulse to hold him physically as there seemed to be no other way of communicating that I was with him. This too could be understood as a countertransference response to his sense of hopelessness and his desire to be held and comforted.

As always I resisted the impulse to touch him. There were several reasons for not holding him which I can articulate now but at the time were mainly intuitively experienced. Firstly, I was fairly sure that James would find such contact confusing. Secondly, if I had held him it would have been primarily for me, an attempt to silence expression of the pain of his aloneness. I was with him emotionally but the feeling would have been extinguished by physical contact. It would have momentarily distracted him from his pain but it would not have saved him from it. Nor would physical contact have made his lonely nights better. In some ways it would have been a lie, a pretense that I could do something to change his situation, which in reality I could not ameliorate. Such a gesture maintains the patient in the child position. It would have prevented him from becoming conscious of his anger: he was furious with me and in the end that became a motivating force. By the end of the session James was very angry. He said he was going away to stay with relatives so he would miss two sessions. As he left he said 'I will drink a bottle of gin tonight.' Thus he let me know that I was useless because I could not or would not rescue him.

There was another occasion when I experienced a bodily reaction that I later understood to be countertransference. This was in response to an existential crisis that James recounted. He had been driving through the town, feeling good and thinking that it was OK to be himself. As he looked at the houses he passed the thought had occurred to him that 'All those houses contain a person or a family who think that they are important.' He reflected that he could not understand why he did not get on with life. The whole of the session was about loneliness and lack of contact with other people, and how pointless his life felt. He said that the spiritual dimension was missing and he feared meeting people.

Whilst he was talking I felt so physically sick that for a moment I thought I would have to excuse myself and leave the room. Then, when I managed to think, I realised that this too was probably a countertransference experience. It seemed that the overwhelming power of the sense of meaninglessness of which he was speaking had affected me physically. My feeling was probably similar to his experience when he drove past the houses and felt the meaninglessness of life. I did consider that this might have been an attack on me, but at that point I did not think it was. However it was not long before such attacks did become evident in his denigration of the analysis.

Silent anger

James's frustration and silent, resentful anger became manifest in the transference. The analysis began to feel static and he questioned why he came. He said that whilst he had once thought about the sessions perpetually during the time between them, now he could not remember the content of the previous session. Sometimes, as he left, he thought that he must remember what had come up, but then it would disappear from his mind. Alongside this was the constant theme of feeling that he should be able to get a job and a house and yet he was unable to do so. He felt at an impasse. He complained that he was unable to motivate himself and it was impossible to find it from outside. This seemed to be a complaint that I was doing nothing actively to help him.

At the same time, and despite the continuous complaints, there was often a strong atmosphere of desire between us. He admitted that he wanted more from me emotionally than he could have, and that this was contributing to his feeling of hopelessness. James reported that he had mentioned that he was in psychotherapy to a friend, who had said knowingly, 'Oh, fantasy relationships.' This had struck him as perceptive, and he now despaired because he had glimpsed what he had been missing, but he could not have it with me. I pointed out that investing in this 'fantasy' relationship might make it possible to find it for real later. The tragedy was that, because of his illness, it was difficult for him to imagine investing in another relationship now.

Dream 26: 29 May, Year 2

> *People were shooting; they were all attacking me and the people I was with. They were nearly all killed and I was alone and hoping not to be caught. I saw a shooting party coming towards me, led by a gamekeeper. He winged five or six pigeons and they fell to the ground, and then a huge fish came at me out of the sky with its vast mouth open.*

James saw this as a positive dream, a sign of hope. I did not see it that way, but refrained from saying so. Firstly, James was being hunted and all the people he was with had been killed. He had not been responsible for their death but he had lost the people he was with. The winged pigeons had been injured but like him they were not dead. The fish seemed to indicate some sort of threat – death perhaps. Perhaps the dream was positive for him because the anger was in the open.

The sense of angry, envious stasis became more obvious over the following weeks. I shall report verbatim from one session that revealed how overwhelming James's lack of motivation was at that time. On his return from staying with relatives he said that he felt like sulking in his room until he died: 'I just don't see what to do or how to do it.' A long and painful silence followed. Then he said, 'Well I don't know what to say.' I said, 'It seems to make you feel uncomfortable.' 'Yes its embarrassing really.' There was another long silence, and then 15 minutes into the session he said, 'Well I guess I should go now – I know only I can get myself out of this – it is me who has to break in – there is no one else to do it; but I just pass time watching the television or sleeping.' Then he said that in the past, when he had got to this point, someone had got him out of it. That was what he needed – someone to set him on the starting line, but this time there was no point in starting. 'I may as well sulk until I die.' It seemed that he was furious with me for not doing something to set him on the starting line.

The next day he was unshaven and referred to the fact that I was going to be away so he would miss one session and then said, 'I feel stuck and it is all pointless. I feel stuck because of the cancer but I'd be like that anyway

I know it. What I was thinking was that there is no point, there is nothing to grow from, without a house or a job there is no growth.' Then he said, 'It is OK being in limbo for now but if I was still here, [alive] in five years time I would be furious with myself for not having got on with it.' Then there was a glimmer of movement when he said he had decided that he must do something: 'I can't just stay around here so I'm taking the opportunity of you being away to go to see some people I used to live with.' This heralded a new and more active phase in his life. The state of utter despair was now replaced by action.

Returning to Life

This was the first of several such forays out into the world to visit family and friends he had not seen for some time. He started attending sporting events and found being part of the crowd very exciting. At last he felt like a part of the world, and at times he looked really well. An ex-girlfriend renewed contact with him and told him that it was time he left home. As well as encouraging him, this induced a sense of panic that she did not realise how serious his illness was. Thus the thought of actually being able to move worried James greatly. He missed more sessions when he went to stay with some friends whom he had not seen for 20 years. It seemed that he was letting me know that missing sessions did not matter to him.

This had the intended effect on me; I felt a tremendous sense of loss that prevented me from recognising his sense of loss at missing sessions. In the normal course of psychotherapy, when people are working towards an ending they begin to withdraw their investment in the analysis. As life's activities become more important there is a gradual letting go, and inevitably a sense of loss. However in James's case the end to which we were working was less optimistic. My sense of loss was probably due to the awareness that James was going to die.

When he returned James explained that he and the couple with whom he had stayed had not seen each other for many years and he had been shocked to realise that neither of them needed to work. This had made him acutely aware of his own situation, and he had become envious. The contrast was striking – he lived in his parents' house and his children lived away from him. If anyone came to visit him he would feel ashamed of how he was living. This brought home to him the realisation that he needed to pack his emotional baggage and leave his parents. Then he recounted how he had helped his friend with a technical problem. He had realised that he was good at this particular task and that he would like to have a job instead of watching TV.

During the next session he told me that he had contemplated cancelling but decided that I would persuade him against it, and anyway 'it gets me out of the house'. In this thinly veiled attack the denigration was clearly active and he said that he still felt just the same – stuck. He sat in the chair and looked furious as he said 'There is no point in going on.' The forays he made out into the world only highlighted the futile nature of his life. He expounded on this at length and on how angry he was with particular women in his life, and then women in general. There were many long and angry silences throughout the session. He sat silently hitting his finger tips together and biting his lip. I acknowledged how painful it must be to see his friends' success. It was similar with me, but I thought that as well as being angry with me he seemed to be in despair.

In retrospect these feelings can be seen as contributing to his eventual move. The envy he experienced in relation to his friends and me was useful; it was so painful that it motivated him. He realised that he aspired to what they and I appeared to have. James was not so different from his friends, and if they could do it so could he. In this way envy can be a motivating force. However there were other aspects of envy that seemed very dangerous to him.

Contamination

When a patient is seriously ill, contamination may be an unconscious fear. For patients with AIDS-related illnesses contamination is obviously a concern. However it is less obvious that patients with cancer, which as far as we know is not transmittable may fear their potential to contaminate others. This is a psychological attitude that might, as in James's case, have a different focus if the person were not physically ill.

James often worried about his power to damage his friends and me. One day he was recounting the mistreatment he had received at the hands of certain doctors. I became aware of envy in the account and suggested that perhaps he was envious of people who, like me, did not as far as they knew, have cancer. Surprisingly this produced an immediate angry response: 'That is what I mean – people are damaged by me – you are now thinking that you might have it – you see what it does!'

It was evident that he could not bear any sign of my vulnerability, but it also unmasked his terror of his potential to damage others. When I asked him about this feeling that he had damaged me he said, 'Well – by talking about what is happening with me – you have to think about it – whether you have it. Smokers don't want me to mention it." Then thoughtfully he reflected, 'Women get breast cancer.' He was clearly worried about his power to damage the part of me/women that he most desired. He explained that when he had mentioned that to one of his friends she had refused to think about it and said 'Stop!' Pointing out that it was not only the cancer, I reminded him of how he often felt damaging if he expressed any feelings. He contemplated this, then said 'Yes you could be right. But look what happens; I talk about it and then you have the problem and think that you may have it. That is damaging.' I responded, 'I don't think it is damaging – it may be a problem but it is one I have to face anyway.' He retorted, 'No you don't.'

At that point I stopped myself. I realised that I was unconsciously denying his effect on me, as well as the importance of what he was trying to convey. I admitted to myself that I was indeed being confronted with my own mortality because of the mere fact that I was working with James. I was evading it because it was uncomfortable to acknowledge, as was his envy of my health. Having become conscious of this I was able to understand. I acknowledged that it must be very lonely to have to bear the sense of being potentially damaging.

This freed James to explain that he felt this separated us; it made him aware of how different we were. In the next session he returned to this topic, saying that I had mentioned something he felt was taboo: 'You might really have cancer.' It seemed as though I knew something that he did not about relationships and that gave me a lot of power; it made him feel in awe of me, and stupid. He said that what was all right in psychoanalysis was not all right in the world. This was like the time when he had felt he wanted to strangle me at the same time as having loving feelings: 'It is OK in psychotherapy but not in the world.' Then he said he felt that women in general knew something that he did not. He did not know the rules – never had. In common with other men who as boys had been banished to boarding school, a community of men where emotions were banned, James was ill-equipped to deal with the adult world and women remained a mystery to him.

Independence

James was due for a check-up at the hospital. He expected to be told that the disease was progressing slowly and that he might have a while longer to live. If that happened he would be faced with the old problem of what to do. He decided to find out more about cancer and so went to a library, where he discovered that no one really knew what would happen in any given case. 'The doctors pretend to know but all it is about is facing up to death; they offer things to avoid death.' As he was discussing this he became upset and then as he recovered he said 'It is about grief.' He was beginning to catch it himself and to understand his own emotions. This is what happens as the conscious attitude is assimilated the analyst's function gradually becomes internalised. A new independence of spirit was beginning to develop.

There was a good deal of humour and some flirtation in the following sessions, on which I commented. This led James to reflect that things had changed. He recalled how, back in October when he had not been able to come, I had written and said I thought he was in the grip of some intense emotions. He said that this had been true, but that had all been mother stuff and now it was different. He felt that he had moved on and was now very aware that I was a woman and was therefore keeping me at arms length. To emphasise the point he extended his arm in a gesture of pushing me away. He said, 'If you get too close you get hurt.' Despite this there was a sense that he was now genuinely relating to me as a whole person. When I offered to be available if he wanted to phone me after the hospital appointment, his new independence was evident. He thanked me but said he would not need to. This felt appropriate as if he was relating to me in a different, more adult way. Perhaps as a result of having discussed his fears of contaminating others he was less afraid of doing so. He was now in more regular contact with his family and friends.

James's positive mood continued and he virtually bounced into the room after the hospital appointment. He was feeling great, the day had gone well and he had told the doctor that he felt fine. The doctor had examined him, found nothing disturbing and said that he would see him again in October. On his return James had gone for a long walk. It had been a wonderful experience; he had climbed to the highest point around and decided that he might live for another five years so he might as well get on with it. Then he had received a phone call from a friend who was willing to help him to find a flat, and another from someone who knew that a mutual friend was moving. There was also a possibility that someone else might help him to find a job. He felt really positive and it appeared that if he would let people help him they were willing to do so.

The next session was the last before the summer break. James looked unwell. He had been for a long walk and had thought that he was going to be late. He recounted a telephone conversation the previous evening with a friend who had tried to give him some advice about treatment for cancer. James felt that she did not understand and that I was the only person he could talk to about it. He then reminded me that the GP had told him that one day he would just fall ill and be dead within two weeks. The message was clear: with me away there was no one to understand him and he might die. This certainly affected me and I was worried that he would die while I was away. He was genuinely anxious and so I voiced what I thought was his fear: that he would not return after this break. He responded, 'Yes I have thought of that. One day it'll be like that – perhaps at Christmas with two or three weeks' break.' Thus as well as the transference material we were both living with the very real uncertainty of the situation. When a patient is as seriously ill as James was there is always the possibility of sudden death, so the breaks in analysis become even more charged than in normal times.

13 The Link Between Psychotherapy and Cancer

During the period described in this chapter, between the summer and winter breaks in the second year, James at last moved into a house of his own. The transition that occurred at that time has implications for the process of psychotherapy in general, when the threat of death does not overshadow it. When the origins of out-of-date patterns of relating become conscious, a form of separation differentiation takes place. It was this that freed James psychologically, enabling him to move on from the point at which he had been arrested. As he began to stand on firmer ground in both psychological and practical terms, he became more confident of his place in the world. He was less avoidant, relating more directly within the analysis and outside. Sadly it was at that point that his health began to fail.

During the summer break there had been a change in James's practical circumstances. The state sickness benefits to which he was entitled were at last being paid. This was the result of a significant emotional shift. As we have seen, James had a serious psychological block that had prevented him from filling in the necessary claim forms. This had suddenly changed. He described how he had been filling in forms and met a potential obstacle: 'There were some daft questions.' In the past, at that point he would have put the form in a drawer and forgotten it, but this time it had been different. He had paused and 'then filled it in anyway, and posted it'. He was buoyant: he had bought a car and told me with excitement of his plan to move; he felt that his life now had a sense of purpose. However this was tempered by two inhibiting factors: he was unable to tell his parents of his plan to move, and there was the ever present fear that he might die before he could achieve his aims.

Psychotherapy and cancer

James was very aware of the cancer; he was intermittently feeling sick and coughing, and there was constant wheezing sound when he breathed. Then one day he said that, on his way to the previous appointment, he had thought that he would like to talk about the link between psychotherapy and cancer, but then he had thought 'No, I can't talk about that!' Although he had not mentioned it during the session he had felt distressed, and this had puzzled him. That night he had had the following dream.

Dream 27: 18 September, year 2

There was this white pus coming out of my side, here where it hurts, and I woke up thinking: Exploding lymph nodes, that is really bad.

Upon waking James had been immensely relieved to realise that it had just been a dream and that he was still alive. Even so the overwhelming sense had been that this was a sign that he was 'finished'. However he had gone back to sleep and awoke the following day with 'no pains, no cough, nothing'. Without even thinking about it he had 'just started to do things'. He had told his parents that he was moving and had been amazed by their response; he had expected them to object, but on the contrary they had been encouraging. This points out the disjunction between expectations based on inner-world perceptions and reality. Thus another practical issue of immense psychological proportions had shifted.

This dream, which had taken place immediately after the session in which James had decided not to speak about the links between psychotherapy and cancer, indicates the psyche's persistence: this connection needed to be made. When the dreamer is ill the physical implications of the dream at first overshadow its symbolic significance. There is little doubt that the exploding lymph nodes in James's dream referred to the reality of his physical state and the ever present awareness that the cancer was spreading. Put simply, lymph is a fluid that carries white blood cells around the body to digest or produce immune response to harmful foreign bodies such as bacteria and toxins. Foreign bodies are removed from the lymph at the lymph nodes, so if cancer should spread to these nodes the outlook is very bad indeed. James's initial diagnosis had confirmed that the cancer had already entered the lymphatic system, so he had known this all along. It seems that he had managed to bury this aspect of the bad news but now the dream had reminded him.

However there is another way of understanding this dream, and that is to attend to its psychological implications. Cancer is thought by some to be associated with unexpressed anger. McDougall's (1989) work on the links between psyche and soma shows the ways in which psychological disturbance manifests itself in physical symptoms. The emergence of the dream pus seems to have had a powerfully liberating effect. This leads to the speculation that this was a consequence of James's recent expressions of anger, which had perhaps purged his system of some of the poison lurking within it. In addition the 'exploding dream lymph nodes' put me in mind of seminal fluid. James admitted that this idea had also occurred to him. If the exploding lymph nodes were like an ejaculation, this could explain the huge burst of energy he had experienced after the dream. Furthermore the physical pain that usually inhibited his movements had gone, indicating that some of it had been due to psychological rather than physical disease. The dream seemed to have had a purifying effect on the psychic system – it was as though a psychological obstacle had shifted and a creative channel had opened up, altering James's attitude towards his family and the tasks that needed attention. Hence this dream appeared to indicate that, despite the cancer, psychotherapy was generating a renewed appetite for life, and this was reflected in the way James's now related to me.

Depth

James became unusually open about what psychotherapy meant to him. He described it as deep and meaningful – even spiritual. It was intimate and very personal, and it made him feel vulnerable and exposed. Despite his previous denial, he admitted recognising that he was able to give something to me. He said, 'This cancer – you are going through it with me and that is important.' At last he was able to accept the depths of the relationship as well as its limits. I was very moved by this recognition that he did have something of worth to give to me. There was a silence and then I told him that I thought he was talking about love. This sensitive topic could have exposed the analysis to the danger of seduction on the one hand or rejection on the other. However the abstinence from physical contact and the analysis that had accompanied it had facilitated an emotional contact that made this acknowledgement possible. Such love is treated with the utmost respect and recognised as a temporary state in which the analyst is privileged to briefly share.

In connection with this the subject of the snowdrops arose again. It had been some months since James had brought them and their little vase was still on my table. James had not referred to it and I had made a mental note to raise the subject when the time was right. When he was discussing the meaning of psychotherapy I queried what it might mean that the vase was still there. James blushed, and after a thoughtful pause said 'Perhaps I'll bring snowdrops again next year.' In the circumstances that was very poignant. James recalled the process that had led him to bring the vase and how it had seemed just right for the snowdrops. The flowers had survived for a long time, but when they died the vase had become a problem and so, as was his usual practice with problems, he had not mentioned it, he had just left it there. Now he said, 'Perhaps I should take it away?'

Because it was I who had raised the topic I was not convinced that James was ready to take the vase away. He admitted that he liked it being there, adding quite seductively, 'Perhaps it's keeping an eye on you.' Then as he left he said 'Maybe I'll take it when I move into my new house.' This seemed appropriate, like withdrawing some of his investment in the analysis, our shared analytic house, and taking it to his own house. He was not yet ready for this, but one day he would be. It seemed that the container for his snowdrops resonated with psychotherapy. The vase was a concrete symbol of the analytic vessel, which was providing the container for his metaphorical 'spring flowering self'.

Reflecting on the countertransference, I was reluctant to agree to him taking the vase away at that stage. This was partly because its meaning had not been fully explored, but that was not all: I had been very moved by the significance, in the present circumstances, of James's comment that he 'might bring snowdrops again next year'. I did not want to give up on that hope. The vase was like a talisman, a concrete manifestation of his desire to remain with me between sessions. It was something meaningful that belonged to him but had been left with me. At some time he would need to reclaim it, but now was not that time.

In the following session James returned to the subject of the vase. It emerged that he felt that he would have to take the vase away eventually, because he could not see me and form a relationship with someone else at the same time. His assumption was that he would have to withdraw his investment in the analysis before he could have a woman in the outer world. When I commented that this sounded as though he felt he had to be faithful to me, he said 'I can only have one woman at a time.' Then, in association, he reflected that he had always been secretive about girlfriends as he feared parental disapproval. Then, just to be sure I did not think he was about to end his therapy, he said 'Psychotherapy is essential to me; the whole pack of cards could collapse if I did not have it.'

Illness

The pack of cards nearly did collapse when James became physically ill. He caught a cold, which developed into bronchitis and he was prescribed antibiotics. In contrast to his previous very positive mood he now became very low and the focus of analysis shifted to concerns about his body. James knew that an infection could kill him very quickly. He reflected that it was 18 months since diagnosis. At that time the consultant had told him that if he survived two years there was a good chance of lasting five. At this point neither of us was convinced of this as he was clearly worried about his condition. Despairingly, he said that as he got older the gap between how very young he felt and his chronological age grew wider.

James was very sad that he could not admit how he really felt to anyone but me. One day during a phone call, when he had thought he was probably dying, he had tried telling one of his women friends but she had become upset. This had made James feel dangerous. I asked what was so bad about being upset, explaining that sometimes it made me sad too, but, I added, that was OK. Reminding James that he had recognised that he gave me something, I suggested that, even when it made them sad, it might be the same with his friends. As he left that day he turned at the door and said that his children were going back to their mother, so perhaps he would be a little sad when he next came. It therefore seemed that he had taken my words as permission to admit to feeling sad.

The move

James started to view houses but none of them was right for him. Everything that was decorated was floral and he said that he would prefer white-washed stone walls and rush matting on the floor. This was a reference to my consulting room, and when I commented on that there was a flash of envious anger. He said, 'Well you don't know what it is like – you are qualified!' He stopped himself, and to repair any potential damage said 'I'm sure you worked hard to get it.' Later, he mentioned that he had an appointment at the hospital the following week. It seemed that as well as my room he envied my health.

This was still present when he arrived flustered and 15 minutes late for his next appointment, saying that he had forgotten he was coming and had driven past the turning. He had found a suitable house and he talked about it in detail. He then came to a stop. I reminded him that at the end of the previous session he had mentioned the appointment at the hospital, and I wondered whether his forgetting might be connected with that. Then he started to yawn repeatedly. When I pointed this out he said that he would fall asleep if he were alone, he would just shut down. It emerged that he was very anxious about this appointment. Consciously he was anxious about finding a parking place. He would be driving himself to the hospital for the first time and dreaded getting news that would make him incapable of driving back. There were pains in his stomach and he suspected secondaries. When he began to talk about his concerns about his body the yawning stopped, so it seemed that the driving and parking problems had been masking his fear about his physical state. When I suggested that he phone after the appointment his response was immediate: 'It would be nice to have someone to tell.' He subsequently phoned from the hospital to tell me there were no secondaries.

When working in psychotherapy with someone who is this ill the link between physical symptoms and the psychological state becomes increasingly obvious. With James it became evident that if I were away his physical state would deteriorate. I had to miss a week unexpectedly and James's GP was also away. The next time I saw him he was obviously unwell. He said that for him it had been a bad time for me to go away because he had moved into his new place. However he had not slept there because the pains in his chest had worried him and he thought he might die. He had thought, 'What have I done?' The awareness that he was going to die was so powerful that he had sat with tears streaming down his cheeks while watching a film on TV. He had not eaten for three days. He now became aware that as soon as he had come into my room he had felt better. Therefore it was he who connected feeling so ill with my being away. My absence, especially at the same time as his GP, had made him feel unsafe. Once the analyst becomes aware of this connection there is an additional sense of responsibility for the person who is so unwell.

James moved into his house and slept there. The first night he felt so ill that he again thought he was dying. He feared that the cancer was rampant. The pain was all around his ribs on the right side but the cancer was on the left, so he worried that it was a secondary, but then told himself that it could not be. I was very aware of how alone he felt at night with such thoughts. I reminded him that perhaps it was a bit like when, as a little boy, alone in bed, he had cried but no one had come. I pointed out that the combination of my being away and his leaving home/his mother, might make him feel as though he were dying even if he were not ill. I explained that children feel like that when they are separated from their parents. His eyes filled with tears. We both sat in silence with the very present sense of his lifelong loneliness.

Deterioration

James could not decide whether it was the chest infection or the cancer that was causing the pains and his general feeling of illness. His GP thought it was a virus and that he was unlikely to die suddenly. James was furious because a year ago she had told him that he could go very suddenly and had given him two months to live. Although the consultant had told him that one lung had completely closed down, when he breathed in he could definitely feel something, as if it were opening up again. He attributed the fact that he had lived longer than expected to a sense of having 'clamped' the cancer. This implies that James considered that his psychological attitude had had an impact.

Then, as he started living independently in his new house, he almost immediately became unwell. He started to lose his voice and speculated that it could be the virus, but it might be due to the cancer – he had read somewhere that this happens in lung cancer. Whilst he was talking he coughed and commented that he had noted that when he had spoken to one of his women friends on the phone the previous night the chest pains had disappeared. He thought that he had 'got something off his chest' with her. Thus it was that he was beginning to take over the analyst's position and make interpretations for himself.

As already stated, this is what happens in the normal course of psychotherapy. The person begins to observe their own patterns. In this analysis many of the normal analytic stages were taking place, but faster than usual. Once a terminal illness is diagnosed it becomes difficult to read the normal workings of the body; nothing is any longer uncomplicated. It is no longer possible to attribute any particular symptom solely to a psychological cause because of the dominant awareness of the seriousness of the physical situation. However it is clear at times like these that there is a link.

The voice

The serious deterioration in James's physical state was shockingly evident when he arrived one day and whispered, 'I have no voice and it won't be coming back.' Because of his move he had had to register with a new GP, who had said that the voice problem might be laryngitis but he thought it was the cancer and referred him immediately to an ear, nose and throat consultant. The latter had confirmed that, because of the cancer, one of the vocal chords was not in use. An operation was possible but it was doubtful whether James was strong enough to withstand the anaesthetic. Now he could only speak in a hoarse whisper. This evidence of the relentless progress of the disease was undeniable and I was aware that James was choking back tears.

I was feeling very sad when he turned to me and said directly, 'You look a bit glum.' I admitted that I felt it. This was clearly threatening to him as he immediately changed the subject. However by now I was very aware of his behavioural pattern, so did not pursue the new topic but instead waited and, at an appropriate moment, drew his attention to this flight. I eventually said that I wondered what happened to him when he saw me looking a bit glum. He reflected in silence, and then looked at me and said sadly, 'Will you miss me?' Surprised, I was nearly overcome with a sense of loss – tears were near the surface and all I could do was nod affirmatively. There was silence between us and then James said, 'There is not much I can say.' It seemed that if I was sad with him, he felt responsible, and that something was expected of him. The tragedy is that all that is possible in such a situation is to acknowledge the immense sadness.

Confronting death

The physical evidence of James's illness brought thoughts of death to the fore. He said that he could not bear to leave his children, and his grief was tangible. As he recovered a little I reminded him that in the previous session he had asked if I would miss him. I commented on the sadness that had passed between us, telling him that I had noticed that when he saw the reply in my face he had cut off. I thought that what felt so dangerous to him was that we might both have cried. He sat silently and nodded in agreement. Then as if to confirm his need to address the reality of his failing health, a dream confronted him starkly with the situation.

Dream 28: 4 December, year 2

> *I was on top of a high hill, watching a football match. I realised that this was the world and it was a boat in the midst of an ocean. I was with a boy from school and the boat was sinking. A man came up and threatened to fight me and I said, 'you can't fight me I have lung cancer. The man said 'Oh yes I can; I invented it.' And he hit me in the balls.*

The fighting theme reminded James of his earlier dreams. At first he had been watching the world from a high place, which was reminiscent of the bull and

chariot dream (dream 10, Chapter 8), in which he had been high up looking
down on the world. Now the world had become a boat in the midst of an ocean,
indicating a connection with the collective, the unconscious as an ocean. The
boy from his school seemed to be a guise for a younger version of him. A man
had threatened to fight him and had not been deterred by what James called his
'cancer power'. This man, who had said that he invented lung cancer, was
similar to figures in previous dreams that seemed to represent death. They too
had threatened the dreamer. There had been the burglar he had chased out of
his house in (dream 3, Chapter 5) and the Tyson figure who had knocked him
down in (dream 23, Chapter 9). That time he had got up, but in this latest dream
the man had hit him where it really hurt.

The next time he came he looked terrible: he was pale and thin, his eyes
had a reddish look and his voice was much worse. He had not expected to
deteriorate so rapidly. He had just been shopping in town and had felt sick
and hot and had started coughing, so he had had to leave. He was giving up
and wanted to be taken to the hospice; he wanted to die alone but not on his
own in his house. James's memories of being cared for were institutional ones
and alone seemed to mean with strangers rather than people that were close
to him. He recalled the sanatorium at his prep school: it had offered respite.
It seemed that he was now considering the hospice as a source of respite.

James said that he had lived alone and now he wanted to die alone. As he
put it, the formal goodbyes had to be brief, he did not want his family
around. At that point I needed to check what he wanted from me. James said
dismissively, 'The same, like the family a brief goodbye.' However I did not
let this pass because I needed to know, not just how angry he was feeling
today, but what he might actually want of me. Therefore I held to my agenda.
James was habitually reluctant to talk about such things but I needed a clear
signal from him. It was very painful and difficult for him to stay with the
topic, and several times tears were very near to the surface. At one point he
started compulsively yawning and then coughing. It seemed that the unshed
tears were choking him.

However I persevered and told him that if he really wanted a brief goodbye I would accept it, but he should know that I was prepared to go to him if
he was no longer able to come to me. At the start neither of us had known
that this was where psychotherapy would lead. I pointed out that even if he
became very ill he might need someone to talk to. I was prepared to continue but we needed to think about how it would be for him if I saw him
away from the room. I insisted on addressing this because it was clear that
the boundaries were going to have to be adapted if psychotherapy was to
continue, and there had to be agreement between us about how to maintain
the frame. James became serious and said that he was worried that he might
not be able to tell me what he wanted. I said that was why I needed to check
with him now. By the end of the session he looked much better.

The winter break was now imminent, and as the link between the
deterioration in his health and my absences had become clearer, it seemed

important to make this explicit. I told James that if his health deteriorated I would like him to let me know, and that this was for my benefit. He was clearly touched by this and went quiet, but then started coughing and yawning. This was now a regular pattern and so I merely acknowledged that it was his repressed tears pressing to the fore.

James commented on the stigma of his dependency on psychotherapy. It made him feel inadequate; it was a relationship he had to pay for and he should instead be forming relationships in the real world. However this was said with conscious regret rather than as an attack. He realised that sometimes I had to be away. Then he said that he felt the need to come for nourishment: 'It is like food and if you are away I am very hungry.' He had had a dream that morning.

Dream 29: 11 December, year 2

> *I was to drive a taxi. I had costed it all out and it was going to be a good job.*
> *Then I realised 'Oh dear I can't do it because my car has a dodgy gearbox.'*

James said that he had thought that this dream was silly until he realised that it was he who had the dodgy gearbox. The job seemed to refer to his new living arrangements, which had been costed out and were going to work, but his gear box was dodgy – he was unwell. He realised he might die at any time because the GP, 'in one of her frank speaking sessions', had told him that the cancer might grow into a main artery and affect his heart, in which case he would die suddenly. Thus he was now able to assimilate and interpret the meaning of his own dream.

James's evident deterioration and the gravity of the situation brought his family closer to him and they became more involved. Despite his difficulty with expressing his feelings to them, it was clear that they were a close family and cared about James. Now they were phoning him every night. Physical separation facilitates psychological distance and so it is likely that his independent living arrangements, the fact that he was now 'housed', made it possible for him to relate to them. He could now admit them to those aspects of his life that he chose and on equal terms. He began to talk to various members of the family and they visited him, helping with the house. In the last session before the break James told me that on his way back from his previous session he had called in on his parents. He and his mother had had the longest talk they had had for a long while, he was relieved, as he had told her everything that he had been told about the state of his health.

James realised that this was likely to be his last Christmas. I pointed out that he sounded alternately angry and sad when he spoke of this. He said 'Yes you are right, I feel both angry and sad. Here I am, I have got my own place and sorted out everything I need to be comfortable and I will probably never use it.' The air of sadness became overwhelmingly present and once again I was nearly overcome by it. It was becoming increasingly evident to me that when James was on the brink of tears, but holding them back, I experienced the sadness as almost overwhelming and had difficulty preventing myself from crying. Thus I came to understand the countertransference implications: I experienced his split-off or unexpressed emotions when he denied them.

We discussed what would happen if during the break he had to go into hospital or the hospice. He said that he would like me to visit, but not 'if it is just your professional duty'. The old theme emerged that he did not want me as a psychotherapist but as a friend he had been seeing for two years. This was appealing and seemed reasonable in the circumstances, but I held to the boundaries. His inner world needed space and I explained this to him. Then he made it clear that he did want me to visit if he went into hospital. I emphasised that, in that case, it would be up to him to try to arrange it.

In this chapter we have seen that when someone is seriously ill during psychotherapy their physical health may be closely affected by the presence or absence of the analyst.

James had been worried that he would not survive the break but now he thought that he would. Reflecting on his state he said that he had less energy than usual, and that, 'The problem is, there is no joy over this Christmas.' He was unaware of the link with my name. However this comment revealed the unconscious implications of his lack of energy: he was again affected by the prospect of my absence.

14 The Problems of Ending When the End is Death

Attention to the ending of any form of psychotherapy is always significant, and this is no less the case when its termination will be brought about by death. In the usual course of analysis, if all has gone well, the ending comes about by mutual agreement. This will be after a suitable length of time and with due consideration of its implications. Fordham (1969) suggests that, when ready to end, the patient's contributions become thinner and both people begin independently to think about termination. He writes that in the ideal prelude to ending:

> The intensity of the transference becomes progressively less and the patient's recognition of the analyst as a real person increases. The patient is able to manage what comes into his mind without much help. Concurrently his life outside analysis becomes richer and more satisfying (ibid., p. 101).

Inevitably this is sad and a mourning process is worked through by both people, before as well as after analysis has finished. Although meetings no longer take place, the patient will continue to learn from what he or she has taken in from the analyst and the analyst takes what she or he has learned from this patient into her or his work with others (ibid.) When the patient is facing death, similar processes occur but their significance may be masked by awareness of the immensity of other impending losses. The analyst too is affected: she or he faces the loss of the patient without the usual sense of continuation.

The dynamic that leads towards this particular form of ending may not bring about a clear resolution of the transference. Even so the real relationship between patient and analyst takes higher priority as the deterioration of the patient's health demands attention. This does not mean that the transference is absent, but awareness of it will need to be balanced with attention to the real situation. Irrespective of whether or not the transference is resolved, the end will come.

The review of the literature in Chapter 1 included descriptions of some of the diverse endings arrived at by psychotherapists who have written about their work with dying patients. In some of the cases described the boundaries were ultimately relinquished in favour of friendship (Lee,

1996). In others, when the patient, was physically absent the solution was telephone sessions (Minerbo, 1998) or contact via a fax machine (McDougall, 2000). Another group maintained face-to-face analysis until the end (Wheelwright, 1981; Bosnak, 1989; Ulanov, 1994). We also saw how, for those who work in the specialist area of palliative care, death is the predictable end of their work (Kearney, 1997; de Hennezel, 1997; Pratt and Wood, 1998.) In the latter environment therapists are trained to work with the terminally ill, which is not usually the case in analytic, psychotherapeutic or counselling practice. Although serious illness may be the reason for the referral, it is more often the case that illness develops after the referral for psychological treatment. The analyst is then faced with what may be, depending on their personal circumstances, a relatively unfamiliar area of work, or even of their life experience. Thus the ending of psychotherapy with the dying demands particular attention.

In the ordinary course of analysis, the presentation of material may intensify when the end is in view. This is because the end of any analysis brings to the fore past losses and bereavements. Sometimes it is even referred to as a symbolic death. A similar pattern may emerge when the anticipated ending is actual death, but, instead of a metaphorical death, it is the end of life itself that has to be faced. Before considering this in relation to the transference I shall turn to Kubler-Ross (1969). She identified stages of coming to terms with a life-threatening illness, all of which have become evident as we have traced James's story. Kastenbaum (2000) puts them succinctly:

1. Denial: this follows the first shock of diagnosis. It usually takes the form of paralysis, followed by disbelief. This stage was evident in Chapter 5.
2. Anger: rage is a common reaction when denial wears off and is usually directed at loved ones or those who are caring for the patient. We have seen this throughout the narrative account, but particularly in the transference and the dreams in Chapters 8 and 10.
3. Bargaining: as the person comes to terms with the fact that they are going to die they make deals with themselves, or with God, that will permit them to live until a certain event has taken place. This reveals a certain amount of hope and the possibility that they might still beat the prognosis.
4. Depression: as the 'patients' physical condition deteriorates and they become physically weaker and less able to function, hope begins to fade and depression sets in. As Kastenbaum (2000, p. 217) suggests, psychologically this is the worst time and 'Fear of death becomes more openly experienced and expressed.' This phase began for James as has been described in the previous chapter.
5. Acceptance: this is the stage where, after all the previous struggles, acceptance comes as relief. James eventually attained that stage, as will be shown in the concluding chapters.

As James's journey has been traced we have seen manifestations of each of these stages, but not always in particular order. With this in mind, we shall consider the relevance of the criteria for ending analysis described by Fordham. We saw in earlier chapters that there were now times when James was able to interpret his own dreams. Although the transference still dominated, his awareness of its patterns was more conscious. He was beginning to be able to differentiate behaviours and responses that belonged to the past from ones that were appropriate in the present. Moreover his relationships were beginning to become more satisfying. If this had been a normal analysis James would probably have continued to develop in this way. Once the material had been integrated, as well as become conscious, the ending would have occurred quite naturally. As other aspects of his life became more rewarding the analyst would no longer have been needed. However at the beginning of the third year the end of life began relentlessly to confront James.

Thus attention to the psychological as well as the practical aspects of the impending end of his life demanded our attention. James was aware of his pattern of abruptly cutting off his feelings when he felt in danger of losing control of his emotions. Now, as he faced the prospect of losing everything, this became an agonising conflict for him. I hope to demonstrate, by close attention to the narrative account, how interpretation of psychological resistance is necessary even when the ending towards which the patient is moving is so utterly final.

At the beginning of the third year of analysis James's health seriously deteriorated and the illness began to affect every facet of his life. Whilst in the early stages, analysis of the past had dominated, now the reality of his present relationships took precedence. This is usual in analysis: as the early material is integrated, attention to the present becomes central. It was now that concerns about how to talk to his family dominated. His children were his main concern and he worried about how they would cope. Although they have been largely absent from the account in this book for reasons of confidentiality, it was they who gave meaning to James's life. With them he enjoyed a mutuality that he had had with no one else, and he could not bear to tell them that he would soon die. Not wanting to interrupt their lives he calculated whether he might manage to wait for this birthday or that exam to be over. This is typical of the bargaining phase described above (Kubler-Ross, 1969). In addition, and very gradually, he began to permit the rest of his family and friends to play a more active part in his life. Even so his inability to cope with their distress continued to inhibit these relationships. This was echoed in the transference and therefore became the focus of much of our work during the first month of the third year. Maintaining the analytic boundaries against internal and external pressure to abandon them was essential if James was to be helped to address the problem of how to talk to others.

During that time my own feelings were in conflict. My genuine affection for James meant that there were times when I wanted to abandon the analysis and befriend him. Meanwhile James was angrily despairing and difficult to be with much of the time. Although he constantly reiterated the futility of analysis, I continued to make transference interpretations as it was evident that his behaviour with me was a reflection of the way he was behaving with others. There were times when I was able to penetrate his defences, which seemed to bring him relief and an understanding of the extent to which he was rejecting those closest to him. Thus much of my work at that time involved mediating his anxiety about his health and interpreting his rejecting behaviour in an attempt to normalise the situation.

This was not easy because the situation was far from normal. His voice was now much worse and he spoke in a rough whisper at all times. This meant that people he talked to on the phone thought that he was finding conversation a struggle and therefore terminated conversations that he would have been quite happy to continue. James failed to explain this to them. In order to give a sense of how the dual problem of mediating his physical and psychological problems functioned at that time I shall recount details of a few of the sessions.

Physical state

James's health was now of grave concern and the first part of most sessions was taken up with his account of the deterioration of his physical condition. He looked unwell and had no energy, which made simple activities such as shopping or going upstairs very difficult. He felt as though there was a bag of rubbish in his chest, and sometimes it took him an hour to recover from changing his position, such as sitting up after lying down. Graphically, James described the sense of his life; it was as if his parachute was coming down. There were times when he felt that he just wanted to let go and die, but then he remembered his children.

This feeling of hopelessness was used to attack the analysis. At the end of one session it was expressed in an angry dismissal when he said, 'I may as well die tonight!' It became clear that this was partly because of the futility of the relationship with me. Awareness of our mutual helplessness in the light of his failing health was ever present for us both. The limits of analysis and the fact that I continued to maintain the boundaries still distressed him. This was confirmed when he recounted that, in a survey of cancer patients who had been in a coma, those with someone to live for survived longer than those without a close relationship. After a pause he questioned why he might have said that. I interpreted this as him telling me how painful it was for him that, although I was the one person in whom he confided, I was not his partner. His apparent relief at this recognition of the situation opened up the topic for further discussion in the following session.

James looked very ill, his skin was quite yellow and his movements were slow. He felt awful and had been coughing until he was nearly sick. Then he said that there was no point in his being at the session because he had nothing to say. When I suggested that it might feel futile because something between us was not being addressed his response was rejecting: 'There is nothing going on between us.' I reminded him of the hopelessness and anger he had experienced in the previous session because of the limits of what I was offering. James denied this, saying 'I don't know – I just feel ill and I don't want hassle – there is nothing between us.' At that point I wondered whether I should stop interpreting the underlying implications and accept that he really did not want me to pursue this topic. There was silence, and then he said 'I think I've upset you.' Non-committally I asked him how that affected him. He replied, 'It surprises me if I affect you.' I told him that I thought that he was pushing me away. This prompted an immediate switch to another topic.

James recounted how his mother had visited him the previous morning, before he was up. He had not answered the door because he had felt too ill to respond. It appeared that he had made a link between the way he was relating to me and the way he had related to his mother. I pointed out that yesterday he had not let his mother into his house, and today he was not letting me into his 'psychological house'. He accepted this thoughtfully.

Then he complained that no one noticed just how ill he was. There were lots of silences and the pace of the session was slow. I suggested that perhaps this was because it was important for him to show me just how ill he was. He still needed me to interpret his state. However his confused anger and sense of futility were ever present and so, at the same time there was tremendous pressure on me not to interpret. The unspoken message was that James was too ill to take my interpretations; they were cruel, so I should leave him alone. I had to remind myself that, despite his resistance, this was what he came for. It was also very similar to the pattern played out when he was depressed, and shut himself in his room. Moreover I realised that my own feeling that I should leave him alone was probably similar to the way his friends and family felt about their approaches to him. Therefore it was imperative to continue to challenge this unstated taboo on upsetting him.

The steel shutter

When James spoke to his friends about his condition they would get upset, which made him so furious that he withdrew from them. This pattern was now evident in the therapeutic relationship. James continued to deny that there was anything happening between us, and I continued to draw his attention to the taboo on upsetting him, suggesting that that was what was going on between us. James responded dismissively, saying that I may think so but he thought that since the break we seemed to be going round and round in circles. He said, 'I tell you my worries and we say – Oh I'm dying – Oh dear!'

This was an attack on the analysis and on me, but most of all it was a dismissal of the importance of his own experience and therefore a form of self-abuse. Hence it was important to counter the attack directly. I pointed out how dismissive he was being and told him that his distress was evident in this comment. It was his tremendous sadness and the fact that we both had feelings about it that worried him. The distress passed between us and it was disturbing for him to notice that I had feelings about what was happening to him.

This got through to him and he became insightful, remembering other endings in his life. He again recalled the times when he had finished with girlfriends, when even though there had been nothing wrong with the relationship he had decided that it must end and had terminated it abruptly. The women had never understood why, but of course nor had he; he just had not known what to do. It became evident that it was when he had realised that they cared that he had rejected them. It reminded him of the film 'Dangerous Liaisons', which he had recently seen. He identified with the central character, who despite his emotional involvement with the female character abruptly cut off the relationship without explanation. James identified with that, and described it as being 'like a steel shutter coming down'.

Considering the ending that lay before us, it seemed that he was now associating the way he was relating to me to finishing with a girlfriend. James was unconsciously attempting to cut me off in order to minimise the pain of the inevitable separation. The end of analysis brings old ways of ending to the fore as they are replayed in the transference; this was what was taking place now and was a way of coping that James had probably learned when his mother had left him at boarding school. Even though she had been upset, it was as though she had cut him off. The cut-off that James and I were facing was even more ruthless; it was death. Little wonder that he was angry as well as distressed.

Now James became more open about the pain evoked by analysis. Sometimes I was the first person he spoke to in a day; talking to me was the only real contact he had with anyone except his doctor. But psychotherapy was not enough – it made him realise what he had missed in life. It was the pain of wanting so much more than he could have that was fuelling his sense of futility. He said 'One or two hours a week isn't enough. Its not much use in the middle of the night.' Thus he conveyed the profound loneliness of his situation and how in the middle of the night, when he most needed someone, no one was with him.

The attacks on the analysis were made because its limits hurt. When I suggested that perhaps he hated me for causing him so much pain, he said 'No I don't hate you, the boundaries of this relationship are very clear and so there is no point in it.' I misunderstood and said 'No point in hating me?' But James had meant no point in the relationship, as became clear when he said, 'Or loving you. This relationship is defined by place. The distance is held by these two chairs. Sometimes I hope that I could get you to break the bound-aries but then anyone looking down could clearly see that it could not be like that.' Referring to an earlier discussion of how it would be if he were in the hospice, I said, 'So is that what you meant about me visiting you as a friend, not a therapist?' He replied, 'Well yes, I realised you wanted to come for you and that touched me. I thought there must be something in it for her then. But there is no point in feeling these things. It all stops no matter what is happening when the time is up.'

Thus James demonstrated how the shutter came down to protect him from feeling too much or wanting too much. James was referring to the end of the sessions, which each time were experienced as a steel shutter. However the comment that 'It all stops no matter what is happening' seemed to be an unconscious reference to death. The cutting off brought about by death would also be cruel and final, so most of all James's sense of futility and depression was because he was dying.

Talking about the end

Now another of his concerns – the disposal of his body – came to the fore. This resonated with his ever present sense of homelessness. His attitude was contradictory: he was anxious about what might happen to his remains, but claimed not to mind because he would not be around. There was a cemetery across the road from his house but he had noticed that it seemed to be full. This was very poignant, as he had also looked in the grave-yard in the city, near his family home. It appeared that there was no room there either. James said that it did not matter; apparently there were more dead bodies in London than live ones and it was a health hazard – it could affect the water supply. Then he said sadly, 'I only want somewhere that my children can go to remember their father.'

He was thinking of talking to his own father about it but could not imagine how to begin. Then dismissively he said that they could do what they liked: 'I thought I'd give my body to medical science and if they can chop it up into little pieces there won't be a problem.' This switch from the feeling level to his cut-off thinking function was another example of the steel shutter. Pointing this out, I suggested that this was very similar to his attempt to find a place to live. This too was about where he belonged and he did not feel that he had a right to be buried anywhere. There was silence, a very sad atmos-phere pervaded the session and there were tears in his eyes. Then he said 'Well that is how it is!' I pointed out that he had again cut himself off when feeling tearful. He sat quietly acknowledging this, and by the time he left he looked better – there was colour in his face and his eyes were brighter.

It became evident that this immensely painful topic was one of the reasons he had been feeling so bad. So it was that the analysis continued in its boundaried form. If I had befriended James he would have missed the opportunity to develop his understanding of processes such as this. The fact that we continued in this way meant that analysis was able to make a difference to James's relationships, even at this late stage in his life. This was borne out in the next session, when he was feeling much better.

He looked very well and was quite lively when he arrived. He had shaved and even looked a little pink cheeked. The tone of the session was humorous. The depression had lifted at the end of the week; he had suddenly felt better. The physical symptoms had ameliorated and the pains in his chest had gone. Describing how it had been before, he said that there had been this awful feeling in his chest when he bent forward and on Friday he had been on the point of going to the doctor to get admitted to the hospice. But now he felt quite the reverse. It was possible that by talking about his funeral and the associated sense of psychological homelessness he had got the topic 'off his chest' for now and was therefore feeling lighter.

Countertransference

Sometimes the countertransference plays perceptual tricks, and this was one such occasion. During this session, whilst James was talking I had a very strange awareness of a visual distortion. As I regarded him, his head seemed to become huge and elongated, whilst his body became tiny and thinned out. It was a rather dizzy and very strong alteration of spacial perception. After the session I wondered whether what I had perceived was the soul separating from the body. It was as though the body was nothing and the head was huge, rather as in Munch's painting 'The Scream'. Unusual experiences of this sort merit attention as a form of countertransference perception. They emerge, very occasionally, as a result of the concentrated gaze; the intent interest in the person. It is as if the state of being is revealed. At that time James was on the edge, hovering between life and death, and perhaps that is what I saw.

The house and the body

By the next session James was again feeling unwell. He had been to the new GP, who had confirmed Dr X's assessment that part of the reason James was feeling so unwell was that he had a virus. As his lungs had been damaged by the radiotherapy they could not deal with even minor infections. This made him realise what would happen if he suffered a proper infection.

Then he switched topics and talked about his house. He was sure there was something wrong with the gas fire because he could not stay in the room without opening the windows. The gas people had tested the chimney with a smoking match to see if it was drawing. They had found nothing wrong but James was still sure there was a problem. I heard this account at two levels:

there was the reality of the problem in the house, and there was the metaphorical level, which I heard in terms of James's body. I pointed this out to him, reminding him of how he had begun the session by describing his breathing difficulties and how his lungs were not functioning properly. Then he had described the ventilation problems in his house. This seemed to indicate that it was his bodily chimney that was blocked. It seems that, as the patient becomes more attuned to the deterioration of his body, the metaphors increase.

One day James reported that the previous night he had thought that he was dying. This had led him to reflect on what would happen if he did die like that, and he had thought it likely that no one would notice until he failed to turn up for his session with me. He had wondered what I would do if he did not turn up. Perhaps I would phone him, and if there was no answer because he was dead, perhaps I would phone his parents or his doctor. He realised that no one had a key to his house.

Clearly this had been a profoundly lonely and frightening experience. As well as the practical aspects of the situation, he was asking me if I would miss him if he died like that – would I notice? Once again the house was relevent as a metaphor. James was genuinely worried about what would happen if he became too ill to contact anyone, or if he died whilst he was alone. This was a lonely situation that merited some practical attention, but his disclosure that no one had a key to his house was also an image of the psychological situation. It seemed that James was telling me that he wanted to be found psychologically, but there was a question over whether he would admit his family or me, whether he would give anyone the key. Perhaps I would have to break in.

Talking to others about dying

A central preoccupation of many people who are facing death is how to talk to their family. It is also a question that exercises family members, who may be unsure whether the person who is dying would prefer them not to mention it. This can become a problem that prevents important aspects of closure taking place. The question of how to talk to his family about dying became a central preoccupation for James. There were days when he just wanted to get it over with and die. That would have been easier than having to discuss it with the family. James said that at first you fight it and tell everyone 'It is not going to get me!' (This is the denial phase – Kubler-Ross (1969)) 'Then gradually you start to realise that it is, but everyone still believes that it isn't.' It seemed as though, because he had said that the cancer would not get him, James was bound, as if by a promise.

James then contacted a cancer charity to seek advice about how to talk to his family. As we discussed this it became clear that the boarding school boy in him had chosen to consult strangers because they were less likely to get upset. It seemed that he did not trust me to hold the emotional line, and was therefore treating me in the same way as he was treating his family. Having explored this I suggested that there might be worse things than both of us crying. The problem was that he had spent his entire life trying to keep everything under control, but the present situation was beyond his control. I added that death is the ultimate loss of control. This clearly moved James, and he fell into silent contemplation.

His next hospital check-up revealed no apparent secondaries, and it was thought that his problem with swallowing was probably being caused by the tumour pressing on the oesophagus. If it got worse he was to let them know, otherwise the next check-up would take place in six weeks' time. When asked, the doctor had said that James could have anything from one to twelve months to live. This was better than he had expected and it freed him to talk to his family without the anticipated sense of urgency. He had awoken that morning with the clear remembrance of the shock he had had when the cancer had been diagnosed. He recalled how he had been in shock and how important it had been that his psychotherapy session was immediately after his hospital appointment. Without it he would have been in trouble.

Now James rehearsed how he might approach his parents. He said that his parents were always there for him when it came to providing a room, but not emotionally – no one had ever been there for him in that way. Now he imagined going back and telling his mother what the doctors had said, and if he timed it right his father would come in and he would speak to both of them. He said that he could tell his mother most of the details but not that he was dying. I pointed out that it was likely she knew already. However there was a huge barrier in acknowledging death. It was as if James felt responsible, even guilty. He said 'Talking about it is rather like jumping across a ravine and suppressing your terror.' Now it seemed that he was talking not just about telling his family, but about death itself. This was the ravine that he would be obliged to cross, suppressing his terror. Perhaps part of the problem with telling others was facing it himself.

Crying and the steel shutter

Gradually this block seemed to lift. James was hugely relieved when he at last managed to speak at length with his children. He talked of how he would speak to the rest of the family, which would be difficult because they avoided pain in the same way as he did. As he was talking about this he started to cough violently. I gave him a drink of water, then reminded him that coughing often indicated that he was upset. He admitted that there was a connection.

Then I suggested that if he did not cut off, he might find tears to be healing. He said that they had been suppressed for 40 years so he could not let them out now. He feared the sound he might make if he did cry. It seemed to me as if it would be a great howl of agony and this made me think not of death, but of birth: perhaps it was coming to life that James feared most. He agreed with this but maintained that he was not going to cry in my consulting room because it was too impersonal. Then pausing he questioned this assumption, which seemed to be a transference to the cold and impersonal school of his childhood. Pointing this out I remarked that if he were to cry he would need to feel held, but at school there had been no one to hold him. This prompted a burst of anger as he recalled being beaten by a huge, sadistic teacher. He became tearful as he recalled how even then he had been expected not to cry. It seemed that James wanted to cry as much as he resisted it. I checked whether he felt my attempts to help him with his grief were intrusive, but he said he wanted me to keep trying.

When James eventually spoke to members of his family they generally managed to hide their emotions, but if any of them became upset he was furious. When I suggested that, as a result, he was shutting them out, he turned his rage on me, saying 'I've had it, I will go to the hospice and die. I've had enough!' The hospice seemed to present a more benign aspect of the school. The imagined hospice would be safer because there he would be looked after by strangers who would not get upset.

As James had raised the topic of the hospice it seemed timely to check what he would want from me if he were admitted. He reflected that if he were in a coma the talking would stop – then what? I offered to be there even if the talking did stop, but only if he wanted it. James said that there would probably be suitable rooms at the hospice and that he would not be the only person who had a psychotherapist, so he would like me to continue to see him.

Coming to the end

The following session James's skin looked rather yellow and papery and he came in slowly. He was in difficulty because he could not eat and had awful stomach cramps from the hunger. The previous night he had been unable to sleep; he had felt dreadful, and had tossed and turned in his bed. He had become increasingly anxious and realised that made it worse. He had thought of phoning his family, but had not wanted them in the house. This indicated the unresolved issues between them – they still did not have the emotional key to his house. Then he had realised that he could phone an ambulance, whereupon he had felt better and fallen asleep. I asked if he had thought of phoning me. He said not at 2.00 am. I said that if things were that bad he could. This was an intuitive response to the realisation that anxiety contributed to his pain. Remembering the previous occasion when he had thought he was dying in the night, I was acutely aware of how dreadful it was for him to feel so alone when he was so very ill.

James had made an appointment to see the GP later that day. He was feeling so weak that he did not know how much longer he could keep coming for his sessions. He asked again, 'What happens when the talking runs out?' He seemed to feel obliged to do something. I suggested that it would be possible just to sit. I pointed out that the lack of food must be part of the problem as it was not possible to keep going without eating.

James was feeling hopeless; he realised that usually when you feel bad the doctor can do something, but now it seemed that his situation could only get worse. Then he said that he was luckier than some people. Thinking of people with arthritis, he said he did not have pain like theirs, 'some cry out if the doctor touches them'. Interpreting this, I said that I thought that he was indeed in pain – not the same pain as people with arthritis, but a form of psychological hurt that made him cry out if I touched him emotionally. Moreover if his family came near to him the pain was nearly intolerable. After that he went quiet and thoughtful. When he left I noted to myself that it felt near the end.

This chapter has demonstrated how the practical and psychological end of psychotherapy needs to be addressed, even when the end that is in prospect is death. This requires mediation of both the emotional and the physical issues that emerge.

Part Four
The Final Phase

15   Breakdown, Boundaries and Hospital

> You can try all you like to establish the right emotional distance, but some-
> times you go under. But doubtless it's also the price you pay for not becom-
> ing desensitised, for simply remaining human (de Hennezel, 1997, p. 78).

Adherence to what we now know as the boundaries and limits of analysis or
psychotherapy has gradually developed over the hundred years since the
first psychoanalysts explored this field of endeavour. Codes of ethics and
guidelines exist to prevent transgressions that would damage the patient,
but when the patient becomes seriously ill the analyst is in relatively
uncharted waters. I am aware that colleagues who work in palliative care
might find my concerns rather unusual as they deal with this type of
situation in their day-to-day work. However psychoanalysts, psychotherapists and counsellors who remain firmly in their consulting rooms for the
major part of their working week will understand that this is a dilemma.
There is no rule book to tell us what to do; and even if there were, each
situation is different. Therefore we need to consider how to handle each set
of circumstances in its own context. For example if a patient is admitted to
hospital for a limited period, do we charge for the missed sessions? When an
illness enters a terminal phase, how do we respond? These were the questions that engaged me as I tried to work out the most human thing to do, as
well as what would be therapeutic for the patient. My own feelings were
involved, so there was also an intuitive response that needed to be closely
monitored. At that point discussions with trusted colleagues were essential.

James was suddenly admitted to hospital one early morning in late
February after phoning to say that he would not be able to attend his session as he was waiting for an ambulance. During the night he had been
unable to breathe. He had phoned his GP, who had come to see him and
immediately called an ambulance. James said he would let me know what
happened. In the middle of the day he left a message, asking me to call the
hospital and telling me the name of the ward. When I got through to him
he sounded faint and quite confused. I was concerned when he asked me
the name of the ward he was in. He had been given oxygen and they were
doing X-rays and tests. When I asked whether he wanted me to go to see
him at the hospital he said he did, so I agreed to go that evening. However
he sounded so strange that I wondered whether he would survive until

then, so I phoned the ward staff to ask whether I should go immediately. They reassured me that matters were not that urgent. Monitoring my own process I realised that my first inclination was to go straight away. However after reflection I took a step back and reminded myself that as I was his analyst it would be more appropriate to go at the end of my working day.

Boundaries: Visit 1

James was alone in a room, sitting up in bed and looking better than I had expected. He had an oxygen mask to hand, but this was now optional as he was feeling a lot better. He explained that he had a temperature and had been prescribed steroids, which would shrink the tumour and thus help with his breathing. Referring to how ill he had been earlier, he explained that when we had spoken on the phone and he had asked me where he was, he had been feeling disorientated. Then he recounted the sequence of events. The previous night he had taken a sleeping pill, and when he awoke in the morning he had been unable to breathe. He had phoned the doctor, who had come immediately and arranged an ambulance without delay.

He then went on to say, with a great deal of relief, that his parents had been to the hospital and several of the issues that had been worrying him had been resolved. He had discussed his worries about the funeral, and been reassured that there would be no problem about the family plot in the city graveyard. His parents had then contacted the vicar, who was coming to see him. So it seemed that once James had broken down and admitted that he needed help, his parents had responded.

The role of the analyst as hospital visitor is rather strange. The perception of the hospital staff is that this is just another visitor, so there is little privacy. This is a good argument for making clear arrangements and letting staff know that such visits are in a professional capacity.

A nurse came in with a drink for James, who was clearly enjoying the attention. Tellingly he said, 'When you've been to the edge and looked over, it is good to come back.' He said that he was pleased I had come, but it was strange to see me in that context. He thought that he would be in hospital for about a week, so we agreed a time when I would visit again. He would make sure that his family knew not to come at that time. Although he was relieved to be receiving care, and was therefore quite bright, talking seemed to be making him tired and he was sweating. I offered to leave if he was finding it exhausting, but he wanted me to stay for the 50 minutes I was offering. Commenting on how odd it was to be talking to me there, he asked 'Do you visit many of your patients in hospital?'

This indicated that he was wondering whether he was exceptional, which of course he was. This fitted with the polarised sense of himself as either 'rubbish' or special. He was referring to having got me out of my room at last, after all his previous failed attempts, so I commented on this. He responded with humour: 'Yes I've got you out of the room and you've got me lying down at last!' This was a reference to the couch, which despite my interpretations he had never used. He continued, 'I suppose you are going to say that I did all this to get you out of your consulting room.' Thus as well as being insightful there was a humorous atmosphere that was tinged with flirtation. It was clearly exciting for James that I had made the effort to visit him. After 50 minutes I drew the 'session' to a close. Then James asked whether I had trouble parking and finding him. Hence there was a subtle change of role: he was being solicitous in a 'patient in hospital with visitor' mode.

This shift in the boundaries, together with my relief that he would not die just yet, contributed to the tremendous impulse I had to touch him as I left. I was drawn to him, and the pull was so strong that it felt as though I was literally tearing myself away. It would have been so simple to give him a hug, as one would a friend in such circumstances, but I did not. Perhaps intuitively I knew that I needed to maintain my role and, that there was still work to do. In reflecting on this I am reminded of Renos Papadopoulos, who talks and writes about working with people traumatised by war. He is often called on to be with them in ways that are beyond the frame of analysis and, in order to preserve his professional role, he carries a diary and wears a tie. It is as much a reminder for himself as for the people with whom he works that he is present as a professional (Papadopoulos, 1998). Intuitively that is what I did: in my mind I maintained a professional persona when it would have been possible to slip into the position of friend.

Snow again: visit 2

I had agreed to see James again, with the intention of maintaining the twice weekly sessions, whilst he was in hospital. Although this meant some extra travelling I did not see it as a problem. However the next visit did present a practical problem: it was the end of February, it was snowing and the hospital in London was some distance from where I lived. The driving conditions were very bad and huge flakes of falling snow were reducing visibility. At one point I seriously considered turning back, but in the end I continued. James was fully aware of how bad the conditions were and he expressed concern that I had made the journey.

It was a year after James had brought the snowdrops, and real snow linked into one of the symbolic threads that were woven throughout this analysis. First it emerged in memory. It will be recalled from Chapter 2 that when, as a small child, James had moved to England it had been a snowy winter and he remembered the cold. This was both a physical and an emotional coldness: he was in a strange country, without his grandparents. Then it emerged in the analysis. There was a time, very early on, when due to a heavy snowfall most of my patients had cancelled their appointments. James had attended his session claiming that it had been a challenge to get through.

Then there was the reference to the heater in my room: noticing that it worked well, James had wondered if it would be effective when it snowed. This indicated the sense of warmth he was already experiencing within the therapeutic relationship. In the context of all these events, it seemed that it was the warmth between us that had kept me going through the snow – I knew how important it was to get to him. James was aware of the symbolism of this. Thus snow continued to be a meaningful symbol of the history and language of this analysis. The snow symbolised its many facets.

James was now feeling quite high, which he attributed to the effects of the steroids, but it was probably also due to the attention he was receiving. He said he had had lots of visitors. He had talked at length with his parents, and he now observed that something seemed to have moved in him. Previously he had been so angry at being stuck in their house for so long that he had not been able to speak to them. Now he could relate to them because he was no longer living in their house. Thus a transition from the trapped child/adult into a more equal relationship with his parents was beginning to take place. The physical separation involved in his move to a place of his own had confirmed his adult status and liberated him from the old pattern. He was beginning to relate to his parents as fallible but loved. This is how the individuation process works, gradually establishing an autonomous identity.

Having told me about his visitors James reflected that not one of them had touched him. He thought he must have been giving off a very strong message not to do so. This was something that I was beginning to understand. I wondered whether the almost irresistible pull towards him that I had felt when I left the previous session had been an embodied response to an unspoken appeal from him, and therefore another facet of the countertransference. I can now see that it might have been helpful if I could have used that understanding to interpret his desire for me to touch him. I missed it, probably because I was not safely installed in my consulting room. I also wonder whether, if I had permitted myself to touch him, it might have been therapeutic for him.

A nurse breezed in, looked at his charts and discussed his fluid intake and outlet. Turning to me, James commented on how he was enjoying being looked after, and then said: 'You know I said, don't you dare suggest I did it intentionally to get you out of your room – but perhaps I did.' I acknowledged this possibility, but then, wanting not to underplay his illness, said that he had been very unwell and stretched to his limits. He agreed, acknowledging that he had no longer been able to cope and his body had just given in. He said that this was the type of care he would have had if there had been someone there for him. Before I left we arranged a time for me to visit later in the week.

Relating: visit 3

On the day of my next visit James had had more investigative tests, and there had been talk of surgery to relieve the constriction in his oesophagus. There had also been a suggestion that radiotherapy might help but the doctors had decided against both courses of action. James too felt that although there was a lump in his throat and it was more of a strain to talk, it was not bad enough for either form of treatment. This symptom of the disease seemed significant considering the metaphorical lump in his throat that he experienced when trying not to cry. James asked if I thought his voice sounded worse. Then he talked a lot about the history of his treatment; he seemed to need to recap at length and without looking at me. Then gradually he warmed up and began to relate more directly. This was similar to the way in which he related in the consulting room, where very often he would first talk about his health, then about the treatment and then moved on to relate more directly. It had been a way of controlling the sessions and me. This was more noticeable in the hospital context.

In the room there were numerous cards, wishing him well, which he pointed out with pleasure. It was strange for me to see him in his pyjamas and in bed, and it seemed important to consider how these visits affected him. I opened up the topic for discussion. James responded, 'Well I know you so well that I quite easily fall into the combination of psychotherapy/hospital visit. It was a bit odd that first day when I realised that I hadn't asked you about you – but I was quite ill that day.' I told him that I had asked because of the transference. James responded freely, 'Well I think it is quite easy – we've been through the mother/child stuff and then a bit of flirtation. Now I think I just trust you; if I need you, you'll come. I expect it – not because it's my due, but because I trust you – I can rely on you.' He said that he liked my visits because I stayed and listened to him – 'Everyone else gets fidgety.' He talked at length about his other visitors, and then about how he would like to write about cancer. There was a silence, then he said 'Well, that is the state of my life at the moment!'

It had been on my mind for some time to write about his analysis and this seemed to be the ideal opportunity to request his permission. He asked me what I had in mind, and I told him it would be for my colleagues. Then he reflected that he must be of interest in a scientific way. It was very important to me to be clear about this, so I said 'I want you to know that is not how I see you.' I then told him that this was unusual. Reminding him that he had asked if I visited all my patients in hospital, I said that I did not. I pointed out that he had come to me because he was depressed, but then we had both had to cope with the cancer. James understood and said he felt flattered that I wanted to write about him. It seemed essential in the light of his earlier comments about writing that I made clear that he would be writing his own story, and that was different. I did not want to detract from his creativity, as had happened so often in his life before. Although I did not put it quite like this at the time, I would be writing my side of our shared story.

After that he told me he had read an article about the most important things in life, and that a close relationship had come top of the list, but he did not have one. He said that his problem now was how to live life, but this had always been his problem. 'I am alive but what to do with it. If I had longer maybe it'd be worthwhile, but I think I can't resolve that now.' It seemed that he was coming to terms with his situation. This could be understood as the 'acceptance' stage identified by Kubler-Ross (1969). James was expecting to be discharged from hospital and would therefore come to me the following Friday.

Back in the consulting room

The next session took place in my room. James explained that he had seen the consultant before being discharged, and had said to the latter that the tumour was malignant and would get him sooner or later. The consultant had raised his hopes by saying that the longer it failed to spread the less likely it was to do so. He should therefore be thinking about symptom control. His steroid intake was gradually being reduced but it needed careful measuring and monitoring, so he was to return in a week. There was an elated feel to the session, as though James was artificially high. At the same time, however, he was feeling very weak. Although he did not want to think about it right now he was relieved to have found out that the hospital and the local hospice worked closely together. If he needed to go there his GP and he Macmillan nurse he had met in the hospital would be involved.

In order to locate himself in the world he had felt the need to travel to me for this session. His parents had fetched him from hospital and he had just dumped his things at home and then come. It was clear that my asking permission to write about him had had a powerful effect. It seemed to have confirmed that what went on between us was important to me. Referring to our conversation in the hospice he said, 'I said about the mother – child stuff but now I'm not sure what else it is – it is not that I want to rape you but it is quite strong. I trust you and it was like I asked you where I was on the ward. I needed to know where I was.' Thus he acknowledged the erotic bond between us; this was not overtly sexual but it was loving. This does not happen in all psychotherapy but when it does – if it is consciously handled, as described in Chapter 7 – it can be good for the analysand. When the patient is dying the therapist may be drawn into a loving bond as part of the resolution of the person's life. This is evident in the work described by de Hennezel (1997).

James continued, saying that I could write about anything he had said. He also seemed to have been spurred on to write himself and he had jotted down a few notes. However he said that I should not wait for him, but get on with it. Thus it seemed that he saw it as a shared project. Although he did not get the chance to write his part of the story I am sure that it is clear to the reader that this was indeed a joint project.

Reflecting on his hospital admission, James thought that he had probably had an anxiety attack because he had felt better before being given oxygen.

He had needed attention and 'they' were not noticing. As I did not think he should dismiss the seriousness of his condition I said that perhaps it was both psychological and physical. As an example I suggested that the lump in his throat might have something to do with his suppressed crying as well as the cancer. James responded almost too readily to that, saying it was so obvious that it must be the case. It seemed that he had gone from being very resistant to almost overly compliant.

The topic of re-establishing boundaries was discussed and I suggested that this might have been one of the reasons he needed to see me back in my room. He reflected on how strange it was that he knew me so well, that there was a real connection, and yet he did not know *about* me. He said that sometimes when he phoned someone else answered and he thought that it might be my daughter, but it might be a lodger. Then he speculated that, if I did have a daughter, perhaps she was at school, or university, or perhaps she was a shopkeeper or a doctor. He continued, 'Perhaps you are married to a vicar or a bricklayer or perhaps you aren't married at all – I don't know.' I pointed out that he had never asked so although he was curious perhaps he preferred not to know. He said that could be true: 'I'm too selfish, I want to talk about me. The focus is on me and I don't need to know the details of your life.' This is a clear reason for maintaining a boundaried approach. James did not know *about* me and did not need to know because, despite the intensity of our involvement, it was a therapeutic relationship in the true meaning of the term. Despite all the appeals, seductions and attacks aimed at getting me to relinquish the boundaries, it now became clear that James needed me to maintain them.

He continued to be emotionally high over the next couple of weeks. This was the effect of the steroids, and as the dose was reduced he gradually came down to earth. Then he noticed that what he ate no longer seemed to affect his weight. He was concerned that his bottom was now nearly non-existent and his chest muscles were wasted; his middle was a little bit fatter, but not much. His clothes were certainly loose on him; he was no longer filling them out. Walking too was more difficult than it had been before he went into hospital. However he claimed that his mind was really clear. This was evident in his increased use of unconscious metaphors, which became rather remarkable. For example one day he told me on his arrival that his car was rattling and he was worried that, if it broke down, he would be unable to get to his sessions. This seemed to be a direct but unconscious reference to his body. If it broke down he would be unable to get to his sessions. The car seemed to symbolise the anxiety associated with his state. Clearly having considered our earlier discussion about his hospital admission, he said he thought he had had a psychological as well as a physical breakdown. I suggested that he might have been, unconsciously, checking that everything would be in place should he be unable to manage. Perhaps he had also been testing what would happen if he were unable to get to see me; whether I would go to him.

James's fear of psychological breakdown was still present; as he expressed it, the wall was still there between him and others and he wanted to get through it. We had often spoken about how I might break in, but now I suggested that perhaps he could choose to come out – it seemed as though he had already removed some of the bricks. He then spoke about other people whose circumstances in life were difficult, and how in comparison he was really lucky because he had a nice house, a psychotherapist, the hospice and parents. It seemed that he was now grateful to be alive. He was also expressing his gratitude to me, as indicated by the fact that as he left that day he used my name, which was something he usually did not do. This seemed to indicate that he was genuinely relating to me – although separate from him, I was someone with whom he was in a relationship. This resonated with his improved relationship with his parents, from whom he seemed at last to feel separate.

Losses and the looming break

The end of March was approaching and my spring break was imminent. Reminded by this break of the end of his marriage, James described it as 'an awful tearing away'. I was impressed with this because it was exactly how I had described my feelings to myself when I had left him in the hospital. I linked this, as well as to his marriage, to his early life and being sent away from home. It seemed that he had probably experienced a dreadful tearing away each time he had gone back to school. James recalled when he was ten or eleven crying for days beforehand. There were broken attachments both ways. He had looked forward to coming home to see his family and then he had looked forward to seeing people at school. 'For some less sensitive boy it was probably OK, but I was vulnerable because it was my very early childhood when the trouble began.'

James missed a subsequent session because he was too weak to get out of bed, and the following session he looked very thin, pale and large-eyed. He had arranged to go into the hospice for a week of rest. He told me that the hospice used to provide only terminal care, but now it also offered palliative care and the focus was on living with cancer rather than dying.

A tirade against doctors warned me that James was being affected by the prospect of my break. When I suggested that he was angry with the doctors because they could not make him better, he admitted that this was part of it. He said that he expected a lot from the doctors, and that this was my fault because he expected the same sort of treatment from them that he had from me. As the break was bothering him I let him know which days I would actually be away from home and asked whether he would like me to phone him at the hospice on my return. He was pleased, but expected to be home by then. We agreed that if he were not at his house I would call the hospice. We were both anxious about the break and some of the material seemed to indicate that he was saying goodbye. As before, I wondered whether I would see him again.

16 The Hospice and Medication

James was admitted to the hospice after his last session before my break. On my return a week later there was a message from him informing me that he was still there. I phoned and he explained that he was worse than he had realised and was therefore remaining at the hospice. I arranged to visit on the Tuesday evening.

The hospice turned out to be a large and once magnificent house. It was situated in its own grounds and its entrance hinted at its past grandeur. This was an appropriate place for James, whose life had been spent in such houses. It was probably also a bit like a boarding school as there was more than one bed to a room. James's room was large, spacious and contained two beds – he was in one and the other was empty. I sat in a chair beside the bed.

That morning James had been very shocked to learn from Dr Z (the hospice doctor) that a secondary cancer had been found in a lymph gland. She had drawn a diagram to show him how it was pressing on the bronchial tube, thus causing the problems he had been experiencing. Although this had been a blow it had also brought relief because it made sense of the symptoms. However it had made James aware that he might not leave this place, except 'in a box'. He was quite well now but he had been very ill with a high temperature. Most evenings he had lain on his side – very often with his father sitting quietly beside him – and wondered what was wrong with him. He said, 'Well now I know.' He speculated about how long he had left, and thought that he might have two or three months and then that would be it. The image of his father sitting with him in this way was striking; it seemed that an emotional bond that had probably always been there was now becoming manifest.

It was clearly distressing to James that everyone else in the place was old. He told me that a man of 92 in the next bed had died on his first night, and that two others had died since. Witnessing this had clearly been very upsetting, and I acknowledged that, unlike these people, he was not old and had not finished living. He said that most of all it had confronted him with the fact that he would not be there for important events in his children's lives, their excursions out into the world.

Then on a more positive note he said that he had had lots of visitors, old friends as well as family. James talked about them and the nurses. Upon my arrival I had told him that he should let me know if he felt tired and wanted me to leave. After a while he did feel tired; it seemed that it was emotionally and physically too much. I offered to return on Thursday and he said that he would appreciate it. Thus the boundaries, the frame of analysis, were adapted to the needs of the present situation.

Facing death and acceptance

The next time it was clear James had been reflecting on our previous conversation. He said, 'All these people in here are dying – several have already died and it makes me face death. I think I've faced it but I don't know, maybe I haven't.' Thus although his family were now available to him, the fact that I had returned had given the space to acknowledge the awefulness, in the true sense of the word, of what he was experiencing. I asked him whether he had been dreaming, thinking that dreams might indicate something of his psychological state. James said that it was funny I asked because he had been dreaming very little but had had a dream the previous night.

Dream 30: 15 April, year 3

> *I was making this big, round, white bed. I was smoothing it out. When I woke I thought 'That is my death bed.'*

James said, 'That is all.' I asked him how he had felt about it and he said 'Nothing much really.' This was quite a stark image, almost like a statement of fact. Perhaps it was merely evidence of the psyche's acceptance of the circumstances.

James said that the nurses were trying to get him to talk about himself, but that they were 'a bit amateur'. They touched him on the shoulder or patted his hand, but he just stared at the floor so that they would go away. The medical director had asked him whether he was feeling a bit twitchy or anxious and offered Diazepam. James had been furious and asked a question to which we would later return: 'What is appropriate anxiety at a time like this?' The medical director had then offered him steroids, and again James had been furious because last time they had given him a false high. Tellingly, he now said that he needed to face things 'without dope'. This was a very important statement and needed to be heard and given weight. This was a choice that James was making and it was his right to do so. I asked if the care team knew why I was visiting him and he said that he expected so. I pointed out that they would not know unless he or I told them, so he agreed that I should write to the medical director and he would tell Dr Z the next time he saw her. Thus I made clear his responsibility for maintaining my role in his treatment.

James said that he thought that he was handling the situation satisfactor-ily. It was important to support him in this, so I told him that I thought that he was handling it well and that I was touched by his courage and determin-ation to face it. However as James had told me earlier that he did not want the nurses to help him bath or shave, I did wonder whether dependency was at issue. It seemed that letting them do these intimate things for him would be tantamount to relinquishing control of his body. James thought for a while and then said, 'Which is what I am doing gradually.' Then he confided that he might be getting bedsores but he would not tell 'them' as he did not want treatment for that yet. He had realised that his sister was the only person he would permit to do things for him, more so than his mother. She had been in the building for five hours the previous day and it was clear that just knowing that had been a great comfort to him. Thus James was now allowing his family to care for him and it was evident that they were pleased to do so when given the chance.

Not wishing to tire James, I had agreed at the start of my visit that I would stay for half an hour and then see how he felt. When the 30 minutes were up he wanted me to stay longer, and so I stayed for 50 minutes. Then he said that he was tired and would lie down.

Monday: the choice about medication

When I arrived at the hospice this time a nurse I met on the stairs said, 'Oh hallo – have you come for James?' She said that he was expecting me, showed me into his room and told me that we would not be disturbed. It felt more official than before – it was recognised as a professional visit.

James was in bed and looking ill. He immediately told me that the medical director had been to see him after I left on Thursday and had said, 'You know your parents are on your side.' James had been furious – he knew that the people there were trying to help, but he experienced it as intrusive. He had not seen the medical director since and therefore did not know whether he had received my letter, but he had told the nurse about me and had asked her to ensure privacy.

James then said that he had very little energy and was feeling low. He had been ill in the night, coughing and sweating so much that they had had to change his sheets. He was permanently on antibiotics. The GP had been in and explained his options regarding medication: he could take steroids for the 'feel good factor', or something to blur the edges, such as morphine. At present he was on painkillers but did not want anything stronger as he wanted to be himself to meet what was happening. Again this was a very clear statement of his intent and wishes. He felt his pulse, got rid of a pillow and lay down on his right side, facing me with his eyes shut and breathing rapidly.

Then he said that if it were not for his children he thought he would let go. After a while I remarked that he seemed worried. He said that he knew he could take steroids and leave the hospice for a while – people were trying to persuade him that it would be better for him if he was at home, but the thought worried him. He had got used to asking the nurses for help and would not have an emergency button at home. I said, 'It seems that you feel safer here.' With some relief he said 'Yes'. My role was clearly still to help him process his feelings, just as it had been all along. It seemed to me that the hospice was probably a bit like the sanatorium at his school: a safe place, a refuge from the outside world.

Considering the vivid dreams he had had in the past, I again asked if he had had a dream. He said:

> Yes, I keep dreaming the same thing, but I can't remember it. When I wake it is very clear as if I understand something. There is something simple I am not doing, like putting bricks in a wall. I can't describe it – it is a sense. I can't recall it now but there are no words to describe it. I can't capture it when I am awake. I dream it when I am sleeping – [laughs] silly that but I am lying here coughing and feeling ill and it is so clear.

I stayed for a full hour and James seemed disappointed when I was ready to go. He said, 'It goes quickly.' That afternoon the deputy medical director phoned in response to my letter. He had wanted to see me at the hospice but had missed me. He invited me to phone Dr Z, the doctor at the hospice, to make an appointment to see her the next time I visited and I agreed. I was aware that preserving the confidentiality of analysis was important, but this had shifted a little as communicating with the care team, with James's permission, would be in his interest. Once again the analytic frame had to be flexible to accomodate the changing situation.

Wednesday: discussing medication

Having discussed the medication with James I felt the need to be better informed. I consulted a colleague who is a physician as well as an analyst, and she explained the potentially positive effects of the medication being offered. On my next visit I was able to approach this topic at a practical as well as an inner-world level.

When I arrived I was again told that James was expecting me and had asked not to be interrupted. When I was shown in he was sitting on the edge of his bed, sweating and mopping himself with a towel. I said that he appeared to be feeling ill and asked whether he wanted me to stay. He said 'Yes – no – I don't know what it can achieve today.' I replied that I had not come to achieve anything. He kept coughing something up and depositing it in tissues. I suggested that he might lie down and he did so, but was restless. I told him about the phone conversation with the deputy director, and that I had made an appointment to see Dr Z, making it clear that I would not talk about the content of our sessions. I explained that she understood that what went on between us was private. He said 'That's fine', but I could tell he was not really able to think about it.

He recounted how the previous day he had felt well and his chest had been clear, but today he felt mentally confused and physically exhausted. He lay down, then sat up, then lay down again, coughing. Clearly he was in considerable discomfort so it seemed timely to discuss medication. I told him about my conversation with my colleague, and explained that she was an analyst as well as a physician and therefore understood both the psychological and the physical aspects of the problem. Then, repeating what she had told me, I explained how the proposed medication could ease his discomfort. It seemed important to confirm that he had a choice, but it was also important to interpret his resistance to accepting help. I pointed out that it seemed that this was transference but this time to the institution. Firstly, it seemed that he was replaying his recent experience of living in his parents' house and refusing their food. Secondly, I thought that his resentment of being looked after by strangers was replaying his boarding school experience. Thus mine was a dual role: whilst I was offering practical information I was also confirming that the choice was his. At the same time I was using my therapeutic knowledge of him to reduce his unconscious resistance so that he was able to make the decision based on the reality of the present situation.

James appeared not to respond. At last he said, 'I think I might just give up soon.' He then lay down. His breathing was laboured but eventually he settled, relaxed and seemed to sleep. I sat there while he slept. He had been sweating and was now uncovered so it seemed to me that he was cold. I covered him up without disturbing him. I continued to sit by his side, and occasionally he opened one eye and looked at me. I was reminded of the way a baby that is apparently asleep seems to be alert to movement and watches occasionally with one eye. After an hour he sat up, coughed a bit and said, 'I don't know – I think I'm just going to crash out now.' After agreeing to see him on Friday morning I left. He was so thin that there was almost no flesh on him – I felt tremendously sad and that I might not see much more of him.

Reflections on the session

James's refusal to take medication was similar to his refusal to take food from his parents – he would rather feed himself than accept help. As we have seen, this had a complex history that went back to the earliest years of his life. However the present situation was complicated because medication is also a poison food. In part he was resisting it for psychologically healthy reasons. He wanted to meet what came, as himself – he wanted to be conscious.

During this session talking had been insufficient; he had needed to show me by his actions just how ill he was. He had terminated the session at the appointed time, so even though it had been rather unusual, it had been a session. Although they were less clear we were both maintaining the boundaries of analysis.

When I left the hospice that day I had felt nothing at all, which was very unusual for me. I later realised that I had been numb; the situation had been just too painful. Such numb reactions are a defensive form of splitting that we all unconsciously employ to some extent in order to protect ourselves from unbearable pain. However, when working as a psychotherapist; they may inhibit ability to be emotionally available, so it is important to understand what is going on and bring it to consciousness. This type of counter-transference experience is the reason why it is necessary for analysts to undergo personal analysis. Later that day I went to see a colleague who was also a friend, and when talking to her I realised that I had unconsciously reached some sort of limit in myself. During this phase colleagues were essential both as a means of support and to help me think about what was going on when it was almost unbearable to do so. This use of one's peers is another means of maintaining a boundaried approach in the face of such intense emotional pressure.

Friday: beginning to accept medication

This time James looked well. He was bright-eyed and relaxed, and said he was feeling a lot better than when I last saw him. Dr Z had had a long talk with him. James asked whether I had seen her yet and I told him that I was going to see her later that morning. When I checked how he felt about that he said that in other situations he would have said 'No', but now it was part of giving up control. He wanted them to accept me as part of the care team. I said that was exactly why I wanted to see her and again I assured him that I would not talk about the content of our sessions.

It emerged that James's more relaxed state was the result of a degree of acceptance of his situation. He had considered what I had said about medication, and the previous night he had taken a sleeping tablet. Dr Z had woken him at 10.30 in the morning so he had slept well – too well. He showed amusement when he said that they had a pharmaceutical solution to every objection he raised. I said that if medication could help, it might be worth considering accepting it. However it was also important to confirm that the likely side effects provided a very valid reason for his reluctance to taking it. It was his right, and in the end only he could decide what was best for him. When I asked whether he thought about dying he replied, 'Well sometimes when I feel really ill I want to get on with it. It feels as if it will be a relief. It's odd really, when you are well, it seems horrific, but when you are ill that changes and it seems like a relief.'

He reflected on the state of his body. Swallowing was difficult but he was still urinating so something was getting through. However his bowel movements were not regular. His body was not functioning well, but he said that, he would have to be approaching death before he would let the nurses help him to bathe. He then admitted that he was now talking to the nurses a bit more, but 'I'm not going to give my soul over to people I don't even know [the nurses] just like that.' He acknowledged that he had talked to Dr Z and was beginning to trust her a bit. I was very moved by the trust in me that this implied: he was prepared to give the care of his soul over to me. He looked tired so I left him and went to see Dr Z.

Meeting with Dr Z

The formation of links with other professionals caring for someone in these circumstances is essential. It is too easy for the analyst to consider the rules of confidentiality as a bar to such co-working. Moreover if I was going to help James in an informed way with decisions about his medication, some communication with the hospice staff was essential.

Dr Z informed me that the changes in James's state were too rapid to be the result of physical deterioration, so they must be psychological. She told me that they had offered him medication and counselling, but he had refused both. The refusal of counselling was hardly surprising as he was already in analysis. However it came as something of a surprise to realise that they were experiencing him as hostile. It seemed that the psychological changes that were taking place in him had not extended to this situation, probably because the hospice evoked regression to a dependent state within an institution that might resemble a boarding school (I thought but did not say this). Dr Z had seen James's relatives and told them that he could live for another few months, perhaps even as much as six months; but he had confounded them before, 'so who knows?' She also thought that it would be good for him to leave the hospice for a while. She had worked with counsellors and therefore understood that while I needed to be informed about his physical condition she accepted the confidentiality of the therapeutic relationship. I said that I could be contacted and left my phone number.

Monday: taking medication

James was in bed looking pale. On Saturday evening he had lost control of his breathing, and had felt so ill and was coughing so much that he had asked for help. He had been given Diazepam, which had knocked him out. His throat was really bad: he was unable to swallow, and even the couple of mouthfuls of water he had taken at breakfast and lunch did not seem to be passing through him. He said that he liked to be left alone so that he could thrash around and spit in his waste bin or the sink.

This led to the subject of visitors. One of his women friends wanted to see him. He had been unable to refuse, but it was a very long drive and he had suggested that it might not be worth it. He had warned her that he might only feel like talking to her for 10 minutes and did not see what could be achieved. I reminded him that he had said a similar thing to me last week, and that perhaps it was not necessary to achieve anything.

He asked if I had seen Dr Z and I told him I had. He lay back and periodically shut his eyes, looking very tired. He talked about his family, and how the previous evening he had been feeling so bad that he had asked them to leave. They had been upset by this. I pointed out that he was always like that. He asked, 'What, hard-hearted?' I said 'No, wanting them close but at the same time pushing them away.' It seemed that James had been cutting the family off and the same pattern was being replayed in relation to me. I noticed that he was tired, and picking up the cue from him, I asked if he wanted me to leave, whereupon he said he was tired and would have to cut the session short. This was a repetition of what had happened with his family the previous evening. I asked if he wanted me to visit on Wednesday. He was off-hand but said he did, if he had not been taken to hospital.

Wednesday

On Tuesday evening I received a message from a nurse saying that James would have to cancel his appointment as he was going to hospital and might still be there on Friday. From that it sounded as though he was being admitted, so I phoned the hospice early on Wednesday. The nurse I spoke to said she thought he would be back at lunchtime; he had only gone to the hospital to see what's what. I asked her to tell him that I had phoned, and that if he felt like seeing me I would be available. I was quite worried as he had told me that he would have to have a permanent tube in his throat to help him swallow. I felt cut off from him; he had been rejecting the last time I saw him and now I could not speak to him directly. However at 1.30 he phoned to say that he was back, and could I come after all?

James was on steroids again, as well as Diazepam. He said that thanks to my words he had decided to accept medication. I felt the responsibility of this and hoped that I had done the right thing. However the steroids had shrunk the tumour and so he was able to eat. The consultant he had seen at the hospital, referring to the steroids, said that if something works, use it. James's mood was clearly being affected by the steroids – he was speeding and appeared a bit high.

Depression and cancer

As mentioned earlier in this chapter, at one point James had asked the rhetorical question, 'What is an appropriate level of anxiety at a time like this?' Now in a similar vein he made a distinction between different types of depression. Critical of the doctor's attitude towards depression, he asked me what Dr Z and I had discussed. He said that he wanted me to tell her where it was at with regard to his depression. 'One day they might give me a shot and I'd be out of it and unable to speak for myself, and I'd want you to tell them what they can do.' I explained that that was not what she and I had discussed. I had asked about his physical condition, and Dr Z had been relieved to learn he had been seeing me prior to the cancer. Then he asked rhetorically, 'What is depression?' He said that when his GP had referred him to me he had been suffering from clinical depression. But that had been different from the anxiety and depression he was now experiencing in connection with this very real situation. This was an insightful distinction.

He then talked about whom he let into his world, saying 'I was ill when my mother visited the other day but perhaps I was less ill than I appeared. I think that I did that with you too.' This was a reference to the events of Monday, and I said that I thought he had wanted me to know how ill he sometimes felt. But, I added, I had felt cut off. He said that this place was like the sanatorium at school. If you needed a rest you would go in there and matron would take your temperature and give you hot chocolate and you would have a rest. I pointed out that what had been missing then was his parents. They had not gone there, but it was different now – they were coming to the hospice, and so were his friends and so was I.

This prompted him to talk about his friend's visit the previous day. He said that he had been feeling awful; he had not slept and so he had taken Diazepam and was feeling drowsy when she arrived. However he had eventually perked up and she had stayed for two hours. He said, 'She drove a huge distance – I don't know why.' I queried this: 'Don't you?' He then reflected on the history of their relationship, realising that it was important to them both. Eventually, after one and a half hours, I stopped him. So I too stayed longer than expected, we both just let it happen, and this time I permitted it. I agreed to see him on Friday. He was seeing the medical director and thought that he might go home at the weekend. Then he showed me his legs, which were shockingly thin – just skin and bone in his jeans.

Before I left I commented on how he was relating to people more openly. He replied, 'I don't want to embarrass you but it's partly because of the last two years. It's made a difference having you during all this.' I said, 'Thank you for saying that.' I had stayed longer than usual that time, which seemed to be linked to this open expression of gratitude and the acknowledgement of the relationship between us.

Friday: talking of love

The beneficial effect of the steroids meant that James was fit to go home, so this was the last time that I visited him at the hospice. He was dressed and sitting in a chair with his bags packed. His mother was going to take him to his house, his children were going to visit him, and his sister was planning to stay with him all week. We agreed to cancel the Monday session but retain the one on Wednesday. If he was unable to make it he would phone and I would go him. He said that he was feeling better, but not bouncing in the way that he had when he left the hospital.

I had been concerned by James's comment in the previous session that if he was unable to speak for himself he wanted me to tell the medical staff what they could do. Now I asked him what he had meant. He replied that if he had been given morphine and was 'out of it' he had hoped I would speak for him. I pointed out that he knew that I was not a medical doctor and would therefore not be able to intervene. It emerged that he was worried about the amount of medication the doctors might give him, and that his family would bow to their authority. An associated concern was that his family might want to take him home when he wanted to stay in the hospice. I said that I thought that he was saying that he wanted me to continue to listen to him. He said seriously, 'Yes – I need someone who knows me better than anyone else, and that is you, to speak for me if necessary. Of course it could be that it gets to a point when you feel, if I can't speak, then you fade out of the picture.'

Once again this was a re-negotiation of the analytic frame as a result of the changing circumstances and so I responded that this was up to him. I told him that I was prepared to see this through if he wanted me to, 'But if you tell me to go away I will.' I pointed out how difficult it was when I received a message from nurses, as I had the previous week. That had made me feel cut off from him and unable to tell what he wanted. He said, 'They may say I'm not well enough but I want you to get through that. I said, 'OK but you need to let them know.' Then I pointed out how well he had done with telling them here in the hospice. James said, 'Yes, I can do it now.' Clearly he was thinking ahead. I was very humbled and moved by his evident trust in me. I hoped that I could do what was needed in this unknown future situation.

James said that he wanted me to know that he had been talking to his father. It seemed that they had found each other again, that James was emotionally coming home to his father. Talking of his children, he said, 'We have never been demonstrative. It is more than that, it can best be communicated when written down.' I remarked that perhaps he was talking about how some sorts of touching happen without touching, like it did between him and me.

He then went on to talk about his two women friends and how they had always stayed in touch over the years. From his words I picked up references to the way he related to me. I said, 'I guess that I am one of them.' He replied very quickly: 'Yes you are. Ever since that time I tried to leave and you stayed with me. I suppose it might have been like them eventually, someone I see once a year but without the intimacy.' I too could imagine that outcome, and in the normal course of events this would have marked a reasonable resolution to psychotherapy. Then he said there was something he wanted to ask me: 'I wonder what it is like having someone who came to you as a knackered, depressed man and then turns into a cancer patient. My problems have changed; they were life problems but cancer has dealt with them. I now have enough money and somewhere to live, but I have cancer. Anyway I wonder about that.'

I thought that he was asking about the nature of the bond between us. We had already established that I was coming to see him because I cared, and I decided to tell him a little about certain overlaps of time and place in our lives. But I was still trying to maintain boundaries so did not go into detail. Thus gradually the real relationship was coming to the fore. As there was little time left it seemed reasonable to tell him a little about me but without burdening him. One of the reasons why psychotherapists do not disclose details of their personal lives is that such information, even when offered with the best of intentions, may be experienced by the patient as a burden.

The common factor between the women in James's life was that sex had broken down but friendship had lasted, with no expectations and no demands. In this session we had talked about what we had in common, but we had also obliquely spoken of our affection for each other. It would probably not have mattered at that late stage to relinquish the boundaries, but we both recognised the need to maintain the analysis. He still needed me to make interpretations that would help him to make sense of his present experiences.

17   Home

This chapter is an account of the final month of James's analysis. Throughout that period he insisted on travelling to see me in my consulting room. He was determined to continue the analysis to the end. Thus the process of individuation continued and even speeded up in this the last month of his life. From my point of view, as his analyst this was an increasingly distressing period. I could do little but witness the inexorable deterioration of this man whom I had come to regard with great affection. However the support I had received from my trusted colleagues throughout the past year continued to sustain me in this last phase, when at times there was no map of the territory.

By the beginning of May it had become an undeniable reality that James was dying and the real relationship now took precedence over interpreting the transference. This is inevitable and totally appropriate when the patient is dying. Much of the transference had been worked through and resolved in the best way possible, given the circumstances. Even so the psychological work continued, and as previously observed James's capacity for metaphor seemed to increase as his body deteriorated. I did not insist on going to see him at his home, although at times I thought that might have been a kindness. Instead, which in some ways was more difficult, I respected his wish to travel to me for as long as he was able. His determination was an aspect of his character that had worked against him for much of his life. It had been behind the defensive psychological pattern described earlier in this book, but now it was mobilised in support of the individuation process. I respected that it was for him to decide, now more than ever, how he wanted to use the analysis.

After his discharge from the hospice James resumed his sessions in my consulting room. A number of physical symptoms had been troubling him and his doctor had prescribed a different antibiotic and some medication to disperse the infection. As a result of this, he had awoken in the middle of the night thinking that he had vomited, only to find that the emission had come from his chest. He had clearly been very distressed and was relieved that he had not been alone in the house. His sister was staying with him and this was making a huge difference to him. He had explained to her about his depression and its origins in childhood, and during breakfast he had said that it was really good to have her there. 'It was a bit like psychotherapy: I said everything that came into my mind and she is a good listener . . . it would have been awful to be alone after that.' At last James was open to communication and was allowing his sister to know him.

James disliked the term 'fighting cancer' but said that all the same he thought there was something in it because he was 'psyching it out'. He told me, 'You are "the first lady" in that, and everyone else is helping: the doctors, the Macmillan nurse, the hospice, the family.' I commented that the expression 'psyching it out' reminded me of the burglar dream (dream 3, Chapter 5). He responded, 'Yes that burglar dream is it!' Then, reflecting on the analytic process, he said that in scientific terms there was no explanation of why talking to me helped him, but perhaps it did open up pathways in his head that affected his body. Recent research has demonstrated that psychotherapy affects the brain in just such a manner, but James's comment was made before this was widely disseminated (see Schore, 1994; Kaplan-Solms and Solms, 2000). In a similar vein, it was now two years since James had been given a maximum of six months to live. There was no hard evidence to suggest that analysis had played a part in extending his life, but James was in no doubt that it had had such an effect.

Plants

In one session James recounted how he had found a plant in his mother's house that he had had for many years and, with help he had repotted it. It had been old and dusty but now it was tall and healthy. He said it symbolised himself: 'I can't be that ill if I look like that.' A long silence followed as I think we were both very aware that although the regenerated plant symbolised his psychological attitude it was far from the reality of his bodily self.

After a while I broke the silence and introduced the topic of the little vase in which he had brought the snowdrops. This represented unfinished business and I pointed out that it was still on the table where he had left it. It seemed to have some symbolic value, so reminding James that he had intended to take it when he moved into his house I asked what he wanted to do with it now. He replied, 'You should regard it as a present.' He continued, 'When I brought those snowdrops back in January last year they were all about growth. I noticed them growing because that was how I was feeling. This year I don't think I noticed them. Then it [the vase] did become a problem because I could not just take it away again – maybe I did not want to. Anyway regard it as a present.' I asked, 'So it stays here?' He said, 'Yes it is me in a way. Like me – well not any more.'

At that point I felt overwhelmingly sad and my eyes filled with tears. He was leaving a bit of himself with me and I was really touched by that. I could not think of anything to say. I noticed that James had started coughing when we began to talk of this. Perhaps because of the huge emotional charge associated with the symbolism of this small vase. We both recognised that one day he would no longer come but the vase would remain; a concrete symbol of the genuine affection that had grown between us. James confirmed this when he linked it to his body, saying 'Its feet are like mine, my ankles are really swollen.' He showed me. I said, 'I suppose that it is the steroids.' He replied, 'Yes – and my cheeks are fatter.' During this exchange it was all I could do not to cry. He continued, 'Otherwise it could be that the lymph nodes aren't functioning.' Before the end of the session James said that he was feeling better now. 'Maybe its because of all the stuff that I brought up – maybe its you.'

The House

In Chapter 3 we explored the symbolism of the house. Now its significance again came to the fore. The tenancy of James's house was now secure, and so with the help of his family, he had collected all his stuff from his parents' house. As he put it, 'Every last stitch of clothing, every book, every pot and pan.' This was his first unconscious symbolic reference to the house. He was moving out of the house of his childhood, his parents' home, and into his own.

In connection with this the topic of plants resurfaced. James had decided to return a plant he had taken from his mother because it was 'too far gone'. He speculated that this was because she kept her plants in a dark room. Then he said, 'I would like you to come to my house and see the plants – perhaps in June. I'm not interested in garden plants but indoor plants, in a room that is light enough, like this one, he indicated my room, this is ideal, they do well in all this light.' This too was an unconscious metaphor. His mother's plants were in the dark but mine flourished in the light. Understood in another way, this was an unconscious reference to his individuation process – his spiritual journey. The dark unconscious state had been transformed into the light of consciousness. He had found the conditions in which to flourish, and as a result his plants were thriving in a home of his own.

A discussion about James's neighbours revealed a similarly intimate psychological connection between the house and his body. Talking of the house where he was now living, he mused about the differences between the neighbours on either side. On the left there was a woman who had put up a fence that blocked him out; but on the right there lived a really friendly couple. He speculated about the woman on the left, who lived alone. He said, 'If I wanted a relationship [with her] I don't think it could happen.' Then without a pause he switched to include me, ' You'd have a job [having a relationship with him] at the moment. I sleep in a double bed because I like it. I sleep on one side but you could not get in there because there are plants all along the other side.' This too was a reference to one side being blocked. Then comparing the neighbours, he continued, 'It is odd really, the left is totally closed, fenced off, and the right totally open and friendly.'

Viewed purely in terms of the psyche this could indicate work still to do. The left – in classical Jungian terms, the unconscious side – was fenced off. The right – the conscious side – was open and accessible. In the course of an ordinary analysis this might have indicated a one-sided development that could over time become balanced. But this was not an ordinary analysis, so it could be understood as a graphic symbolic description of James's state: whilst his psyche was developing, his body was becoming more and more closed off.

Alternatively it could be viewed as an unconscious, metaphorical reference to James's body. His left lung was completely blocked, fenced off, whilst the right one was open and friendly. I pointed this out. At first he was taken aback but then grew excited by the link, which now seemed obvious to him. He said, 'Things like this give me hope. I will confound them all yet!' There was a long thoughtful pause, and then I voiced the unspoken thought that hovered in the silence between us: 'But there is always the concern that you might not.' This was followed by more silence, then James said that he had everything mobilised and perhaps would die tomorrow. When he said that, I again, felt very sad.

Earlier he had asked permission to put his tissue in the bin. Now he apologised for going on about his body. I said, 'That sounds similar to asking if you can put your tissue in the waste bin.' He replied, 'Well you aren't here to deal with my body; and it is infected.' I commented that although he felt able to leave his vase here and celebrate the metaphorical aspects of the body, he seemed worried about contaminating me with the unpleasant physical aspects of his illness. I added that the two were intimately connected.

The hospice and the school

James reflected on how ill he had been at the hospice. He thought that he had had to be admitted so that everyone would know just how ill he was. I agreed that he had been very ill and said that it seemed important that I had witnessed this. Reminding him of the time when I had covered him up, I said that that was what he had needed when he was young and ill and there had been no one there. He said, 'Yes I think that's right. When I was at school I used to get a chest infection, preceded by a high temperature, and that is exactly what happened in the hospice.' Except that this time the people he needed had seen him: 'My family and you, you all saw how ill I was.' It seemed that he was saying that now there were witnesses who cared about him.

The conversation we had had in the hospice, when I had told him a little about myself, now came to mind. I wondered how that had affected him. He said, 'Well I was dying and it was about farewells.'

Body and psyche

Each session I was increasingly aware of how very thin he was. His clothes hung loosely off him, and I noticed that his legs were just skin and bone;

there was no muscle. Sometimes he had trouble getting out of the chair and needed help to regain his balance. As I watched him make his way to his car, I realised just how sick he was and the tremendous reversal from when he first came. Then he had been relatively physically fit but there had been little room in his life for psyche. Now the spirit was alive and strong but the body was quickly deteriorating.

This contrast was particularly evident in one session when James was very frail and coughing frequently. He talked at length about his body, and then in marked contrast to the awfulness of his physical deterioration he expressed, his delight in things that were growing. He described the beauty of the May blossom, explaining that when the snowdrops had been out this year he had not noticed them, but now it was really spring and he was enjoying it. At a symbolic level it was his own rebirth to which he was referring. Earlier in the year, when the snowdrops had been out, James had been expecting to die, so this time was like a reprieve – a renewal and spring time.

However the previous day he had asked the doctor if he was right in thinking that the common cold could kill him. He had been taken aback by the response. The doctor had said ' "That's right" – straight out! I asked to have it straight and I got it.' He did not know if he had taken it in yet, but when he had seen his naked body in the mirror he had thought that he looked positively starving. It would be too late if he did not start to build himself up, so he had planned a programme of rest and eating, as well as doing things. Thus the alternating facets of optimism and despair were his constant companions.

One day James's mother went to his house for lunch, which pleased him. He talked about getting better, about dying and about his children; he seemed to be concerned about continuity. In the discussion of his plants, his children and leaving the little vase with me, it seemed he had been planting seeds. If they grew, then a bit of him would continue. James liked that, he said 'Yes, earth, roots and seeds that's it.' Then he thought about it and corrected himself: 'Earth, roots and leaves – not seeds – is what growing is about.'

In the Jewish tradition immortality lies in what we leave behind – in our children, trees we have planted, and books. It seemed that all these threads of meaning were manifest in the material in these sessions. James was considering how he would live on after his death. In that regard this book is his legacy.

Deterioration

James's physical deterioration became more apparent with each passing day. He was very unsteady and often needed my help to get into the room. Each time he arrived or rose to leave I carefully monitored his progress and it necessary saw him safely to his car. Sometimes he needed a little help, but mostly he managed. Writing about it now, it is a wonder that he continued to come to me. However whenever I suggested visiting him at home he rejected the offer, indicating that one day I would go to him, but as long as he was able he would come to me. I think that this was because of his fierce independence combined with an unspoken intention to continue to keep me separate from his family.

However, throughout this month he seemed to be demanding too much of his body. One day he carefully lowered himself into the chair and explained that when he had been shaving that morning he had put his back out. This was causing him pain and he had spent much of the day in bed. He said, 'You've no idea the lengths I have gone to to get here.' Then he described in detail the difficulty of getting out of bed, and then out of the house and finally into his car. It had clearly taken a supreme effort of will. He was also concerned that, although he felt well and had eaten a lot, his body was wasting and he had lost even more weight. The irony was that everything else in his life was working for the first time: he had a place to live, enough money and could even let people in emotionally. He said that psychotherapy had made a big difference. In the last two years some blocks had been removed so relationships were better. It seemed that James was again saying thank you.

The next session was the last he was able to attend, and he was feeling down. He had been to see the doctor about medication because his back was worse and he was constipated; the latter represented one more thing that was now out of control. I commented on how the process seemed to be relentless. James took that up and talked rapidly about his body for five or ten minutes. Then he said, 'That's the update but I'm not sure if that is what I should be talking about. I feel that there is something else.' I thought about this and then pointed out that we were not talking about what would happen if all this wasting continued: death. James said, 'Yes I think that's it.'

Then he reflected on how he had wanted to die twice in his life – once in the October before last and once in the hospice. However he did not feel that way now. Life had never been better, his affairs were in order and the children were as prepared as they could be. When the time did come he wanted to die in peace. But, he said, 'I do not feel ready.'

The last session

Before the next session James phoned to say that he could not get out of bed because his back had seized up. The GP had been called out and he would phone me when he knew what was happening. We agreed that I would visit on Monday if he were unable to get to me. He phoned the following day to say that he was still in bed and would not be able to come, and then again on Saturday evening to tell me that the doctor had said he would have to stay in bed until Tuesday at least. His back muscles had wasted and therefore he could not get up. We talked for a while and I agreed to visit him at home on Monday at his usual time.

When I arrived at James's house his sister, who was caring for him, intro-duced herself and showed me to his room. He was propped up in his bed, unable to move. I sat beside the bed as he told me that he had 'hospital at home' nurses who came in regularly. The doctor had been in and James was now taking morphine. The reason the pain was so bad was because he had no flesh on him so his bones were crunching on his nerve ends. He said, 'Morphine is last rites.'

His sight was deteriorating and he was unable to focus. Although he was sleeping well he was aware that whilst he slept, instead of his body being restored, the cancer was eating away at him. As he put it, the steroids he was taking were villains as well as heroes: they were probably causing the wast-ing. The women friends with whom he had regular phone contact were both coming to visit him that week; with irony he said he thought that was an ominous sign. Mentally James was very alive and lively and emotionally very connected. It was then that he said, 'I feel more alive now than I have ever been.' (see Chapter 2, p. 21)

James talked about his body, the nurses and medication, and then said he felt good and wondered whether he was avoiding something. He seemed to veer off so I asked him what he might be avoiding. He did not know, but said perhaps I'd get my tears. I was so near to tears myself that I thought he meant that I would cry, but then recovering, I realised he meant that he might cry. He said that he thought that he would, but not until the goodbyes at the end. It sounded as though something would dissolve. A prayer remembered from school kept going through his mind: 'Lord, let this thy servant go in peace.' As he recited it he seemed near to tears, but when I asked whether he felt like crying he said 'No' and looked at his watch. This was something he often did when tearful.

As I left at the end of the session I looked back and was shocked at just how ill he appeared I thought that I might not see him again. Again I experienced the now familiar tearing sensation. Having driven away from the house I stopped and parked and the tears flowed. I realised that, as well as being expression of my own grief, these were James's unshed tears. I wanted to tell him that I would never forget him. I think he wanted me to know what I meant to him and he wanted to cry. We were avoiding crying together; I could not help him to cry because I was so near to tears myself. Physical contact would have facilitated it, and I now question what would have been so wrong with that. Was it necessary to maintain the boundaries to the end? I think that it was, because intuitively I knew that I must not burden James with my emotion. I knew that he would have found my distress impossible to deal with. Moreover it seemed that he was still controlling me as well as himself at some unspoken level.

James phoned to cancel his next session. It proved very difficult to make another appointment: I suggested the next morning but he had physiother-apy and the nurse and doctor were calling, so the afternoon would be better; I could not make the afternoon so offered the evening, but that was not good for him. He said to leave it until Monday. He then said, 'If you came and the physiotherapist came I would not know how to prioritise. You might have to wait and spend time downstairs drinking tea.' This comment suggested that he still wanted to keep me apart from his family. He went on to say that yesterday had been a bad day. The painkillers were working so in theory he could move, but he did not have the strength to do so. He said 'The Lord giveth and the Lord taketh away.'

During this period discussions in supervision were essential. My colleague kept in focus the meaning of what was happening when I might otherwise have lost sight of it. The substance of our discussion was that it appeared as though James did not need me so much at that time. He had his family. My colleague suggested that this was a reflection of the successful outcome of the analysis. James was in his own house with his family and friends. Letting him go was part of the conclusion of the work.

The final visit

Before going to see James the following Monday as agreed, I phoned and told his sister that I was planning to visit and enquired whether that would be all right. She told me that he was sleeping, and that while she was sure he would like to see me it would be best to go in the evening. I gave her my phone number.

That evening I went alone into his room. He was asleep, so I sat beside him, touched his hand and told him I was there. He raised himself as if temporarily coming back to life. Unable to speak, he mumbled a bit and smiled. I expressed acknowledgement of the fact that he felt poorly, and he seemed to agree. I said, 'Just rest – I'll sit here.' He fell back to sleep. Then disturbed by a sound he raised himself and muttered that he felt confused. I acknowledged this and he again fell asleep. I stayed a while and then left. The following morning his sister phoned to say that he had died three hours later.

The funeral

The analyst works with the inner world and the funeral is the territory of the family. However when they phoned to invite me to the funeral I was relieved – I needed to be there for my own sake. The funeral took place in the city church near his parents' home. Inevitably I met members of his family but I left immediately after the service, declining their invitation to join them later. It would not have been appropriate for me to go with them, nor was it what James would have wanted.

18 Supervision, Countertransference Bereavement and Research Questions

The purpose of writing this book was dual. Clearly it was an attempt to make sense of the complex countertransference engagement I faced when working in psychotherapy with this dying man. However my ultimate aim is far more ambitious than that: my hope is that this book will offer help, a kind of map of the territory, to others travelling a similar path. Therefore in this brief concluding chapter, I address some practical questions arising out of this account. Firstly I turn to supervision.

Supervision

I have indicated in previous chapters that my colleagues were important in helping me to maintain the analytic boundaries, but I have only briefly alluded to supervision. In the early stages of working with James my usual peer group supervision was sufficient. However when the illness became a dominant factor, combined with the erotic countertransference, it became clear that more was needed so I sought individual supervision. While the content of these discussions is not an explicit part of this story, the professional reader might be interested to know that its function was to help me to think about the meaning of some of the communications that took place within the analytic context. It gave space to consider practical decisions about the extension of the analytic boundaries. Although there was never any question of my breaking the analytic frame, supervision provided a forum to discuss the wish to do so and to process its meaning in the context of this analysis. Most of all, supervision was a general source of support.

Reflecting on the point at which I sought individual supervision, it is now clear that I was seeking a place to express and understand the combination of affection and loss engendered in this therapeutic relationship. It could be argued that supervision provides a combined parental couple to think about the analysand. This strengthens the container of the analysis and is therefore particularly important when it is under the intense pressure engendered by physical illness. Very often the presence of hate and other negative emotions is seen as an indication that serious analytic work is taking place. Love and more positive emotions are sometimes viewed as avoidance of the negative. However I hope that, in the narrative account, I have shown that these are two sides of the same coin. The erotic is not merely about love – it is messy, sometimes violent, and at times terrifying for patient and analyst alike. Nor is hate merely about negative feelings – its counterpart is need, desire and love. The intensity of such material is totally engaging for both people.

For this reason when, in the process of analysis or psychotherapy, the analysand becomes fatally ill and then dies the analyst is faced with a rather unusual form of bereavement. We might call this 'countertransference bereavement'. Because it takes place within the framed and confidential setting of analysis it would be inappropriate to discuss such bereavement outside the professional context. Analysts, psychotherapists or counsellors working in private practice may feel defensive or ashamed of being so deeply affected, especially as they are aware that medically trained colleagues and those working in palliative care are confronted with these issues every day. While they appear to cope well enough, I know from my own work as a supervisor that this countertransference bereavement sometimes overwhelms people working in palliative care. In de Hennezel's (1997) words, this is the price we pay for remaining emotionally alive in this difficult human situation. Supervision is essential in facilitating this. Supervision is different from personal analysis, which in this context is only necessary if the analyst's personal bereavements and losses have been insufficiently analysed in the past.

It is evident that I learned a great deal from working with James, and it seems to have been a lesson learned for a purpose as a year later another of my patients developed a cancer. This man was of a similar age to James, and I had been working with him for four years when we came to the realisation that he too was dying. While no two cases are the same, my experience with James meant that I was a little more prepared for some of the boundary issues that arose. The intensity was less pressing due to his personal circumstances, but also because, as a result of my experience with James, I was more confident about my role. Home visits and negotiating a reduced fee were now part of a familiar process. However in this case I did not visit as frequently as I had with James.

Home visits

It would be quite wrong to imagine that all sick patients want to be visited by their analyst – many prefer their analyst to stay in the consulting room. Therefore it is important not to assume that hospital or home visits are the only solution; there are many other options that are less time consuming and less demanding for both people. It is therefore important to clarify, firstly, what it means for the analyst, and then whether or not she or he wishes to visit, and if so why? If she or he does not want to visit there is no obligation to do so. In most of my cases where the analysand has become ill, especially for a short time, I have not visited. Therefore it was important for me to question my own motives for visiting James.

Having considered whether or not the analyst is prepared to visit it is necessary to consider whether the visit would benefit the analysand. It is important to analyse, as I did with James, what it would mean – psychologic- ally and practically – for the patient to have their analyst at their hospital bedside or in their home. Arrangements for privacy need to be considered as well as how it might be managed with relatives. Even if the patient appears to want the visit, in practice, it might be experienced as intrusive.

The fee

When a patient faces a life-threatening illness, and is consequently unable to work, the fee may have to be reduced. Unless the patient has other financial resources the alternative may be to end the analysis. This raises questions about the analyst's ethical responsibility when a patient is no longer able to pay due to illness. Clearly those working in the statutory sector are at an advantage over analysts who have to live from their private practice income. Haynes and Wiener (1996) discuss the real and symbolic meanings of money in the context of 'soul work' and the difficulty many ana- lysts have in confronting their own need to be paid. In order to accommo- date the patient who becomes too ill to work it might be worth considering making provision in a practice, for one patient who needs to be seen for a limited period irrespective of their ability to pay. However even when someone is seriously ill, reduction of the fee needs careful consideration. As with home visits, offering a reduced fee may be experienced as intrusive. Again thought needs to be given to why the reduction is being offered: is it for the benefit of the patient or merely to make the analyst feel better? Thus any decision that is made to accommodate a patient's altered state needs to be analysed before action is taken.

Questions for future research

We turn now to questions that have arisen from this account that merit further attention. The question raised in the previous chapter about whether analysis might prolong the life of someone with a terminal illness is one on which there seems to be little hard evidence. McDougall (2000, p. 48) writes of an analysand who was suicidal before becoming ill, and makes the general point, quoted in Chapter 1, that the psychoanalyst cannot cure a patient's cancer but 'when the patient is helped both somatically and psychically her chances of survival are notably increased' (McDougall 2000:48). This concurs with my sense that James's life may have been prolonged as a result of psychotherapy. It also raises the question of whether there is a link between clinical depression and the onset of cancer. Cancer is considered by some to be the result of repressed anger turned inwards; a somatic manifestation of a psychological problem. There appears to be little evidence, to substantiate this idea, but the question would benefit from detailed research.

The comment made by James when he was considering how odd it was that talking to me seemed to make a difference prompts another question. He suggested that perhaps it opened up pathways in his head that affected his body. This leads us to consider the study of brain function in relation to psychoanalysis. Findings seem to indicate that psychotherapy could indeed open up areas of the brain that have been damaged by early emotional trauma, permitting them to function again (Schore, 1994; Kaplan-Solms and Solms, 2000).

Dreaming

Analysts sometimes dream of their patients, and such dreams may clarify or reveal the meaning of a particular situation. Despite my intense involvement with James, I only once dreamed about him. As we have seen, James dreamed vividly in the middle phase of the work, but towards the end, as death became a reality, the dreams lessened. Others have noticed a similar reduction in dreams of the dying (Bosnak, 1989). However, at the same time as James's dreams decreased, his ability to make metaphorical links increased. Could there be a connection here? Perhaps it was to do with relinquishing of defences, but another possibility is that the life of the unconscious may become less opaque as the body deteriorates. This too merits further research.

In conclusion, it has been my aim to show how working with the dying patient in psychotherapy may be an enriching, as well as challenging, experience for the analyst. It is hoped that this account has given a sense of the meaning and purpose of desire, dreams and individuation mediated within the context of a bounded therapeutic relationship.

References

Aldridge, D. (ed.) (1999) *Music Therapy in Palliative Care*, London and Philadelphia: Jessica Kingsley.

Astor, J. (1995) *Michael Fordham: Innovations in Analytical Psychology*, London and New York: Routledge.

Bach, S. (1990) *Life Paints its Own Span: On the Significance of Spontaneous Pictures by Severely Ill Children*, Einsiedeln, Switzerland: Daimon Verlag.

Bachelard, G. (1960) *The Poetics of Reverie: Childhood, Language and the Cosmos*, trans. from the French by Daniel Russell, Boston: Beacon Press, 1969 edn.

———(1964) *The Poetics of Space*, trans. from the French by Maria Jolas, Boston: Beacon Press, 1969 edn.

Beaver, V. (1998) 'The butterfly garden: art therapy with HIV/AIDS patients', in M. Pratt and M. Wood (eds), *Art Therapy in Palliative Care: The Creative Response*, London and New York: Routledge.

Benjamin, J. (1988) *The Bonds of Love*, London: Virago.

Bertoia, J. (1993) *Drawings from a Dying Child: Insights into Death from a Jungian Perspective*, London and New York: Routledge.

Bion, W.R. (1968) *Experience in Groups*, London and New York: Taylor & Francis.

Blum, H.P. (1973) 'The concept of eroticized transference', *Journal of the American Psychoanalytical Association*, 21, pp. 61–76.

Bonasia, E. (2001) 'The countertransference: erotic, eroticised and perverse', *International Journal of Psychoanalysis*, 82(2), pp. 249–62.

Bosnak, R. (1989) *Dreaming with an AIDS Patient*, Boston and Shaftesbury: Shambala.

Bowers, M., Jackson, E., Knight, A. and Leshan, L. (1964) *Counselling the Dying*, Northvale, NJ and London: Jason Aronson, 1994 edn.

Bowlby, J. (1974) *Attachment:* Volume One *of Attachment and Loss*, London: Hogarth.

———(1980a) *Separation, Anxiety and Anger:* Volume Two of *Attachment and Loss*, London: Hogarth.

———(1980b) *Loss, Sadness and Depression:* Volume Three of *Attachment and Loss*, London: Hogarth.

Cassirer, E. (1955) *The Philosophy of Symbolic Forms: Volume 2, Mythical Thought*, New Haven: Yale University Press.

Chasseguet-Smirgel J. (1984a) *Creativity and Perversion*. London: Free Associations Books.

———(1984b) 'The femininity of the analyst in professional practice', *International Journal of Psychoanalysis*, Volume. 65, p. 169.

Chodorow, N. (1978) *Reproduction of Mothering: Psychoanalysis and the Sociology of Gender*, Berkeley: University of California Press.

Circlot, J.E. (1962) *A Dictionary of Symbols*, London: Routledge, 1990.

Connell, C. (1998) *Something Understood: Art Therapy in Cancer Care*, London: Wrexham.

Cooper, J.S. (1978) *An Illustrated Encyclopaedia of Traditional Symbols*, London: Thames & Hudson.

Covington, C. (1996) 'Purposive aspects of the erotic transference', *Journal of Analytical Psychology*, 41(3), pp. 339–52.

de Hennezel, M. (1997) *Intimate Death: How the Dying Teach Us to Live*, trans. from the French by Carol Brown Janeway, London: Warner Books.

Diamond, J. (1998) *'C' Because Cowards Get Cancer Too*, London: Vermillion, 1999 edn.

Dollimore, J. (1998) *Death, Desire and Loss in 'Western Culture'*, London: Penguin Books.

Duffell, N. (2000) *The Making of Them: The British Attitude to Children and the Boarding School System*, London: Lone Arrow Press.

Dumas, A. (1944) *The Count of Monte Cristo*, London: Oxford University Press, 1990 edn.

Eichenbaum, L. and Orbach, S. (1983) *What do Women Want?*, London: Michael Joseph.

Eissler, K.R. (1955) *The Psychiatrist and the Dying Patient*, New York: International Universities Press.

Feinsilver, D.B. (1998) 'The therapist as a person facing death: the hardest of external realities and therapeutic action', *International Journal of Psychoanalysis*, 79(6), pp. 131–50.

Field, N. (1989) 'Listening with the body', *British Journal of Psychotherapy*, Vol. 5(4).

Fordham, M. (1969) 'On terminating analysis', in M. Fordham, R. Gordon, J. Hubback and K. Lambert (eds), *Technique in Jungian Analysis*, London: Karnac, 1989.

———(1976) *The Self and Autism*, London: Library of Analytical Psychology, Vol. 3.

———(1985) *Explorations into the Self*, London: Library of Analytical Psychology, Vol. 7.

Fordham, M., Gordon, R., Hubback, J. and Lambert K. (eds), (1989) *Technique in Jungian Analysis*, London: Karnac.

Freud, A. (1965) *Normality and Pathology in Childhood*, London: Hogarth.

Freud, S. (1900) *The Interpretation of Dreams*, Standard Edition IV, London: Hogarth.

———(1912) 'The dynamics of transference', Standard Edition, XII, London: Hogarth, 1963 edn.

———(1915) 'Observations on transference love', *Introductory Lectures on Psychoanalysis*, Standard Edition, XII, London: Hogarth.

———(1917) 'Transference', Standard Edition, XVI, London: Hogarth.

———(1920) "Letter to Ferenzi', in M. Schur, *Freud Living and Dying*, London: Hogarth.

Gilligan, C. (1982) *In A Different Voice*, London and Cambridge, MA: Harvard University Press, 1993 edn.

Goldberger, M. and Evans, D. (1985) 'On transference manifestations in male patients with female analysts', *International Journal of Psychoanalysis*, Vol. 66, pp. 295–310.

Goldstein, R. (ed.) (1999) *Images, Meanings and Connections: Essays in Memory of Susan Bach*, Einsiedeln, Switzerland: Daimon Verlag.

Gordon, R. (1971) *Dying and Creating: A Search for Meaning*, London: Library of Analytical Psychology, Vol. 4.

Greenson, R. (1967) *The Technique and Practice of Psychoanalysis*, London: Hogarth.

Guggenbuhl-Craig, A. (1971) *Power in the Helping Professions*, New York: Spring.

Guttman, H.A. (1984) 'Sexual issues in the transference and countertransference between female therapist and male patient', *Journal of the American Academy of Psychoanalysis*, 12(4), pp. 187–97.

Hall, J.A. (1977) *Patterns of Dreaming: Jungian Techniques in Theory and Practice*, Boston and London: Shambala, 1991 edn.

Harlow, H.F. (1959) 'Love in infant monkeys', *Scientific American*, 200(6), pp. 64–74.

Haynes, J. (1996) 'Death of the analyst: the end is where we start from', *Harvest*, 42(1), pp. 27–44.

Haynes, J. and Wiener, J. (1996) 'The analyst in the counting house: money as symbol and reality in analysis', *British Journal of Psychotherapy*, 13(1), pp. 14–25.

Heimann, P. (1949) 'On countertransference', *International Journal of Psychoanalysis*, 31, pp. 81–4.

Hillman, J. (1977) *The Myth of Analysis*, New York: Harper.

Hinshelwood, R. (1989) *A Dictionary of Kleinian Thought*, London: Free Associations Books.

Horney, K. (1932) 'The dread of woman', *International Journal of Psychoanalysis*, 13, pp. 348–60.

Hubback, J. (1996) 'The archetypal senex: an exploration of old age', *Journal of Analytical Psychology*, 41(11), pp. 3–18.

Irigaray, L. (1974) *Speculum of the Other Woman*, trans. by Gillian C. Bell, New York: Cornell University Press.

Jaffe, A. (1958) *An Archetypal Approach to Death Dreams and Ghosts*, Einsiedeln, Switzerland: Daimon Verlag, 1999 edn.

Judd, D. (1989) *Give Sorrow Words: Working with a Dying Child*, London, 2nd edn, now published by Whurr, 1995.

Jukes, A. (1993) *Why Men Hate Women*, London: Free Associations Books.

Jung, C.G. (1913) *Psychological Types*, CW6, Princeton: Bollingen, 1989 edn.

———CW is *The Collected Works of Carl Gustav Jung*.

———(1928) *Dream Analysis Part 1*, London and New York: Routledge, 1965 edn.

———(1930) 'The Stages of Life', in *The Structure and Dynamics of the Psyche*, CW8, London: Routledge.

———(1935a) 'The Tavistock Lectures', in *The Symbolic Life*, CW 18, London: Routledge.

———(1935b) 'The Soul and Death', in *The Structure and Dynamics of the Psyche* CW8, London: Routledge.

———(1946) 'The Psychology of the Transference', in *The Practice of Psychotherapy* CW16, Princeton: Bollingen.

———(1955) 'Synchonicity: An Acausal Connecting Principle', in *The Structure and Dynamics of the Psyche* CW8, London: Routledge.

———(1956) *Symbols of Transformation*, CW5, Princeton: Bollingen.

———(1959a) 'The Transcendent Function', CW8, in *The Structure and Dynamics of the Psyche* London: Routledge.

———(1959b) *The Archetypes and the Collective Unconscious*, CW9, Part 1, Princeton: Bollingen.

———(1963) *Memories, Dreams and Reflections*, London: Fontana.

———(1964) *Man and His Symbols*, London: Aldus Books.

Kaplan-Solms, K. and Solms, M. (2000) *Clinical Studies in Neuro-Psychoanalysis*, London: Karnac.

Karme, L. (1979) 'The analysis of a male patient by a female analyst', *International Journal of Psychoanalysis*, Vol. 60, pp. 253–61.

Kast, V. (1992) *The Dynamics of Symbols: Fundamentals of Jungian Psychology*, trans. Susan A. Schwarz, New York: Fromm International.

Kastenbaum, R. (2000) *The Psychology of Death*, London: Free Associations Books, first published 1972.

Kearney, M. (1996*) Mortally Wounded: Stories of Soul, Pain, Death and Healing*, New York: Touchstone Books, 1997.

———(2000) *A Place of Healing: Working with Suffering in Living and Dying*, Oxford: Oxford University Press.

Klein, M. (1946) 'Notes on some schizoid mechanisms', in M. Klein, *Envy and Gratitude and Other Works*, London: Hogarth, 1975.

———(1975a) *Envy and Gratitude and Other Works*, London: Hogarth.

———(1975b) *Love, Guilt and Reparation*, London: Hogarth.

———(1980) *The Psycho-Analysis of Children*, London: Hogarth.

Kristeva, J. (1983) *Tales of Love*, New York: Columbia University Press.

———(1989) *Black Sun: Depression and Melancholia*, New York: Columbia University Press.

Kubler-Ross, E. (1969) *On Death and Dying*, London and New York: Tavistock, 1984 edn.

Kulish, N.M. (1984) 'The effect of the sex of the analyst on the transference', *Bulletin of the Meninger Clinic*, 48(2).

Lacan, J. (1977) *The Four Fundamental Concepts of Psycho-Analysis*, London: Penguin.

Lambert, K. (1981) *Analysis, Repair and Individuation*, London: Society of Analytical Psychology/Academic Press.

Lawrence, G. (2000) *Tongued with Fire*, London: Karnac Books.

Lawton, J. (2000) *The Dying Process: Patients' Experiences of Palliative Care*, London and New York: Routledge.

Lee, C. (1996) *Music at the Edge: The Music Therapy Experiences of a Musician with AIDS*, London and New York: Routledge.

Lester, E.P. (1985) 'The female analyst and the eroticised transference', *International Journal of Psychoanalysis*, 66, pp. 283–93.

Little, M. (1950) 'The analyst's total response to his patient's needs', in M. Little, *Towards Basic Unity*, London: Free Associations Books, 1986 edn.

Mahler, M., Pine, F. and Bergman, A. (1975) *The Psychological Birth of the Human Infant*, New York: Basic Books.

Mann, D. (1997) *Psychotherapy: An Erotic Relationship*, London and New York: Routledge.
McDougall, J. (1989) *Theaters of the Body*, New York: Norton.
——(1995) *The Many Faces of Eros: A Psychoanalytic Exploration of Human Sexuality*, London: Free Associations Books.
——(2000) 'Theatres of the psyche', *Journal of Analytical Psychology*, 45(1).
McLeod, J. (1994) *Doing Counselling Research*, London: Sage.
——(2000) *Qualitive Research in Counselling and Psychotherapy*, London: Sage.
Meltzer, D. (1992) *The Claustrum: An Investigation of Claustrophobic Phenomena*, The Clunie Press.
Minerbo, B. (1998) 'The patient without a couch: an analysis of a patient with terminal cancer', *International Journal of Psychoanalysis*, 79(1), pp. 83–93.
Mitchell, J. (2000) *Mad Men and Medusas*, London and New York: Allen Lane the Penguin Press.
Morrison, B. (1993) *And When Did You Last See Your Father?* London: Granta Books.
Murray Parkes, C. (1972) *Bereavement: Studies of Grief in Adult Life*, Harmondsworth, Penguin, 1980 edn.
Neumann, E. (1955) *The Great Mother*, Princeton University Press.
Olivier, C. (1980) *Jocasta's Children: The Imprint of the Mother*, trans. by George Craig, reprinted London: Routledge, 1989.
Orbach, A. (1999) *Life, Psychotherapy and Death*, London and Philadelphia, Jessica Kingsley.
Papadopoulos, R.K. (1998) 'Destructiveness, atrocities and healing: epistemological and clinical reflections', *Journal of Analytical Psychology*, 43(4), pp. 455–77.
Perry, C. (1991) *Listen to the Voice Within: A Jungian Approach to Pastoral Care*, London: SPCK.
Peters, R. (1990) *Living with Dreams*, London, Sydney, Auckland and Johannesburg: Rider.
Picardie, R. (1998) *Before I Say Goodbye*, Harmondsworth: Penguin.
Pratt, M. and Wood, M. (eds) (1998) *Art Therapy in Palliative Care: The Creative Response*, London and New York: Routledge.
Racker, H. (1974) *Transference and Counter-Transference*, International Psycho-Analytical Library, No. 73, London: Hogarth.
Rutter, P. (1989) *Sex in the Forbidden Zone*, London: Tarcher Mandala, 1990.
Samuels. A. (1985a) 'Symbolic dimensions of Eros in transference–countertransference: some clinical uses of Jung's alchemical metaphor', *International Review of Psychoanalysis*, 12, p. 199.
——(1985b) *The Father: Contemporary Jungian Perspectives*, London: Free Associations Books.
——(1993) *The Political Psyche*, London and New York: Routledge.
——(2001) *Politics on the Couch*, London: Profile Books.
Saunders, C. (1959) *Care of the Dying*, London: Macmillan.
Scaife, S. (1993) 'Sickness, health and the therapeutic relationship', *Inscape*, Summer.
Schaverien, J. (1991) *The Revealing Image: Analytical Art Psychotherapy in Theory and Practice*, London and Philadelphia: Jessica Kingsley Publishers [1999 edition].
——(1995) *Desire and the Female Therapist: Engendered Gazes in Psychotherapy and Art Therapy*, London and New York: Routledge.
——(1996) 'Desire and the female analyst', *Journal of Analytical Psychology*, 41(2), pp. 261–87.
——(1997) 'Men who leave too soon: reflections on the erotic transference and counter-transference', *British Journal of Psychotherapy*, 14(1), pp. 3–16.
——(1998) 'Jung, the transference and the psychological feminine', in Seu, I.B. and Heenan, M.C. (eds), *Feminism and Psychotherapy*, London: Thousand Oaks and Delhi: Sage.
——(1999a) 'The death of an analysand: transference, countertransference and desire', *Journal of Analytical Psychology*, 44(1), pp. 3–28.
——(1999b) 'Art within analysis: scapegoat, transference and transformation', *Journal of Analytical Psychology*, 44(4), pp. 479–510.
Schore, A. (1994) *Affect Regulation and the Origins of the Self*, Hillsdale, NJ and Hove: Lawrence Erlbaum Associates.

Searles, H. (1959) 'Oedipal love in the countertransference', in H. Searles, *Collected Papers on Schizophrenia and Related Subjects*, London, Maresfield, 1986 edn.

Sedgwick, D. (1994) *The Wounded Healer: Countertransference from a Jungian Perspective*, London and New York: Routledge.

Sourkes, B.M. (1995) *Armfuls of Time: The Psychological Experiences of the Child With a Life-Threatening Illness*, London and New York: Routledge.

Spector Person, E. (1985) 'The erotic transference in women and men: differences and consequences', *Journal of the American Academy of Psychoanalysis*, 13(2), pp. 159–80.

——(1999) *The Sexual Century*, New Haven and London: Yale University Press.

Stern, D. (1985) *The Interpersonal World of the Human Infant*, New York: Basic Books.

Stevens, A. (1995) 'Jungian psychology, the body, and the future', *Journal of Analytical Psychology*, 40(3), pp. 353–64.

Storr, A. (1999) *The Art of Psychotherapy*, London and New York: Routledge.

Tower, L.E. (1956) 'Countertransference', *Journal of the American Pscychoanalytic Association*, 4, pp. 224–55.

Ulanov, A.B. (1994) *The Wizard's Gate: Picturing Consciousness*, Einsiedeln, Switzerland: Daimon Verlag.

Von Franz, M.L. (1984) *On Dreams and Death: A Jungian Interpretation*, Chicago and La Salle, IL: Open Court, 1998 edn.

Watkins, M. (1976) *Waking Dreams*, Dallas, TX: Spring.

Welman, M. and Faber, P. (1992) 'The dream in terminal illness: a Jungian formulation', *Journal of Analytical Psychology*, 37(1), pp. 61–81.

Wharton, B. (1996) 'In the last analysis: archetypal themes in the analysis of an elderly patient with early disentegrative trauma', *Journal of Analytical Psychology*, 41(1), pp. 19–36.

Wheeler, S. (1996) 'Facing death with a client: confrontation or collusion, countertransference or compassion?', *Psychodynamic Counselling*, 2(2), pp. 167–78.

Wheelwright, J.H. (1981) *The Death of a Woman: How a Life Became Complete*, New York: St Martin's Press.

Wiener, J. (1994) 'Looking out and looking in: some reflections on "body talk" in the consulting room', *Journal of Analytical Psychology*, 39(3), pp. 331–50.

Wilber, K. (1991) *Grace and Grit: Spirituality in the Life and Death of Treya Killam Wilber*, Golden Bridge, Dublin: Gill & Macmillan/Boston: Shambala.

Wilde, O. (1896) 'The Ballad of Reading Gaol', in *Oscar Wilde: Complete Poetry*, Oxford: World's Classics, 1997 edn.

Winnicott, D.W. (1958) *Through Paediatrics to Psycho-Analysis*, London: Hogarth, 1982 edn.

——(1965) *The Maturational Processes and the Facilitating Environment*, London: Hogarth, 1985 edn.

——(1971) *Playing and Reality*, Harmondsworth: Penguin.

Wood, M. (1990) 'Art therapy in one session: working with people with AIDS', *Inscape*, Winter, pp. 27–33.

——(1998) 'The body as art: individual session with a man with AIDs', in M. Pratt and M. Wood (eds), *Art Therapy in Palliative Care: The Creative Response*, London and New York: Routledge.

Wright, E. (ed)1992 *Feminism and Psychoanalysis: a Critical Dictionary* Oxford: Blackwell.

Wrye, H.K. and Welles, J.K. (1994) *Narration of Desire*, Hillsdale, NJ: The Analytic Press.

Young, M. and Cullen, L. (1996) *A Good Death: Conversations with East Londoners*, London and New York: Routledge.

Young-Eisendrath, P. (1997) *Gender and Desire: Uncursing Pandora* A and M University College station: Texas.

——(1999) *Women and Desire: Beyond Wanting to be Wanted*, London: Piatkus Books.

Index